W9-BEJ-921

MASTER THE GED

GED

LANGUAGE ARTS, WRITING

2 0 0 2

TEACHER-TESTED STRATEGIES AND

TECHNIQUES FOR SCORING HIGH

Sharon Sorenson

ARCO™

THOMSON LEARNING

Australia • Canada • Mexico • Singapore • Spain • United Kingdom • United States

An ARCO Book

ARCO is a registered trademark of Thomson Learning, Inc., and is used herein under license by Peterson's.

About Peterson's

Founded in 1966, Peterson's, a division of Thomson Learning, is the nation's largest and most respected provider of lifelong learning resources, both in print and online. The Education Supersite^{SM} at www.petersons.com—the Internet's most heavily traveled education resource—has searchable databases and interactive tools for contacting U.S.-accredited institutions and programs. In addition, Peterson's delivers unmatched financial aid resources and test-preparation tools. Peterson's serves more than 100 million education consumers annually.

Peterson's is a division of Thomson Learning, one of the world's largest providers of lifelong learning. Thomson Learning serves the needs of individuals, learning institutions, and corporations with products and services for both traditional and distributed learning. Headquartered in Stamford, Connecticut, with offices worldwide, Thomson Learning is a division of The Thomson Corporation (www.thomson.com), one of the world's leading e-information and solutions companies in the business, professional, and education marketplaces. For more information, visit www.thomsonlearning.com.

For more information, contact Peterson's, 2000 Lenox Drive, Lawrenceville, NJ 08648;
800-338-3282; or find us on the World Wide Web at: www.petersons.com/about

Third Edition

ISBN 0-7689-0793-4

Printed in the United States of America

10 9 8 7 6 5 4 3 2 1   04 03 02

Contents

Introduction

Congratulations! Taking this first step toward passing the GED test is indeed a big step—one that can lead to increased job potential and tremendous self-satisfaction.

This book is designed to help you succeed on the GED Language Arts, Writing test. As you probably know, the Language Arts, Writing test is in two parts, one part with multiple-choice questions and the other requiring an essay response. You must be successful with both parts in order to pass the test.

To help you, this practice book

- presents the subject matter you need to answer the multiple-choice questions.

- includes subject-specific practice with every chapter.

- offers GED practice material for the Language Arts, Writing multiple-choice questions.

- shows you how to prepare a successful essay response.

- gives specific guidelines for writing the GED essay.

- furnishes GED practice material for the essay response.

As you work through the practice book, you will find cross references to remind you of things you already know. Be sure to check the references for review. The more carefully you practice, the more successful you will be on the test.

Best wishes to you. May you join the thousands before you who have found passing the GED test to be the stepping stone to new careers, new lives, and new personal satisfaction.

Note to the Teacher

This practice book addresses both parts of the GED Language Arts, Writing, test—the multiple-choice questions and the essay response. In Section I, Fundamentals of Edited American English, students study the rules and examples for grammar, usage, and mechanics. Practice follows each chapter, including frequent GED applications. Students are told that the GED test will not ask them to identify the parts of speech of all the words in a sentence or underline phrases or identify the kinds of clauses in a sentence. Rather, the test will ask them to *apply* their understanding of the rules in order to correct sentence errors. Answers to practice questions include an explanation for the correct responses, with references to specific chapters and rules. The references permit students to review topics that are still causing difficulty.

In Section II, Writing Sentences, Paragraphs, and Essays, students study how to write effective essays, especially the kinds of essays that generally appear on the GED test. The models for each kind of essay include marginal notes pointing out specific components of an effective essay. Research shows that careful study of models and their analyses is the most effective instructional technique for GED preparation. In addition, that portion of the practice book also includes multiple GED practices.

The book concludes with a chapter that walks students through a sample GED essay question, from the planning stage to the completed essay, with marginal notes analyzing the completed essay response. Step-by-step suggestions show students how to plan, write, and check the essay response. The hints include suggestions on how to allot the forty-five-minute time limit most effectively and how to remember important points to check.

Now you can find in one text everything you need to help your students prepare for the GED Language Arts, Writing test.

SECTION I

Fundamentals of Edited American English

The first portion of the GED Language Arts, Writing exam is made up of fifty multiple-choice questions that ask you to correct errors in grammar, usage, mechanics, sentence structure, unity, and coherence. To help you prepare for the GED Language Arts, Writing exam, this book starts with the fundamentals. Of course, that's where you start when you learn anything. Once you understand the basics—in this case words and sentences—then you'll be able to make sense of the explanation for writing a powerful GED essay. And that, of course, is the second part of the GED Language Arts, Writing exam.

In order to pass the GED exam, however, you need some background. Like any other subject that you study, writing has a vocabulary that is peculiar to the subject. So we'll start off slowly, teaching you the vocabulary, giving you the background you need. We'll talk about the parts of speech and the parts of a sentence. Once you understand those building blocks of writing and can solve the common problems that crop up there, you'll have the fundamentals for creating a good paragraph. And once you have paragraphs under control, you're ready to master the essay. So it's one step at a time. That's the easiest way to prepare for the GED Language Arts, Writing exam.

So let's get started with the fundamentals of parts of speech and parts of a sentence, followed by usage and mechanics.

Classification of Words

A word is the smallest part of the English language. When strung together, words are the nuts and bolts that express your ideas and hold your sentences together. Fortunately, however, all of these thousands of nuts and bolts are classified into only eight groups. We call these eight groups of words "parts of speech." In short, that means they make up all the parts of anything we say or write.

The eight parts of speech include (1) nouns, (2) pronouns, (3) verbs, (4) adjectives, (5) adverbs, (6) prepositions, (7) conjunctions, and (8) articles. You don't need to know everything there is to know about all parts of speech. In fact, we'll look in depth at only six of them (nouns, verbs, adjectives, adverbs, prepositions, and conjunctions) and address the others in passing. So let's get started.

PART 1: NOUNS

A. Definition

A noun is the name of a person, place, or thing. Sometimes a substitute name, called a pronoun, names the person, place, or thing. (But this traditional definition is not always adequate.)

Example: *Singing* in the *shower* is not for *me*.

>   (*Singing* is the name of a thing; *shower* is the name of a place; and *me* is the substitute name of a person.)

Often, definition alone won't let you identify part of speech accurately. For instance, you may have looked at *singing* in the sentence above and thought at first that it looked like a verb. Without considering *function*, you may not recognize all nouns.

IMPORTANT: Don't panic! It's okay if you don't understand everything we say here about function. In the second part of this chapter, "Parts of the Sentence," you'll learn more that will help you understand function. After you've worked through "Parts of the Sentence," come back to "Classification of Words." The two parts are very closely related. For the time being, we'll give you hints to help you get started.

B. Function

A noun most commonly functions in one of three ways:

1. As the subject of a verb

    Example: Some *lawnmowers* cut a four-foot swath.

    >   (*Lawnmowers*, a noun, is subject of the verb *cut*.)

    >   Ask "who?" or "what?" in front of the verb to find the subject.

ROAD MAP

- *Nouns*
- *Verbs*
- *Adjectives*
- *Adverbs*
- *Prepositions*
- *Conjunctions*

3

2. As an object

     a. As direct object of the verb

        Example: Some lawnmowers cut a four-foot *swath*.

            (*Swath*, a noun, is the direct object of the verb *cut*.)

            To find the direct object of the verb, ask "who?" or "what?" after the verb.

     b. As an indirect object of the verb

        Example: The banker gave my *coworker* a loan.

            (*Coworker*, a noun, is now the indirect object of the verb *gave*.)

            To find the indirect object of the verb, ask "to whom?" or "for whom?" after the verb.

     c. As object of the preposition

        Example: My coworker needed the loan for a *car*.

            (*Car* is the object of the preposition *for*.)

            To find the object of a preposition, ask "who?" or "what?" after the preposition. We'll tell you later exactly how to recognize a preposition.

3. As a predicate word

     Example: My coworker is a sharp *businesswoman*.

         (*Businesswoman*, a noun, is the predicate noun after the linking verb *is*.)

         To find a predicate word, ask "who?" or "what?" after a linking verb. We'll tell you later exactly how to recognize a linking verb.

C. Characteristics

A noun's characteristics will also help you separate it from other parts of speech. A noun may have the following characteristics, but also remember that not all nouns will have every one of the following characteristics.

1. Certain endings indicate nouns:

     a. Nouns can be made plural, usually by adding -*s* or -*es*.

        Examples: *worker, workers; banker, bankers; lawnmower, lawnmowers; grass, grasses*

     b. Nouns can be made possessive by adding either an apostrophe and -*s* or an apostrophe only. When the noun is possessive, it functions as an *adjective*.

        Examples: tree, tree's leaves; leaves, leaves' colors

2. Certain words often appear in front of nouns:

     a. Articles: *a*, *an*, and *the*

        Examples: *the* tree, *a* tree, *an* earring, *a* ruby earring

     b. Adjectives (words that describe shape, size, appearance, or number)

        Examples: *tall cone-shaped* tree (describes size and shape of tree) *three golden maple* trees (describes number, kind, and appearance of trees)

NOTE

Some nouns have peculiar plural forms, like woman, women; mouse, mice; he/she, they; but most nouns can be made plural.

In other words, certain characteristics will serve as a test to help you decide whether or not a word is a noun. If that word can be made plural (that is, you can count them), or if that word can show ownership, or if that word can have *a, an,* or *the* in front, you can bet it will be a noun.

Look at the following nonsense sentence. If you can recognize the nouns among these nonsense words, you really understand nouns!

> When the jibjam quots the flitstat after a purdletroe warkled the clatterstrow, the barmel praesslebrow was strottled by an ubby warkened.

Certain words in the sentence above are obviously nouns. Can you recognize them? Consider *characteristics.* Find all the articles (*a, an,* and *the*). You know that a noun has to follow an article, although maybe not immediately. (There may be an adjective or two between the article and the noun.) If you still do not know whether or not a word is a noun, check for plural forms. Then consider *function.* When you think you have found all the nouns, check your answers with those below.

Nouns in the nonsense sentence:

> *jibjam* (*The* appears in front, and it is the subject of the verb *quots.*)
>
> *flitstat* (*The* appears in front, and it is the direct object of the verb *quots.*)
>
> *purdletroe* (*A* appears in front, and it is the subject of the verb *warkled.*)
>
> *clatterstrow* (It is the direct object of *warkled.*)
>
> *praesslebrow* (*The*, as well as the adjective *barmel*, appears in front, and it is the subject of the verb *strottled.*)
>
> *warkened* (*An*, as well as the adjective *ubby*, appears in front, and it is the object of the preposition *by.*)

NOTE

For every article appearing in a sentence, there will be a noun following, although that noun may not be the very next word.

PART 2: VERBS

A. Definition

A verb shows action or state of being. This definition tells you that there are two kinds of verbs. As a result, there are also two basic functions:

B. Function

1. Some verbs show action.

    Example: Some employees *chatter* constantly.

    > (*Chatter* shows action on the part of the employees.)

2. Some verbs link the subject to the predicate word.

    Example 1: Some employees *are* noisy.

    > (*Are* is a state of being or linking verb and links *employees* to *noisy.*
    >
    > *Noisy* describes *students. Noisy* is a predicate adjective.)

    Example 2: These young men and women *are* job applicants.

    > (*Are* now links *men* and *women* with *applicants. Applicants* renames *men* and *women. Applicants* is a predicate noun.)

NOTE

You will often need to try both *yesterday* and *tomorrow* if you do not know in which time (or tense) the sentence is written.

C. Characteristics

Verbs show the following characteristics:

1. A verb changes time (or *tense*).

    To test for a verb, insert the words *yesterday* or *tomorrow* in front of the sentence. The word that changes is the verb.

    Example: They were singing in three-part harmony.

    Yesterday, they were singing in three-part harmony. (no change)

    Yesterday, they sang in three-part harmony.

    Tomorrow, they will sing in three-part harmony.

    From this simple test, you know that the words that changed, *were singing*, is the verb.

    a. Because a verb changes time, it has certain endings: *-s, -ed, -en, -ing*.

        Examples: The boss *ambles* down the hallway.

        The boss *ambled* down the hallway.

        The boss *will amble* down the hallway.

        The boss *is ambling* down the hallway.

        Do not confuse the *-s* ending on verbs with the *-s* ending on nouns. We add an *-s* to *nouns* to make them *plural*; we add an *-s* to *verbs* to make them *singular*.

        Examples: The managers (plural *noun*) amble (plural *verb*).

        The manager (singular *noun*) ambles (singular *verb*).

    b. Because a verb changes time, it also may have certain helping verbs (or *auxiliaries*):

do	have	could	may	will
does	has	would	might	shall
did	had	should	must	
	is	was	be	
	am	were	been	
	are		being	

        The helper plus the main verb equals the complete verb phrase:

        helper(s) + main verb = complete verb phrase

        $$\left. \begin{array}{c} could \\ + \\ have \\ + \\ been \end{array} \right\} + promoted = could\ have\ been\ promoted$$

        Some of the helping verbs can be used alone as main verbs; but when they appear with other verbs after them, they are helpers.

Example 1: Marty and Jo have their application forms.

  (*Have* is the entire verb.)

Example 2: Marty and Jo *should have* their application forms.

  (*Should* is a helper for the main verb *have*.)

Example 3: Marty and Jo *have finished* their application forms.

  (*Have* is a helper for the main verb *finished*; *finished* appears after *have*.)

Example 4: Gerry *should have finished* her application forms.

  (*Should* and *have* are both helpers; *finished* appears after *have* and *should* and therefore is the main verb.)

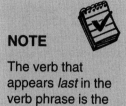

NOTE

The verb that appears *last* in the verb phrase is the main verb.

So the first characteristic of a verb is that it changes time. Now you are ready for the second and third characteristics:

2. Most verbs show action.

  a. The subject does something. (The verb is in active voice.)

  Example: That personnel manager *interviewed* me.

  b. The subject has something done to it. (The verb is in passive voice.)

  Example: I *was interviewed* by the personnel manager.

3. Some verbs are linking. There are two kinds of linking verbs:

  a. Verbs that are always linking verbs:

is	was	be
am	were	been
are		being

  These verbs are always linking when they are the *main* verbs. If they are merely *helping* verbs, they are *not* linking.

  Example 1: She *could have been* an outstanding secretary.

    (*Been* is the main verb, so the verb is linking.)

  Example 2: Linda *is being treated* for a serious illness.

    (*Is* and *being* are only helpers for the main verb *treated*, so the verb is action, not linking.)

  b. Verbs that can be linking verbs or action verbs:

seem	appear	remain
become	grow	stay

  look
  smell
  taste   } verbs of the senses
  sound
  feel

  The trick of it, of course, is to be able to recognize when these verbs are action verbs and when they are linking verbs.

Check: Substitute some form of *to be* (*is, am, are, was, were, be, been,* or *being*) for any one of these eleven verbs. If the substitution makes sense, that verb is linking.

Example 1: He *felt* miserable.

He *was* miserable.

(A form of *to be* works, so *felt* is a linking verb.)

Example 2: She *felt* the fabric.

She *was* the fabric.

(No! *Felt* in this sentence is *not* a linking verb.)

Example 3: He *tasted* the cake.

He *was* the cake.

(No! *Tasted* here is *not* a linking verb.)

Example 4: The cake *tasted* delicious.

The cake *was* delicious.

(A form of *to be* works, so *tasted* is a linking verb.)

Be aware that a form of *to be* can substitute for other verbs that will *not* be linking:

Example: The pictures *hung* on the wall.

The pictures *were* on the wall.

But *hung* is *not* a linking verb. It is not one of the eleven verbs listed in (b) above.

Sometimes, it is difficult to know whether the verb is a linking verb followed by a predicate word or if the verb is, in fact, a verb phrase.

Examples: The author was dedicated to his work.

The book was dedicated to the author's students.

The author is dedicating the book to her students.

In the first sentence, *was* is the linking verb, and *dedicated* is a predicate adjective. In the second sentence, the verb is *was dedicated*. In the third sentence, the verb is *is dedicating*. How can you tell? Where there is some form of *to be* (*is, am, are, was, were, be, been,* or *being*) plus another word that looks like a verb, insert the word *very* after the verb *to be*. If *very* makes sense, the verb is a linking verb with a predicate word. If *very* does *not* make sense, then you have a verb phrase.

Example 1: The author was [very] dedicated to his work.

(Because *very* works here, you know that *was* is a linking verb.)

Example 2: The book was [very] dedicated to the author's students.

(Because *very* does not make sense, you know the verb phrase is *was dedicated*.)

Example 3: The author is [very] dedicating the book to her students.

(*Very* does not work; the verb phrase is *is dedicating*.)

HINT

When words like *hung* appear in a sentence, you may wish to check your dictionary to see whether or not the verb can function as a linking verb.

PART 3: ADJECTIVES

A. Definition

An adjective describes or modifies a noun.

B. Function

An adjective will answer one of these questions about a noun:

1. *Which one?*

    Example: The *broken* chair was in the *south* hall.

    (*Broken* describes which *chair*, and *south* tells which *hall*.)

2. *What kind?*

    Example: Her *wool* sweater kept out the *biting* cold.

    (*Wool* describes what kind of *sweater*, and *biting* describes what kind of *cold*.)

3. *How many?*

    Example: *Seven* employees attended the meeting.

    (*Seven* tells how many *employees*.)

4. *Whose?*

    Example: The supervisor's chair was outside *her* door.

    (*Supervisor's* describes whose *chair*, and *her* describes whose *door*.)

    Remember that one of the characteristics of a noun is that adjectives can appear in front of it. This means that each of the words being described above is a noun:

    the *broken* (adjective) *chair* (noun)

    the *south* (adjective) *hall* (noun)

    the *wool* (adjective) *sweater* (noun)

    the *biting* (adjective) *cold* (noun)

    seven (adjective) *employees* (noun)

    the *supervisor's* (adjective) *chair* (noun)

    her (adjective) *door* (noun)

Recognizing adjectives will help you recognize nouns—and vice-versa! Finally, you will want to recognize the characteristics of adjectives.

C. Characteristics

1. Certain endings on adjectives enable you to compare one thing with another.

    Example 1: Andrea is a *brave* girl.

    (We are talking about only one girl, so we use the plain form of the adjective, *brave*.)

    Example 2: Betty, however, is *braver* than Andrea.

    (Now we are talking about the comparison of two girls, so we use the comparative form, the *-er* form, *braver*.)

Example 3: But Priscilla is the *bravest* of the three.

> (Since we are now comparing three, we must use the superlative form, the *-est* form, *bravest*.)

We often misuse these three forms—usually substituting the *-est* form for the *-er* form. For instance, if you have only one brother and he is taller than you, then he is the *taller* of the two; you are the *shorter* (not *shortest*). If you have a sister two years younger than you and you have no other brothers or sisters, then you are the *older* sibling (not *oldest*) in your family. If, on the other hand, you have *two* siblings, both of whom are older than you, then you are the *youngest* of the three. To summarize:

one person = brave, short, old, young

one of *two* persons = braver, shorter, older, younger

one of *three* or more persons = bravest, shortest, oldest, youngest

The endings *-er* and *-est* will work for short adjectives, but if the adjective has three or more syllables, use another word instead of the ending:

brave   braver   bravest
beautiful   more beautiful   most beautiful

Use *more* like *-er* and *most* like *-est.*

Of course, there are some words that have their own peculiar comparisons, but you are no doubt familiar with them. You would not say *good, gooder, goodest,* now, would you! So you recognize *good, better,* and *best* as the usual comparisons. But the point remains: comparisons are characteristic of adjectives.

2. Placement also helps to identify adjectives.

   a. Adjectives usually appear in front of the nouns they modify.

      Example: The *brave* fireman rescued the child from the burning house.

      > (*Brave* describes *what kind* about the noun *fireman.*)

   b. The adjective can appear after a linking verb. That adjective is called a predicate adjective.

      Example: He is *brave.*

      > (*Brave* describes *what kind* about the noun substitute (or pronoun) *he* and comes after the linking verb *is.*)

PART 4: ADVERBS

A. Definition

An adverb modifies a verb, an adjective, or another adverb.

B. Function

An adverb will answer the following questions about verbs, adjectives, or other adverbs:

1. *Where?*

   Example 1: He walked *home.*

      > (*Home* tells *where* about the verb *walked.*)

   Example 2: The lumberjack cut *down* the tree.

      > (*Down* tells *where* about the verb *cut.* That sentence could also read this way: The lumberjack cut the tree *down.* Adverbs are movable!)

Since adverbs are movable, try that moving test when you do not know whether *down* is an adverb or a preposition. Prepositions cannot be moved.

Example 1: The fireman ran *down* the hall.

(Since we cannot say, "The fireman ran the hall down," we know that *down* is a preposition.)

Example 2: The wrestler knocked *down* his opponent.

(We can say, "The wrestler knocked his opponent down," so we know the movable word is an adverb, not a preposition.)

2. *When?*

Example 1: He walked to work *yesterday*.

(*Yesterday* tells *when* about the verb *walked*.)

Example 2: The alarm rang *late*.

(*Late* tells when about the verb *rang*.)

3. *How?*

Example 1: The flag swayed *gently* in the wind.

(*Gently* tells *how* about the verb *swayed*.)

Example 2: The flag swayed *very gently* in the wind.

(*Very* tells *how* about the adverb *gently*.)

4. *To what extent?*

Example 1: He tried *quite* hard to finish the job.

(*Quite* tells *to what extent* about the adverb *hard*. *Hard* tells *how* about the verb *tried*.)

Example 2: He was *absolutely* certain about the answer.

(*Absolutely* tells *to what extent* about the predicate adjective *certain*.)

C. Characteristics

Adverbs have two characteristic endings that help identify them:

1. Adverbs, like adjectives, can be compared using the endings *-er* and *-est* or the words *more* and *most*.

Example 1: The men work *hard*.

Example 2: The men worked *harder* today than they did yesterday.

(Comparison of how *hard* the men worked on *two* days requires the comparative, or *-er*, form.)

Example 3: Of all the days in the week that they worked, the men worked *hardest* on Saturday.

(The comparison of how *hard* the men worked on six days requires the superlative *-est* form.)

Example 4: The children behaved *properly*.

Example 5: These children behaved *more properly* than those.

(Comparison of how *two* groups behaved requires the comparative, or *more*, form.)

Example 6:   Of the three groups of children, the neighbor's children behaved *most properly*.

(The comparison of how *three* groups behaved requires the superlative *most* form.)

Since both adjectives and adverbs have the characteristic of comparison, you will have to go back to consider *function* to distinguish between the two. Adjectives will make comparisons about *nouns*. Adverbs will make comparisons about *verbs*, *adjectives*, and other *adverbs*.

Consider, too, this additional characteristic ending of adverbs:

2.   Adverbs often end in *-ly*.

Example: He worked rapid*ly*, ate hungri*ly*, and slept sound*ly*.

Warning: Not all words that end in *-ly* are adverbs. Some are adjectives. Be sure to check function.

Example: He was a *friendly* man who had a *burly* physique.

(*Friendly* tells what kind of *man* [noun], and *burly* tells what kind of *physique* [noun], so both are adjectives by *function*.)

HINT

Adjectives make comparisons about nouns; adverbs make comparisons about verbs, adjectives, and other adverbs.

PART 5: PREPOSITIONS

A. Definition

A preposition shows the relationship of its object to another word in the sentence. (That definition probably does not help much, but don't give up yet!)

B. Function

The preposition, with its object, functions as a single word.

NOTE: To find the object of the preposition, ask *who?* or *what?* after the preposition.

Example 1:   The poodle frisked *through the room*.

Ask: through what?

Answer: through the room

(*Room* is the object of the preposition *through*. The preposition and its object form the prepositional phrase *through the room*. *Through* shows the relationship between the noun *room* and the verb *frisked*.)

Example 2:   The terrier barked at the *frisky little poodle*.

Ask: at *who* or at *what*?

Answer: at *the poodle*

(*Poodle* is the object of the preposition *at*. The prepositional phrase begins with the preposition and ends with its object: *at* (preposition) *the frisky little poodle* (object of the preposition). The phrase includes, therefore, any modifiers of the object. In the sentence above, *frisky* and *little* both modify *poodle* and so are parts of the prepositional phrase.)

To summarize, then, the prepositional phrase functions as a single word. It functions in one of two ways:

1. As an adjective

    Example: The woman *with red hair* is my friend.

    > (*With* shows the relationship of *hair* to *woman*, and *with red hair* tells *which* about the noun *woman*. The whole phrase *with red hair* functions as a single word, as an adjective modifying *woman*.)

2. As an adverb

    Example: The workman who fell *into the bucket* of wet cement needs a hose.
    (*Into* shows the relationship between *fell* and *bucket*. *Into the bucket* says *where* about *fell*, and the whole phrase functions as a single word, as an adverb modifying the verb *fell*. Incidentally, *of wet cement* functions as an adjective describing *what kind* about *bucket*.)

C. Characteristics

The following characteristics indicate prepositions:

1. A preposition will always be followed by an object, which must be a noun. (Remember, *all* objects are nouns.)

    Since prepositions are rather peculiar words that we use frequently, you really need to be able to recognize them easily. Prepositional phrases cause all sorts of problems later if you fail to learn to recognize them. Since the definition doesn't really help you pick out prepositions easily, think of this final characteristic, peculiar though it may be, as one that will help you find those prepositions:

2. A preposition is "any place a rat can run." (The preposition *of* is the only exception!)

    Strange? Yes, but look at the following list of prepositions, written here with objects (forming prepositional phrases), to see how this strange idea works:

NOTE

A preposition is always followed by an object, which must be a noun.

A rat can run **about** the room,	**for** many hours
above the window,	**from** now until 3:30 p.m.!
or **across** your desk	He can also run **from** the
any time **after** 8:00 p.m.,	exterminator
even **against** your wishes.	**in** a panic
He can run **along** your foot,	**into** hiding
among your books,	**like** a flash
or **around** your shoulders	**of** lightning.
at an easy pace.	He can run **off** the window ledge
That same rat can run **before**	**on** the east side **of** the room,
your very eyes	**over** the wall,
or **behind** your back,	**through** the meadow and **to**
below the bookcase	the woods
or **beneath** the door.	**toward** Grandmother's house!
He can run **beside** your notebook,	He can even run **under** her door,
between your boots,	and **up** the attic stairs
or **beyond** your reach	**with** great haste
by the file cabinet.	**without** a sound.
This wily little rat can run **down**	He can run as well as walk
your arm	**as far as** Tennessee
during coffee break	**in spite of** his short legs
except on Saturdays and Sundays	**because of** his great energy.

And so, you see, some prepositions are even made of more than one word; but the rat, ambitious little creature that he is, can still run!

PART 6: CONJUNCTIONS

A. Definition

A conjunction is a connecting word. The most common conjunction is called a *coordinating conjunction*. These conjunctions include the words *and*, *but*, *or*, *nor*, and *for*.

B. Function

1. Most conjunctions join two equal parts of a sentence.

    Example: Rodney *and* Jose put in 20 hours of overtime last week.

    (And joins the two subjects *Rodney* and *Jose.)*

    Example: Rodney worked 15 hours of overtime, *but* Jose worked only 5 hours.

    (But joins two main clauses: *Rodney worked 15 hours of overtime* is the first clause, and *Jose worked 5 hours* is the second clause. We'll talk more about clauses later.)

    Example: Edward will work in the mailroom *or* drive the delivery truck.

    (Or joins two verbs and their objects: *will work in the mail room* is the first part, and *drive the delivery truck* is the second.)

    NOTE: Writers who use coordinating conjunctions incorrectly (or forget to use them at all) will have difficulty with some parts of the GED exam. Remember three points:

    1. Use coordinating conjunctions to join *equal* parts of a sentence. (We'll talk more about parallelism in Chapter 16.)

    2. When you use a coordinating conjunction to join two complete sentences, also use a comma. (We'll talk more about run-on sentences in Chapter 16.)

    3. If you run two sentences together without a comma and a conjunction, you will lose points on the GED exam. (We'll talk more about comma splices in Chapter 16.)

2. Some conjunctions start *subordinate clauses*. These are called *subordinating conjunctions*. We'll talk more about them in Chapter 12, but here are a couple of examples:

    Example: *When* employees take vacation time, the company hires substitutes.

    (When starts the subordinate clause *when employees take vacation time.)*

    Example: The employee evaluation form was revised *after* two supervisors found errors on it.

    (The subordinating conjunction *after* connects the subordinate clause *after two supervisors found errors on it* to the main clause.)

C. Characteristics

Conjunctions show the following characteristics:

1. Coordinating conjunctions connect two parts of a sentence, like two subjects, two verbs, two prepositional phrases, or two clauses.

2. Subordinating conjunctions show relationships or connections between the subordinate clause and the main clause. Common subordinating conjunctions include words like *when*, *where*, *while*, *after*, *because*, *since*, and *others*. We'll talk more about subordinating conjunctions in Chapter 12.

PRACTICE
EXERCISE 1

Directions: You now have the basic information about the six important parts of speech: nouns, verbs, adjectives, adverbs, prepositions, and conjunctions. Use the following practice to see if you understand this basic information. Determine the part of speech of the italicized word. When you have finished, check your answers against the correct answers provided on the next page; try to figure out *why* you went wrong—*if* you did.

1. The football fans cheered the first *down*.
2. *Down* jackets keep the wearer quite warm in very cold weather.
3. Climbing carefully *down* the ladder, he felt more and more relief as he neared the bottom.
4. The champion wrestler will *down* his opponent easily.
5. That little imp knocked *down* my carefully stacked grocery display!
6. The manager is working *outside* his realm of authority.
7. As he stepped *outside*, the wind blasted him in the face.
8. To conserve energy, we planned to insulate all the *outside* walls.
9. Those two boys really *like* baseball!
10. The Wargels painted their house green; we plan to paint ours in a *like* manner.
11. At my suggestion of a date at the movies, her face lit up *like* a neon sign.
12. I watched as my colleague *neared* the podium.
13. The burglary occurred *near* the intersection of Third and Main Streets.
14. Time draws *near*!
15. Having been involved in a *near* accident, Joyce drives more carefully now.
16. The winter's supply of firewood is *nearly* gone.
17. The horse *nearing* the finish line is being ridden by the youngest jockey here.
18. History studies the *past*.
19. His *past* actions are a good indication of what to expect in the future.
20. Thank goodness, I *passed* the course!
21. Yesterday, my sister slept *past* noon.
22. The jogger runs *past* the post office every afternoon.

EXERCISE 1—ANSWERS

1. *Noun.* The clues are the article *the* and the adjective *first. Down* functions as a direct object of the verb *cheered.*

2. *Adjective.* It describes *what kind of* about the noun *jacket.*

3. *Preposition.* A rat can run *down the ladder. Down* has a noun-object: *ladder.*

4. *Verb. Will* is a helping verb, so its presence indicates a verb phrase.

5. *Adverb.* It tells *where* about *knocked*, the verb. (If you were tempted to call this one a preposition, note that the sentence can be rearranged to read, "That little imp knocked my carefully stacked dominoes down." Because *down* can be moved about in the sentence, you can guess that it functions as an adverb.)

6. *Preposition.* A rat can run *outside his realm of authority! Realm* is a noun, the object of the preposition.

7. *Adverb.* It tells *where* about the verb *stepped.*

8. *Adjective.* It tells *which ones* about the noun *walls.*

9. *Verb.* You can change the time: Yesterday, those boys really *liked* baseball.

10. *Adjective. Like* tells *what kind of* about the noun *manner.*

11. *Preposition. Like* has a noun object: *sign.* The whole phrase tells *how* about *lit.*

12. *Verb.* You can change the time: Tomorrow my colleague *will near* the podium.

13. *Preposition.* A rat can run *near the intersection. Intersection,* a noun, is the object of the preposition *near.* As a phrase, *near the intersection* tells *where* about the verb *occurred.*

14. *Adverb. Near* tells *where* about *draws*, the verb.

15. *Adjective. Near* tells *what kind of* about the noun *accident.*

16. *Adverb.* The *-ly* ending is a clue. So is the fact that *nearly* tells to *what extent* about *is gone*, the verb.

17. *Adjective.* Bet you goofed on that one! Did you call it a verb? *Nearing* here tells *which* about *horse:* the one *nearing the finish line.*

18. *Noun. The* is the first clue that you have a noun. *Past* also functions as the object of the verb *studies.*

19. *Adjective. Past* tells *which ones* about *actions.*

20. *Verb.* The *-ed* ending is a clue, but you need to see if that word will, in fact, change time: Tomorrow, I *will* pass the course.

21. *Preposition.* Can't a rat run *past noon*?

22. *Preposition.* Rats can run *past the post office*, too!

EXERCISE 2

Directions: Now try these nonsense sentences. By applying all the clues, you should be able to determine the part of speech of each of the words in these sentences! When you finish, check your answers with those below.

1. The quargle fotterstadt with yankop in its zedtop doppled lommily down the prufhoth.
2. A rewant at the moldud prampted the wobats.
3. After gundernt, an uprezeted flingle was omkled into the vifertt.
4. A langly priffert under the croddertz humphered and wekkened ikingly until eddstodt.
5. During a dedderft in the bockfert, the okkendult's caedt is gunrothing.

EXERCISE 2—ANSWERS

Sentence 1: The quargle fotterstadt with yankop in its zedtop doppled lommily down the prufhoth.

The—article, determines that a noun follows
quargle—adjective, modifies *fotterstadt*
fotterstadt—noun, subject
with—preposition
yankop—noun, object of the preposition *with*
in—preposition
its—adjective, modifies *zedtop*
zedtop—noun, object of the preposition *in*
doppled—verb
lommily—adverb, modifies the verb *doppled*
down—preposition
the—article, determines that a noun follows
prufhoth—noun, object of the preposition *down*

Sentence 2: A rewant at the moldud prampted the wobats.

A—article, determines that a noun follows
rewant—noun, subject
at—preposition
the—article, determines that a noun follows
moldud—noun, object of preposition *at*
prampted—verb
the—article, determines that a noun follows
wobats—noun, object of the verb *prampted*

Sentence 3: After gundernt, an uprezeted flingle was omkled into the vifertt.

After—preposition
gundernt—noun, object of the preposition *after*
an—article, determines that a noun follows
uprezeted—adjective, modifies *flingle*
flingle—noun, subject
was omkled—verb
into—preposition
the—article, determines that a noun follows
vifertt—noun, object of the preposition *into*

Sentence 4: A langly priffert under the croddertz humphered and wekkened ikingly until eddstodt.

> *A—article*, determines that a noun follows
> *langly—adjective*, modifies *priffert*
> *priffert—noun*, subject
> *under—preposition*
> *the—article*, determines that a noun follows
> *croddertz—noun*, object of the preposition *under*
> *humphered—verb*
> *and—joining word*
> *wekkened—verb*
> *ikingly—adverb*, modifies verbs *humphered* and *wekkened*
> *until—preposition*
> *eddstodt—noun*, object of the preposition *until*

Sentence 5: During a dedderft in the bockfert, the okkendult's caedt is gunrothing.

> *During—preposition*
> *a—article*, determines that a noun follows
> *dedderft—noun*, object of the preposition *during*
> *in—preposition*
> *the—article*, determines that a noun follows
> *bockfert—noun*, object of the preposition *in*
> *the—article*, determines that a noun follows
> *okkendult's—possessive noun*, functions as adjective, modifies *caedt*
> *caedt—noun*, subject
> *is gunrothing—verb*

EXERCISE 3

Directions: Apply what you know to determine the part of speech of each of the words in these sentences. If you were generally successful with nonsense sentences above, you will do well with these.

1. The frozen tundra offered little of interest to me.
2. Bratwurst is traditional food at the German festival.
3. Joo Ree works easily with domestic animals.
4. In the middle of the floor lay four pairs of brown shoes.
5. Ironically, eating sometimes makes me hungry!

EXERCISE 3—ANSWERS

Sentence 1: The frozen tundra offered little of interest to me.

article, adjective, noun, verb, noun (object of the verb), preposition, noun (object of the preposition), preposition, pronoun (noun substitute)

Sentence 2: Bratwurst is traditional food at the German festival.

noun, verb, adjective, noun, preposition, article, adjective, noun

Sentence 3: Joo Ree works easily with domestic animals.

noun, verb, adverb, preposition, adjective, noun

Sentence 4: In the middle of the floor lay four pairs of brown shoes.

preposition, article, noun (object of preposition), preposition, article, noun, verb, adjective, noun (object of the verb), preposition, adjective, noun

Sentence 5: Ironically, eating sometimes makes me hungry!

adverb, noun (subject of verb), adverb (modifies verb), verb, pronoun (noun substitute), adjective (modifies pronoun)

If you made reasonable progress with these sentences, you are well on your way toward mastery. Keep in mind that Chapter 2, *Parts of the Sentence*, will help you sort out and understand some specifics that may at present be unclear.

Parts of the Sentence

A SENTENCE ATTACK PLAN

Because it is important later in being able to determine correct usage, you must be able to find the major parts of the sentence:

  subject

  verb

  direct object

  indirect object

  predicate word

There are seven steps to a sentence attack plan that will help you recognize the principal parts of the sentence. As you study any sentence, follow these steps to analyze it.

STEP 1: PREPOSITIONAL PHRASES

Mark out all the prepositional phrases. Remember that the prepositional phrase is the preposition *plus* the noun that is its object *plus* any words in between. (The words in between are modifiers of the object.) In other words:

  preposition
    +
  modifiers   } = prepositional phrase
    +
  noun (object)

Since prepositional phrases can function only as modifiers, they cannot function as any major part of the sentence. As a result, you will keep yourself out of trouble by eliminating them from the beginning.

  Example: A dish of grapes was sitting on the dining room table.

        After the prepositional phrases are marked out: A dish . . . was sitting.

  NOTE: By eliminating *of grapes*, the prepositional phrase, you will eliminate any confusion between the nouns later when you must select the subject of the sentence.

STEP 2: VERBS

Find the word that changes *time*. That word will be the verb. (Be sure to find the whole verb phrase.) Remember that to make finding the verb easier, you can add the words *yesterday* or *tomorrow* in front of the sentence.

Example: A dish of grapes **was sitting** on the dining-room table.

Step 1: A dish . . . **was sitting**. . . .

Step 2: A dish was sitting.

Tomorrow, a dish *will be* sitting.

(Helper verbs *will* and *be* are joined with the main verb, *sitting*.)

Was sitting is the whole verb.

STEP 3: ACTION VERB OR LINKING VERB

Determine whether the verb is an action verb or a linking verb. (You may need to review verb characteristics in Chapter 1, Part 2, Section C.)

Example: Some of the patients in the hall are friends of mine.

Step 1: Some . . . are friends. . . .

Step 2: Some are friends.

Yesterday, some *were* friends.

Are is the verb.

Step 3: *Are* is a linking verb. (It is one of the verbs *to be* that are always linking.)

STEP 4: SUBJECTS

Ask *who?* or *what?* in front of the verb to determine the subject.

Example: Most of the people at the circus reacted with surprise at the clown's antics.

Step 1: Most . . . reacted. . . .

Step 2: Most *reacted*.

Tomorrow, most *will react*.

Reacted is the verb.

Step 3: *Reacted* is an action verb.

Step 4: *Who* or *what* reacted?

Answer: *most*

Most is the subject.

Two warnings are necessary as we talk about subjects:

Warning 1:   Sometimes the subject does not appear in front of the verb. Asking *who?* or *what?* in front of the verb will still determine the subject, but you may have to look *after* the verb in the sentence in order to find the answer.

Example: Onto the field ran the coach and his team.

Step 1: . . . ran the coach and his team.

Step 2: Ran the coach and his team.

Tomorrow *will run* the coach and his team.

Ran is the verb.

Step 3: *Ran* is an action verb.

Step 4: *Who* or *what* ran?

Answer: *coach and team.*

Coach and *team* are the subjects.

Warning 2:   The words *here* and *there* can never be subjects. (They tell *where* and usually function as adverbs.) In sentences that begin with *here* or *there*, you will have to look *after* the verb to find the subject.

Example: There are two bowls of shelled peanuts in the cabinet.

Step 1: There are two bowls. . . .

Step 2: There are two bowls.

Yesterday, there *were* two bowls.

Are is the verb.

Step 3: *Are* is a linking verb.

Step 4: *Who* or *what* are?

Answer: *bowls* (*Here* and *there* can never be subjects.)

Bowls is the subject.

STEP 5: DIRECT OBJECTS

If you have a *linking* verb, skip to Step 7. If you have an *action* verb, ask *who?* or *what?* after the verb to find the direct object. (Remember, the direct object must be a noun.)

Example: A few of the children brought their toys with them to the birthday party for my son.

Step 1: A few . . . brought their toys. . . .

Step 2: A few brought their toys.

Tomorrow, a few *will bring* their toys.

Brought is the verb.

Step 3: *Brought* is an action verb.

Step 4: *Who* or *what* brought?

Answer: *few* (subject)

Step 5: Since *brought* is an action verb, ask:

Few brought *who* or *what?*

Answer: *toys*

Toys is the direct object.

Two warnings follow:

Warning 1: Not all action verbs will have a direct object. Consider, for example, the sentence in the example for Step 4: *Most of the people at the circus reacted with surprise at the clown's antics.* After all the prepositional phrases were crossed out, nothing was left except *most reacted. Most* is the subject, and *reacted* is the verb. Even though *reacted* is an action verb, there is nothing to answer the questions *who?* or *what?* for the direct object. Consider this additional example:

Example: The dark, ominous clouds moved steadily toward us from the western horizon.

Step 1: The dark, ominous clouds moved steadily....

Step 2: The dark, ominous clouds moved steadily.

Tomorrow, the dark, ominous clouds *will move* steadily.

Moved is the verb.

Step 3: *Moved* is an action verb.

Step 4: *Who* or *what* moved?

Answer: *clouds* (subject)

Step 5: Since *moved* is an action verb, ask:

Clouds moved *who* or *what?*

Answer: none (*Steadily* tells *how*, not *who* or *what*.)

There is no direct object.

Warning 2: There can be no direct object after a linking verb.

Example: The water seemed deep along the bank.

Step 1: The water seemed deep. . . .

Step 2: The water seemed deep.

Tomorrow, the water *will seem* deep.

Seemed is the verb.

Step 3: *Seemed* is a linking verb.

Step 4: *Who* or *what* seemed?

Answer: *water* (subject)

Step 5: You cannot complete this step because the verb is *linking.* Go to Step 7.

NOTE: If you did ask the questions for the direct object (water seemed *who* or *what?*) you would get an answer: *deep.* But there are two problems here:

1. You cannot have a direct object after a linking verb.

2. *Deep* is not a noun. Direct objects must be nouns.

You can see, then, why Step 3 is so important. If you neglect to determine whether the verb is an action verb or a linking verb, you will probably get into trouble at Step 5.

Sometimes you will find a sentence that has words that seem to answer both *who?* and *what?* after the verb. Compare these two sentences:

Example 1:   John bought ice cream and cookies.

John bought *what?*

Answer: *ice cream and cookies*

(You have two direct objects joined with *and*.)

Example 2:   John bought Sue candy.

John bought *who* or *what?*

Answer: *Sue* and *candy?*

(It appears that *Sue* answers *who?*, and *candy* answers *what?* But did John buy Sue? Not quite! That leads us to Step 6.)

STEP 6: INDIRECT OBJECTS

If you have a direct object, ask *to whom?* or *for whom?* to find the indirect object. You cannot have an indirect object if there is no direct object.

Example: For Christmas, Barbara bought her family airline tickets to England.

Step 1: . . . Barbara bought her family airline tickets. . . .

Step 2: Barbara bought her family airline tickets.

Tomorrow, Barbara *will buy* her family airline tickets.

Bought is the verb.

Step 3: *Bought* is an action verb.

Step 4: *Who* or *what* bought?

Answer: *Barbara* (subject)

Step 5: Barbara bought *who* or *what?*

Answer: *tickets* (direct object)

Step 6: Since we have a direct object, ask:

Barbara bought tickets *to whom* or *for whom?*

Answer: *family*

Family is the indirect object.

NOTE: In Step 5 you could have had two answers:

1. Barbara bought *who?*

Answer: *family* (Of course, that does not really make sense. Barbara did not buy her family!)

2. Barbara bought *what?*

Answer: *tickets*

Even though *family* was not a sensible answer for Step 5, if you were not thinking carefully, you could have stumbled at that point. So consider these three warnings:

Warning 1:   If there appear to be two words, one of which answers *who*? and another of which answers *what*?, the first one (which answers *who*?) is the indirect object, and the second one (which answers *what*?) is the direct object.

Example: Laura taught her friends a new dance step.

Step 5: Laura taught *who* or *what*?

Answer: *step* (direct object)

Step 6: Laura taught step *to whom* or *for whom*?

Answer: *friends* (indirect object)

Friends answers *who*? and *step* answers *what*?, so the answer to *who*? is the indirect object and the answer to *what*? is the direct object.

Warning 2:   The indirect object will always appear in the sentence between the verb and the direct object. It cannot appear after the direct object. If the sentence pattern is

noun/verb/noun/noun

then the pattern may be

subject/verb/indirect object/direct object

Warning 3:   If the word *to* or *for* actually appears in front of the word you think is the indirect object, you have a prepositional phrase, not an indirect object. And you should have crossed out all prepositional phrases in Step 1!

Example: Madelyn bought tickets for us for Saturday's concert.

Step 5: Madelyn bought *who* or *what*?

Answer: *tickets* (direct object)

Step 6: Madelyn bought tickets *to whom* or *for whom*?

Answer: none

The *for* in front of *us* makes *for us* a prepositional phrase. You can see once again the importance of Step 1. Be sure to eliminate all prepositional phrases!

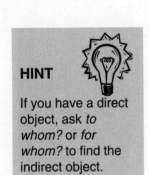

HINT

If you have a direct object, ask *to whom?* or *for whom?* to find the indirect object.

STEP 7: PREDICATE WORDS

If you have a linking verb, the word that answers *who*? or *what*? after the verb is the predicate word. The predicate word may be a noun or an adjective.

NOTE: You are asking the same questions that you did in Step 5, but now you are asking them after a *linking* verb, not an action verb.

Example 1:   The chocolate cake on the right end of the table is especially well decorated.

Step 1: The chocolate cake . . . is especially well decorated.

Step 2: The chocolate cake is especially well decorated.

Yesterday, the chocolate cake *was* especially well decorated.

Is is the verb.

Step 3: *Is* is the linking verb.

Step 4: *Who* or *what is*?

  Answer: *cake* (subject)

Step 5: If you have a linking verb, skip to Step 7.

Step 7: Cake is *who* or *what*?

  Answer: decorated

  Decorated is the predicate word. It is a predicate adjective.

Example 2: The red-haired man in the third row probably will be foreman of the jury.

Step 1: The red-haired man . . . probably will be foreman. . . .

Step 2: The red-haired man probably will be foreman.

  Yesterday, the red-haired man probably *would have been* foreman.

  Will be is the verb.

Step 3: *Will be* is a linking verb.

Step 4: *Who* or *what* will be?

  Answer: *man* (subject)

Step 5: If you have a linking verb, skip to Step 7.

Step 7: Man will be *who* or *what*?

  Answer: *foreman*

  Foreman is the predicate word. It is the predicate noun.

COMPOUND PARTS

Now that you have considered the seven steps of the sentence-attack plan, you need to deal with one more concept that can apply to all seven steps:

Any part of the sentence can be compound. The compound parts may be joined by the words *and*, *but*, *or*, or *nor*. (These words are called *coordinating conjunctions*.)

The following examples illustrate:

Step 1: Compound object of the preposition

  Example: The sunbeams reflected through the *goblets and vases* in the jewelry store's *windows and showcases*.

Step 2: Compound verb

  Example: Shop owners *advertise* their products *and solicit* our business.

Step 3: Compound verb, one of which is an action verb and the other of which is a linking verb

  Example: The track team *represented* young people from many backgrounds *and was* a melting-pot for their differences.

  (*Represented* is an action verb and *was* is a linking verb.)

Step 4: Compound subject

  Example: *Most* of her friends *and* a few *acquaintances* showed up for the open-house in her honor.

Step 5: Compound direct object

Example: The chemist was awarded a bronze *plaque and* a $1000 cash *prize* for his work in cancer research.

Step 6: Compound indirect object

Example: The guide offered *Dan or me* a free two-day fishing trip.

Step 7: Compound predicate-adjective

Example: That cold lemonade tasted *sweet but refreshing.*

Sometimes a sentence can have several compound parts:

Example: The groundskeeper and his assistants built the young boys and girls a long-needed bicycle path and foot trail and, as a result, are both excited and gratified by the children's positive reaction and steady use of the new facilities.

Step 1: compound object of preposition:

reactions and *use* (also *facilities*)

Step 2: compound verb:

built and *are*

Step 3: compound verb, one action and the other linking:

built (action) and *are* (linking)

Step 4: compound subject:

keeper and *assistants*

Step 5: compound direct object:

path and *trail*

Step 6: compound indirect object:

boys and *girls*

Step 7: compound predicate adjectives:

excited and *gratified*

SUMMARY FOR THE SENTENCE-ATTACK PLAN

Step 1: Mark out the prepositional phrases.

Step 2: Find the verb, the word that changes time.

Step 3: Determine whether the verb is an action verb or a linking verb.

Step 4: Ask *who?* or *what?* in front of the verb to determine the subject. (*Who* or *what* [verb]?)

Step 5: If you have a linking verb, skip to Step 7. If you have an action verb, ask *who?* or *what?* after the verb to find the direct object. ([Subject][verb] *who* or *what?*)

Step 6: If you have a direct object, ask *to whom?* or *for whom?* after the direct object to find the indirect object.

Step 7: If you have a linking verb, ask *who?* or *what?* after the verb to find the predicate word.

PRACTICE
EXERCISE 1

Directions: For practice, consider the following questions about the general ideas in the sentence attack plan. Check your answers with those at the end of these questions.

1. Can you have a compound subject?
2. Can you have a direct object after a linking verb?
3. Must you have an indirect object after a direct object?
4. Do action verbs take predicate words?
5. Will most linking verbs have predicate words?
6. Will all action verbs have direct objects?
7. Can you have an indirect object without a direct object?
8. Can a sentence have both a predicate word and a direct object?
9. Can the verb be more than one word?
10. Can there be more than one verb in a sentence?
11. Can there be both a linking verb and an action verb in the same sentence?
12. Can direct objects appear after action verbs?
13. Can there be two direct objects in a sentence?
14. Can prepositional phrases serve as subjects or objects?
15. Can a sentence have both a direct object and an indirect object?
16. Must a sentence have a subject?
17. Will the subject appear in front of the verb?
18. Will all sentences have a verb?
19. Will all sentences have either a direct object or a predicate word?
20. Are all subjects, direct objects, indirect objects, and predicate words nouns?

EXERCISE 1—ANSWERS

1. *Yes.* Example: My *sister* and *Georgette* are going shopping.

2. *No.* Direct objects must follow action verbs.

3. *No.* A direct object may exist without an indirect object.

4. *No.* Predicate words follow linking verbs.

5. *Yes.* Most linking verbs will have a predicate word, but sometimes that predicate word is implied. Example: Is Sue your sister? Yes, she is. (*My sister* are the implied predicate words.)

6. *No.* Example: Joanne jogs after work every day. Joanne jogs *who* or *what*? Answer: none.

7. *No.* There must be a direct object before there can be an indirect object.

8. *Yes,* but only if there is *both* an action verb and a linking verb.

9. *Yes.* The verb often has helpers.

10. *Yes. Example:* Barbara *bought* and *delivered* the flowers herself.

11. *Yes. Example:* The young athlete *ran* seven miles and *was* exhausted.

12. *Yes.* Not every action verb, however, must have a direct object.

13. *Yes. Example:* Our members read both newspaper *reports* and magazine *articles* about the dispute.

14. *No.* Prepositional phrases function only as adjectives or adverbs. Example: The receptionist *behind the desk now* works *only on weekends*. The first prepositional phrase functions as an adjective telling "which one?" about the noun *receptionist*, and the second functions as an adverb telling "when?" about the verb *works*.

15. *Yes.* A sentence must have a direct object before it can have an indirect object, but the direct object may exist without an indirect object.

16. *Yes,* of course!

17. *Not always.* Remember that *here* and *there*, for instance, cannot be subjects; the subject will have to come after the verb in that case. There are other situations, too, of course, in which the subject comes later.

18. *Yes!*

19. *No.* Since an action verb may exist without a direct object and since, in some cases, linking verbs have only implied predicate words, a sentence may exist—and often does, in fact—with only a subject and a verb.

20. *No.* Predicate words and objective complements may be nouns or adjectives.

EXERCISE 2

Directions: Now that you have practiced the sentence attack plan, try applying the seven steps to the following sentences. You will need to apply, also, the information you learned in Chapter 1. Label the following items in these sentences:

subject
verb
direct object, if any
indirect object, if any
predicate word, if any

When you finish, check your answers on the following pages.

1. The professor, with some help from his niece, found his car keys behind the cushion.
2. A couple of my friends seemed especially pleased with their respective successes at the track meet.
3. One of the cheerleaders fell during the half-time show and twisted his left ankle.
4. The mayor sent the City Council her ideas for improving city traffic flow.
5. We bought three back issues of *National Geographic* for your use.
6. Do you really understand these solutions to the problem?
7. The essay-contest winners were a young man in my neighborhood and a woman in the next town.
8. Funds from the state government financed local road improvements.
9. With his courage, he will win a medal for bravery.
10. Most young speakers appear nervous but usually steel themselves with determination.
11. The basketball referee called a personal foul on Roberto.
12. Some of these civic-minded people have been buying their out-of-town friends souvenirs from our city.

EXERCISE 2—ANSWERS

Sentence 1: The professor, with some help from his niece, found his car keys behind the cushion.

Step 1: The professor . . . found his car keys. . . .

Step 2: The professor found his car keys.

Tomorrow, the professor *will find* his car keys.

Found is the verb.

Step 3: *Found* is an action verb.

Step 4: *Who* or *what* found?

Answer: *professor* (subject)

Step 5: Professor found *who* or *what*?

Answer: *keys* (direct object)

Step 6: Professor found keys to *whom* or *for whom*?

Answer: none

Sentence 2: A couple of my friends seemed especially pleased with their respective successes at the track meet.

Step 1: A couple . . . seemed especially pleased. . . .

Step 2: A couple seemed especially pleased.

Tomorrow, a couple *will seem* especially pleased.

Seemed is the verb.

Step 3: *Seemed* is a linking verb.

Step 4: *Who* or *what* seemed?

Answer: *couple* (subject)

Step 5: If you have a linking verb, skip to Step 7.

Step 7: Couple seemed *who* or *what*?

Answer: *pleased* (predicate word)

Sentence 3: One of the cheerleaders fell during the half-time show and twisted his left ankle.

Step 1: One . . . fell . . . and twisted his left ankle.

Step 2: One fell and twisted his left ankle.

Tomorrow, one *will fall* and *twist* his left ankle.

Fell and *twisted* are the verbs.

Step 3: *Fell* and *twisted* are both action verbs.

Step 4: *Who* or *what* fell and twisted?

Answer: *one* (subject)

Step 5: One fell *who* or *what*?

Answer: none

One twisted *who* or *what*?

Answer: *ankle* (direct object)

Step 6: One twisted ankle *to whom* or *for whom*?

Answer: none

Sentence 4: The mayor sent the City Council her ideas for improving city traffic flow.

Step 1: The mayor sent the City Council her ideas. . . .

Step 2: The mayor sent the City Council her ideas.

Tomorrow, the mayor *will send* the City Council her ideas.

Sent is the verb.

Step 3: *Sent* is an action verb.

Step 4: *Who* or *what* sent?

Answer: *mayor* (subject)

Step 5: Mayor sent *who* or *what*?

Answer: *ideas* (direct object)

Step 6: Mayor sent ideas *to whom* or *for whom*?

Answer: *City Council* (indirect object)

Sentence 5: We bought three back issues of *National Geographic* for your use.

    Step 1: We bought three back issues. . . .

    Step 2: We bought three back issues.

          Tomorrow, we *will buy* three back issues.

          Bought is the verb.

    Step 3: *Bought* is an action verb.

    Step 4: *Who* or *what* bought?

          Answer: *we* (subject)

    Step 5: We bought *who* or *what*?

          Answer: *issues* (direct object)

    Step 6: We bought issues *to whom* or *for whom*?

          Answer: none (Remember, *for your use* is a prepositional phrase.)

Sentence 6: Do you really understand these solutions to the problem?

    Step 1: Do you really understand these solutions. . . .

    Step 2: Do you really understand these solutions?

          Yesterday, *did* you really *understand* these solutions?

          Do understand is the verb.

          (Did you remember that *do* is usually a helping verb?)

    Step 3: *Do understand* is an action verb.

    Step 4: *Who* or *what* do understand?

          Answer: *you* (subject)

    Step 5: You do understand *who* or *what*?

          Answer: *solutions* (direct object)

    Step 6: You do understand solutions *to whom* or *for whom*?

          Answer: none

          (You didn't answer with *problems*, did you? Remember, you crossed that out in the prepositional phrase in Step 1.)

Sentence 7: The essay-contest winners were a young man in my neighborhood and a woman in the next town.

    Step 1: The essay-contest winners were a young man . . . and a woman . . . .

    Step 2: The essay-contest winners were a young man and a woman.

          Tomorrow, the essay-contest winners *will be* a young man and a woman.

          Were is the verb.

    Step 3: *Were* is a linking verb.

    Step 4: *Who* or *what* were?

          Answer: *winners* (subject)

    Step 5: If you have a linking verb, skip to Step 7.

    Step 7: Winners were *who* or *what*?

          Answer: *man* and *woman* (compound predicate words)

Sentence 8: Funds from the state government financed local road improvements.

Step 1: Funds . . . financed local road improvements.

Step 2: Funds financed local road improvements.

Tomorrow, funds *will finance* local road improvements.

Financed is the verb.

Step 3: *Financed* is an action verb.

Step 4: *Who* or *what* financed?

Answer: *funds* (subject)

Step 5: Funds financed who or *what*?

Answer: *improvements* (direct object)

Step 6: Funds made improvements *to whom* or *for whom*?

Answer: none

Sentence 9: With his courage, he will win a medal for bravery.

Step 1: . . . he will win a medal. . . .

Step 2: He will win a medal.

Yesterday, he *won* a medal.

Will win is the verb.

Step 3: *Will win* is an action verb.

Step 4: *Who* or *what* will win?

Answer: *he* (subject)

Step 5: He will win *who* or *what*?

Answer: *medal* (direct object)

Step 6: He will win medal *to whom* or *for whom*?

Answer: none

Sentence 10: Most young speakers appear nervous but usually steel themselves with determination.

Step 1: Most young speakers appear nervous but usually steel themselves. . . .

Step 2: Most young speakers appear nervous but usually steel themselves.

Tomorrow, most young speakers *will appear* nervous but usually *will steel* themselves.

Appear and *steel* are the verbs.

Step 3: *Appear* is a linking verb. (Substitute *are* to test the verb.)

Steel is an action verb.

Step 4: *Who* or *what* appear?

Answer: *speakers* (subject)

Who or *what* steel?

Answer: *speakers* (subject)

Step 5: (Here is the tricky part. You have *both* an action verb and a linking verb. So you will need to do Step 5 with the verb *steel* and skip to Step 7 with the verb *appear*.)

Speakers steel *who* or *what*?

Answer: *themselves* (direct object)

Step 6: Speakers steel themselves *to whom* or *for whom*?

Answer: none

Step 7: Speakers appear *who* or *what*?

Answer: *nervous* (predicate word)

Sentence 11: The basketball referee called a personal foul on Roberto.

Step 1: The basketball referee called a personal foul. . . .

Step 2: The basketball referee called a personal foul.

Tomorrow, the basketball referee *will call* a personal foul.

Called is the verb.

Step 3: *Called* is an action verb.

Step 4: *Who* or *what called*?

Answer: *referee* (subject)

Step 5: Referee called *who* or *what*?

Answer: *foul* (direct object)

Sentence 12: Some of these civic-minded people have been buying their out-of-town friends souvenirs from our city.

Step 1: Some . . . have been buying their out-of-town friends souvenirs. . . .

Step 2: Some have been buying their out-of-town friends souvenirs.

Yesterday, some *had been buying* their out-of-town friends souvenirs.

Have been buying is the verb.

Step 3: *Have been buying* is an action verb.

Step 4: *Who* or *what* have been buying?

Answer: *some* (subject)

Step 5: Some have been buying *who* or *what*?

Answer: *souvenirs* (direct object)

(Remember, they did not buy their friends!)

Step 6: Some have been buying souvenirs *to whom* or *for whom*?

Answer: *friends* (indirect object)

3

Agreement of Subject and Verb

Now that you have grasped the basics of general "grammar," we are ready to talk about the real problems with writing and speaking: usage. The first of these usage problems deals with agreement of a subject with its verb.

Agreement of subject and verb is, for the most part, a learned speech pattern. Many of us grew up saying "the boy walks" and "the boys walk." Sometimes, however, problem situations occur in which our learned patterns defeat us. These situations are what we need to talk about in this chapter.

BASIC PREMISES

Let us start with three basic premises:

1. Subjects can be singular (referring to one) or plural (referring to more than one).

    Examples: The *apple* (singular) is rotten.

    The *apples* (plural) are rotten.

2. Verbs can be singular or plural.

    Examples: The child *talks* (singular) constantly.

    The children *talk* (plural) constantly.

    NOTE: Subjects add *-s* to form the *plural,* and verbs add *-s* to form the *singular.*

    Apple is singular. *Talks* is singular. *Apples* is plural. *Talk* is plural.

3. Subjects must agree in number with their verbs. Singular subjects must have singular verbs. Plural subjects must have plural verbs.

    Examples: *He* (singular subject) *walks* (singular verb).

    They (plural subject) *walk* (plural verb).

    With these basic premises in mind, let us now consider the problems that occur in subject-verb agreement.

ROAD MAP

- *Basic Premises*
- *Choosing the Subject*
- *Indefinite Pronouns*
- *Compound Subjects*
- *Collective Nouns*
- *Nouns Plural in Form*
- *Practice*
- *GED Practice*

PROBLEM 1: CHOOSING THE SUBJECT

A problem occurs when the writer is confused about choosing the subject. Since the verb must agree with its subject, not recognizing the subject will result in a glaring error! (A review of Chapter 2 may help here.) Three specific situations seem to cause the most frequent problems among GED candidates:

Situation A

Sometimes the writer has difficulty locating the subject when words come between the subject and its verb. These words may be prepositional phrases, verbal phrases, or clauses. Such words cause a problem because the writer's "natural" patterns make him want the verb to agree with the nearest noun—which may not be the subject.

Example 1:   The box of apples is beginning to rot.

(Is beginning must agree with its subject *box,* not with *apples* in the prepositional phrase.)

Example 2:   The cars, washed and shined with care, sit ready for the parade.

(Sit must agree with its subject *cars.* The verbal phrase *washed and shined with care* cannot alter the subject-verb agreement.)

Example 3:   Those motorcycles that roar up and down the street cause disturbance for the hospital.

(Cause must agree with its subject, *motorcycles.* The clause *that roar up and down the street* cannot alter the subject-verb agreement.)

Warning: Some prepositional phrases logically make a subject appear to be plural:

with   as well as
along with   in addition to
together with

But prepositional phrases *cannot* alter the noun-subject.

Example 1:   The doctor, together with his two assistants, is working desperately.

(Is working must agree with its subject, *doctor.* The prepositional phrase *together with his two assistants* cannot alter the subject-verb agreement, even though logic wants you to call that verb plural.)

Example 2:   My neighbor, along with her two German shepherds, walks across the pasture daily to visit.

(Walks must agree with its subject, *neighbor.* Do not let the prepositional phrase *along with her two German shepherds* interfere.)

Example 3:   The television set, in addition to the water heater and the furnace, was damaged by the lightning.

(Was agrees with the subject *set.* Ignore those prepositional phrases!)

Situation B

Sometimes the writer may have difficulty locating the subject when the subject comes after the verb. If, for instance, the sentence begins with *here* or *there,* the subject comes *after* the verb.

Example 1: There are three seats empty.

(Seats *are.*)

Example 2: Here is the letter I was looking for.

(Letter *is*).

Other sentences may also have the subject appearing after the verb:

Example 1: Into the office charge the supervisor and her assistant.

(Supervisor and assistant *charge.*)

Example 2: Where are the old newspapers?

(Newspapers *are.*)

Example 3: Who are the girl in the ski outfit and the girl in the tennis dress?

(Girl and girl *are.*)

Situation C

Sometimes the writer is confused by the choice of subject if the subject is singular and the predicate word is plural—or vice-versa. He may think the verb *sounds* wrong; but the verb must agree with its subject, not its predicate word.

Example 1: Physical conditioning and mental attitude are the winning combination.

(Conditioning and attitude *are.*)

Example 2: The winning combination is physical conditioning and mental attitude.

(Combination *is.*)

WARNING

A verb must agree with its subject, not its predicate word.

PROBLEM 2: INDEFINITE PRONOUNS

A problem occurs when indefinite pronouns appear. (Remember from Chapter 1 that pronouns are merely noun substitutes.) There are three groups of indefinite pronouns:

Group A

Indefinite pronouns that are always singular:

someone	anyone	everyone
somebody	anybody	everybody
each	one	either
nobody	no one	neither

The easiest way to remember these singular words is to think *single one* or *one* with each:

some [single] *one*
some [single] *body*
every [single] *one*
each [single one]
neither [one]

Example 1: *Everyone* in the office is too warm to work effectively.

(Think, "every [single] one *is.*")

Example 2: *Neither* of the mechanics wants to work on Sunday.

(Think, "neither [one] *wants.*")

Example 3: *Everybody* seated in the last two rows resents being asked to move forward.

(Think, "every [single] body *resents*.")

Example 4: *Each* of my friends calls me once a week.

(Think, "each [one] *calls*.")

Group B
Indefinite pronouns that are always plural:

several
few
both
many

These words are especially easy to remember since they all *mean* "more than one."

Example 1: Both of the books require careful reading.

(Both *require*.)

Example 2: Several of the fielders regularly run 4 or 5 miles a day.

(Several *run*.)

Group C
Indefinite pronouns that can be singular or plural:

some   all
any   most
none

To determine whether these words are singular or plural, look at the prepositional phrase that follows.

Example 1: Some of the sugar is on the floor.

(Since *some* can be singular or plural, look at *sugar* to decide: *sugar is*.)

Example 2: Some of the apples are in the sink.

(Since *some* can be singular or plural, look at *apples* to decide: *apples are*.)

PROBLEM 3: COMPOUND SUBJECTS

A problem occurs when there are compound subjects. Three kinds of compound situations occur:

Situation A
Two subjects joined by *and* will always take a plural verb:

1 and 1	=	2
doctor and nurse		work
1 and 2	=	3
doctor and nurses		work
2 and 1	=	3
doctors and nurse		work

NOTE: Some peculiar combinations occur that are logically singular. For these, use the singular verb.

Example 1: *Peaches and cream is* my favorite desert.

Example 2: *My sister and best friend is* Mary Ann.

Situation B

Two singular subjects joined by *or* or *nor* will take a singular verb:

1 or 1	=	1
doctor or nurse		*works*
1 nor 1	=	0
doctor nor nurse		*works*

Situation C

A singular subject and a plural subject joined by *or* or *nor* will take a singular or plural verb, depending on which subject is nearer the verb:

1 or 2	=	2
doctor or		*nurses work*
2 or 1	=	1
doctors or		*nurse works*
1 nor 2	=	2
doctor nor		*nurses work*
2 nor 1	=	1
doctors nor		*nurse works*

Consider the following examples for all three compound-subject situations:

Example 1: Neither Ellen *nor* her *cousins are* planning a vacation.

(1 nor 2 = 2)

Example 2: Neither her cousins *nor Ellen is* planning a vacation.

(2 nor 1 = 1)

Example 3: Both her cousins *and Ellen are* planning a vacation.

(2 and 1 = 3)

Example 4: Ellen *or* her *cousin is* planning a vacation.

(1 or 1 = 1)

PROBLEM 4: COLLECTIVE NOUNS

A problem occurs when the subject is a collective noun that can be singular or plural. Collective nouns are nouns that represent a group: *team, jury, cast, class, crew, audience.*

Situation A

Collective nouns are *singular* when the group works together as a unit.

Example 1: The *team runs* enthusiastically onto the floor.

(The team works together as a unit.)

Example 2: The *jury has reached* its verdict.

(The jury functions as a unit in reaching a verdict.)

Situation B

Collective nouns are *plural* when the members of the group are acting individually.

Example 1: The *team are putting* on their uniforms.

(Each team member acts individually to put on his own uniform. If we said, "The team *is* putting on its uniform," we would have the entire team in one uniform! How unhandy!)

Example 2: The *jury have argued* for three hours.

(Each individual jury member is presenting his point of view.)

Hint: Often the meaning of the sentence will tell you whether the collective noun is singular or plural, but sometimes additional hints appear—like plural pronouns.

Example 1: The jury reaches *its* decision after much deliberation.

(The singular *its* gave a hint that *jury* is singular.)

Example 2: The crew take *their places* five minutes before curtain time.

(The plural *their* and *places* give a hint that *crew* is plural. Of course, the entire crew could not be in one spot anyway!)

PROBLEM 5: NOUNS PLURAL IN FORM

A problem occurs when words look plural but are not. Three such situations occur.

Situation A

Some words end in -*s* but represent a single thing: *news, measles, mumps*. These words need singular verbs.

Example 1: The six o'clock *news is* about to begin.

Example 2: *Measles* sometimes *has* rather serious side effects.

Warning: Some words end in -*s* and *seem* to represent a single thing, but there are two *parts* to that single thing. Then the verb is plural. Consider words like *pants, scissors, trousers, shears,* and *pliers.*

Example 1: The *scissors are* on the desk.

Example 2: Here *are* the *pliers.*

Situation B

Words that end in -*ics* are usually singular: *politics, mathematics, civics, ethics, economics, athletics.* These words are *singular* when they refer to a study, science, or practice.

Example 1: *Politics is* an interesting avocation.

Example 2: *Mathematics is* his favorite subject.

Example 3: *Economics is* a course required for high school graduation.

Warning: These words are *plural* when they have modifiers in front of them.

Example 1: *His politics are* somewhat divided.

(The singular modifier *his* makes *politics* plural.)

Example 2: *The mathematics* of the tax return *are* flawless.

(*The* makes *mathematics* plural.)

Example 3: *The school's athletics are* all for both males and females.

(The modifiers *the school's* make *athletics* plural.)

HINT

Words that end in -*ics* are usually singular.

Situation C

Some words that have become part of our language retain their original foreign plural forms:

Singular	Plural
datum	data
alumnus	alumni
memorandum	memoranda

Because we usually see these words in the plural form, we sometimes forget the singular form and thereby use the wrong verb form. Consider these examples:

Example 1: The *data were collected* by a licensed agency.

Example 2: The *memoranda are* easily *read and understood.*

Situation D

Titles that are plural still represent a single thing, so the title needs a singular verb.

Example 1: *Great Expectations presents* universal themes for all of us to consider.

Example 2: *A Man for All Seasons is playing* at our local theater.

Situation E

Some nouns in the plural form represent an amount, a fraction, or an element of time. Those nouns are considered *singular.*

Hint: Try substituting the words *that amount* for the phrase. If the substitution works, the phrase is singular. If you need to substitute with *that number,* for countable items, then the phrase is plural.

Example 1: *Sixty minutes is* too much time to spend eating.

(*That amount* of time is too much time to spend eating.)

Compare: *Sixty minutes seem* to be passing rapidly on the timer's clock!

(*That number* of minutes—countable—is passing.)

Example 2: *Five dollars is* what that hamburger costs.

(*That amount* is what that hamburger costs.)

Compare: *Five one-dollar bills are* all he had with him.

(*That number* of bills—countable—is what he had.)

Example 3: *Three-fourths* of the pie is gone.

(*That amount* of the pie is gone.)

Compare: *Three-fourths* of the cars are gone from the parking lot.

(*That number* is gone. Cars are countable.)

Example 4: *Sixty pounds is* an excessive weight to mail.

(*That amount* is an excessive weight.)

Compare: *Sixty pounds* of cornmeal were sold to sixty customers yesterday.

(*That number* of pounds were sold.)

If you can master the solutions to these five problems, chances are you will have little or no difficulty in using the correct verb form to agree with the subject, and you'll sail through the GED questions about subject-verb agreement!

PRACTICE
EXERCISE 1

Directions: Try the following sentences to test yourself for understanding of all ten rules. Check your answers with those that follow. Problem and situation references are given so that you can review anything you may not have mastered yet.

1. An Indian headdress and two beaded moccasins (was/were) in the museum window.
2. The boss's memoranda (is/are) filed away safely.
3. The neighbor, along with three of his friends, (is/are) going to Canada for a fishing trip.
4. Few of the trees (lose/loses) their leaves in spring.
5. *Three Faces of Eve* (is/are) a study in psychology.
6. Someone in one of these neighborhoods (is/are) on the mayor's investigative committee.
7. His ethics (requires/require) scrutiny.
8. All his friends (wishes/wish) him well and hope that all happiness (is/are) his.
9. None of the sunshine (seeps/seep) into the inner part of the house.
10. Everybody (knows/know) his part!
11. We thought five dollars (was/were) a fair donation.
12. Neither of the young men (was/were) recognized for outstanding contributions.
13. Neither the managers nor the supervisor (understands/understand) the complexity of the situation.
14. The crew (was/were) working at their respective jobs.
15. The bowl of bananas (is/are) tempting.
16. Everyone in the room (sees/see) opportunity knocking.
17. The baby and his mother (is/are), according to all reports, doing well.
18. Any of the nails that you don't use (is/are) returnable.
19. Although it is usually thought of as a childhood disease, measles (is/are) even more serious as an adult disease.
20. Mathematics (is/are) his favorite subject.
21. I hope somebody (sings/sing) the national anthem.
22. His hobby (is/are) butterflies.
23. Neither the carpenter nor the cabinet maker (was/were) willing to build the fancy shelves.
24. Both (is/are) excellent lecturers.
25. The city's economics (is/are) unsettled.
26. The financial advisor, in addition to the City Council members, (plans/plan) to complete additional reports for the year's end.
27. Their team usually (has/have) a successful season.
28. Miss Altheide or her two nieces (plans/plan) to attend the card party.

29. Some students (is/are) hoping that some achievement (is/are) forthcoming.

30. His tractor, as well as the plows, discs, and drills, (needs/need) regular maintenance.

31. Oil lamps (is/are) a good source of light.

32. Either crickets or minnows (makes/make) good fishing bait.

33. Three-fourths of his chickens (is/are) good layers.

34. Onto the rodeo grounds (charges/charge) a wild bull.

35. Politics (enters/enter) nearly everyone's life.

36. Seven one-dollar bills (brings/bring) him luck, he thinks.

37. Two cats and a dog (sleeps/sleep) together at my house.

38. That tree, which has heart-shaped leaves, (is/are) especially ornamental.

39. *60 Minutes* usually (airs/air) on Sunday evening.

40. Neither the roll-top desk nor the two electric typewriters (belongs/belong) to him.

41. As soon as the data (is/are) collected, the administration can give the results.

42. Athletics (is/are) a major part of her life.

43. The cast (performs/perform) admirably.

44. Either the scrubber or the precipitator (is/are) not functioning properly at the power-generating plant.

45. There (is/are) three people waiting to talk with the congressman.

EXERCISE—ANSWERS

1. headdress and moccasins *were* (Problem 3, Situation A)

2. memoranda *are* (Problem 5, Situation C)

3. neighbor *is* (Problem 1, Situation A)

4. few *lose* (Problem 2, Group B)

5. *Three Faces of Eve is* (Problem 5, Situation D)

6. someone *is* (Problem 2, Group A)

7. ethics *require* (Problem 5, Situation B)

8. all (friends) *wish and hope* (Problem 2, Group C) all (happiness) *is* (Problem 2, Group C)

9. none (sunshine) *seeps* (Problem 2, Group C)

10. everybody *knows* (Problem 2, Group A)

11. five dollars (that amount) *was* (Problem 5, Situation E)

12. neither *was* (Problem 2, Group A)

13. neither managers nor supervisor *understands* (Problem 3, Situation C)

14. crew *were* at *their* jobs (Problem 4, Situation B)

15. bowl *is* (Problem 1, Situation A)

16. everyone *sees* (Problem 2, Group A)

17. baby and mother *are* (Problem 3, Situation A)

18. any (nails) *are* (Problem 2, Group C)

19. measles *is* (Problem 5, Situation A)

20. mathematics *is* (Problem 5, Situation B)

21. somebody *sings* (Problem 2, Group A)

22. hobby *is* (Problem 1, Situation C)

23. neither carpenter nor cabinet maker *was* (Problem 3, Situation B)

24. both *are* (Problem 2, Group B)

25. economics *are* (Problem 5, Situation B)

26. advisor *plans* (Problem 1, Situation A)

27. team *has* (Problem 4, Situation A)

28. Miss Altheide or nieces *plan* (Problem 3, Situation C)

29. some (students) *are* (Problem 2, Group C) some (achievement) *is* (Problem 2, Group C)

30. tractor *needs* (Problem 1, Situation A)

31. lamps *are* (Problem 1, Situation C)

32. either crickets or minnows *make* (Problem 2, Group A)

33. three-fourths (that number of chickens) *are* (Problem 5, Situation E)

34. bull *charges* (Problem 1, Situation B)

35. politics *enters* (Problem 5, Situation B)

36. bills (that number) *bring* (Problem 5, Situation E)

37. cats and a dog *sleep* (Problem 3, Situation A)

38. tree *is* (Problem 1, Situation A)

39. *60 Minutes airs* (Problem 5, Situation D)

40. neither desk nor typewriters *belong* (Problem 3, Situation C)

41. data *are* (Problem 5, Situation C)

42. athletics *is* (Problem 5, Situation B)

43. cast *performs* (Problem 4, Situation A)

44. either scrubber or precipitator *is* (Problem 3, Situation B)

45. people *are* (Problem 1, Situation B)

GED PRACTICE

Since this is your first opportunity to practice with the GED Language Arts, Writing exam format, notice what the format includes. For all of the multiple-choice questions on the exam, you will be given informational text. The text will be 200–250 words and include twenty or fewer sentences. Then you'll be asked questions about how those sentences should be corrected.

In this first practice, you'll find a shorter text. You'll also find only three possible answers. As you work your way through this practice book and become more comfortable with the GED format, we will increase the length to that typically found on the GED exam. By the time you finish this book, you will have had ample practice with the full-length format.

> **Directions**: Now that you have worked your way through isolated sentences in the exercise above, apply your understanding to the following passage. First, read the entire passage, and then choose the letter of the correct subject-verb agreement. Note that this segment is set up in the same manner as the GED exam. When you finish, check your answers below.

Lewisport Art Exhibit

(1) When the artists and Ms. Karl comes to Lewisport to exhibit their work, spectators will see a wide variety of styles and media. (2) For instance, the paintings from the student group shows works in oil and tempera. (3) Pastels or ink drawings show representative works by the master herself. (4) Because the media Ms. Karl uses is widely varied, her most successful students' work shows a blend of techniques, all learned from Karl's examples. (5) Neither the students nor Ms. Karl, however, is recognized for work in sculpture, and works in any kind of wood tends to be primitive at best. (6) Nevertheless, a visitor to the exhibit, like the art critics themselves, is likely to find something impressive. (7) Since ethics are not part of the exhibit, however, some critics may find certain artistic subject matter to be in poor taste.

1. Sentence 1: When the artists and Ms. Karl comes to Lewisport to exhibit their work, spectators will see a wide variety of styles and media.

   What correction should be made to the sentence?

   (1) Change <u>comes</u> to <u>come.</u>
   (2) Change <u>see</u> to <u>sees.</u>
   (3) No correction is necessary.

2. Sentence 2: For instance, the paintings from the student group shows works in oil and tempera.

   What correction should be made to the sentence?

   (1) Change <u>shows</u> to <u>show.</u>
   (2) Change <u>works</u> to <u>work.</u>
   (3) No correction is necessary.

3. Sentence 3: Pastels or ink drawings show representative works by the master herself.

   What correction should be made to the sentence?

   (1) Change <u>drawings</u> to <u>drawing</u>.
   (2) Change <u>show</u> to <u>shows</u>.
   (3) No correction is necessary.

4. Sentence 4: Because the media Ms. Karl uses is widely varied, her most successful students' work shows a blend of techniques, all learned from Karl's examples.

   What correction should be made to the sentence?

   (1) Change <u>uses</u> to <u>use</u>.
   (2) Change <u>is</u> to <u>are</u>.
   (3) Change <u>shows</u> to <u>show</u>.
   (4) No correction is necessary.

5. Sentence 5: Neither the students nor Ms. Karl, however, is recognized for work in sculpture, and works in any kind of wood tends to be primitive at best.

   What correction should be made to the sentence?

   (1) Change <u>is</u> to <u>are</u>.
   (2) Change <u>tends</u> to <u>tend</u>.
   (3) Change <u>is</u> to <u>are</u> and change <u>tends</u> to <u>tend</u>.
   (4) No correction is necessary.

6. Sentence 6: Nevertheless, a visitor to the exhibit, like the art critics themselves, is likely to find something impressive.

   What correction should be made to the sentence?

   (1) Change <u>critics</u> to <u>critic</u>.
   (2) Change <u>is</u> to <u>are</u>.
   (3) Change <u>find</u> to <u>finds</u>.
   (4) No correction is necessary.

7. Sentence 7: Since ethics are not part of the exhibit, however, some critics may find certain artistic subject matter to be in poor taste.

   What correction should be made to the sentence?

   (1) Change <u>are</u> to <u>is</u>.
   (2) Change <u>critics</u> to <u>critic</u>.
   (3) Change <u>find</u> to <u>finds</u>.
   (4) No correction is necessary.

GED PRACTICE—ANSWERS

1. (1) artists and Ms. Karl *come* (Problem 3, Situation A)
2. (1) paintings *show* (Problem 1, Situation A)
3. (3) (correct)
4. (2) media *are* (Problem 5, Situation C)
5. (2) works *tend* (Problem 1, Situation A)
6. (4) (correct)
7. (1) ethics *is* (Problem 5, Situation B)

Using Nouns Correctly

Nouns cause a few headaches for beginning writers. Mostly the headaches come from making nouns plural and/or possessive. And nouns that name specific people, places, or things are capitalized. So let's look at all the rules for using nouns correctly.

PART 1: RULES FOR PLURALS

Rule 1

Make most nouns plural by adding –s or –es.

Compare these nouns and their plurals:

an application form	two application forms
my desk	all desks
a delivery truck	both delivery trucks
a cleaning brush	two cleaning brushes
your stop watch	our stop watches

Rule 2

Some nouns have odd plural forms.

Compare these nouns and their plurals:

businessman	two businessmen
your child	her children
a computer mouse	two computer mice
a white-tailed deer	two white-tailed deer
one piece of datum	all of the data

Most people probably can't remember all the odd plural forms. When in doubt, check your dictionary. If a word has an odd plural, the dictionary will note that form after the abbreviation *pl.*, for *plural*.

(For more information about forming possessives, see Chapter 13, Part III.)

PART 2: RULES FOR POSSESSIVES

We use possessive forms to show ownership. Forming the plurals correctly, however, can be a bit confusing. Here are the simple rules:

Rule 1

For most singular nouns, add an apostrophe followed by an –s to show possession.

Example: The *driver's* clipboard lay on the *truck's* dashboard.

ROAD MAP

- *Rules for Plurals*
- *Rules for Possessives*
- *Rules for Capitalizing*
- *Practice*
- *GED Practice*

Rule 2

For most plural nouns, add an apostrophe after the *–s* to show possession.

Example: The *drivers'* clipboards lay on their respective *trucks'* dashboards.

Compare these additional examples:

Singular Possessive	Plural Possessive
hard drive's data	hard drives' data
computer's memory	computers' memories
Web site's address	Web sites' addresses

Rule 3

With nouns that have odd plural forms, treat them like singular nouns. Add an apostrophe followed by an *–s* to show ownership.

Example: The security guard found a *man's* sport coat in the *men's* locker room.

(*Man's* is singular possessive and *men's* is plural possessive.)

Compare these additional singular and plural possessives:

the goose's feathers	two geese's feathers
the memorandum's message	several memoranda's messages
a child's mother	both children's mother

Now that you have studied how to make nouns plural and possessive, study this chart, which puts together all the rules:

Singular	Singular Possessive	Plural	Plural Possessive
a computer file	a computer file's data	several computer files	several computer files' data
a file box	a file box's labels	both file boxes	both file boxes' labels
the boss	the boss's orders	too many bosses	too many bosses' orders
one workman	one workman's rights	all workmen	all workmen's rights

PART 3: RULES FOR CAPITALIZING

The following four rules for capitalization cover most common needs.

Rule 1: Capitalize the First Word in Sentences

Example: *The* news anchor reported the disputes.

Rule 2: Capitalize Titles

Titles of people: *Dr.* Karla Jeffers, *Mrs.* Todd, *President* Bush, *Senator* Lugar, *Uncle* Bob, *Grandmother* Dixon, *Father* Mason

> **Warning:** Do *not* capitalize common nouns: *Mother,* but *my mother; Grandmother Dixon,* but *his grandmother; Senator Lugar,* but *a senator.*

Titles of Publications, Works of Art: "Stress in the Work Place," *Gone with the Wind, U.S. News and World Report,* the *Mona Lisa.*

> **NOTE:** Book and magazine titles are italicized (or underlined) and article and chapter titles are enclosed in quotation marks.

> **Warning:** Do *not* capitalize *a, an,* and *the* or prepositions in titles *unless* they come at the beginning or end of the title: *From Here to Eternity, The Comedy of Neil Simon*

WARNING

Do *not* capitalize titles that appear *after* names: *Dr.* Karla Jeffers, but Karla Jeffers *the doctor.*

Rule 3: Capitalize Proper Names and Words Made From the Proper Names

Names of days, months, holidays: *Monday, February, Thanksgiving* (but not seasons: *spring, autumn*)

Geographic names: *Scott County, Miami, Alaska, Lake Michigan, Missouri River, Rocky Mountains, France,* the *Midwest,* the *South* (but not *midwestern* or directions: *north, south*), *Williams Street* (but not *street* and not *streets* as in *the corner of Williams and Main streets*)

Business names: *Ford Motor Company, Kleenex, Pepsi, Scotch* tape

School names and subjects: *Oakland City College, World Economics 202* (but not *economics*), *Geography I* (but not *geography*)

Religious names and pronouns: *Trinity Lutheran Church,* the *Koran, God, His* teachings, *Buddha, Mennonite*

Names of people and languages: *Roman, Chinese, Vietnamese*

Abbreviations of proper names: *CST* (Central Standard Time), *NATO* (North Atlantic Treaty Organization), *FBI* (Federal Bureau of Investigation)

Rule 4: Capitalize the First Word and All Nouns in the Salutation of a Letter and the First Word in the Closing of a Letter

Example: *Dear Mr. Warner, My dear Miss Sarah; Fondly yours, Sincerely*

PRACTICE
EXERCISE 1

Directions: From the words in parentheses, choose the correct noun form for the following sentences.

1. Home medical (supplyers, suppliers, supplier's, suppliers') allow many people to continue to live at home, even after they face serious medical (problem's, problems, problems').

2. The delivery (truck's, trucks, trucks') logo said "Home Medical Services, Inc."

3. For the route driver who makes (delivery's, deliveries, deliveries'), the job may seem routine.

4. For home-bound (patient's, patients, patients'), however, an on-time delivery can mean life or death.

5. Four (memorandums, memoranda, memorandas) announced various new (positions, position's, positions') within the delivery system.

6. Several oxygen (tanks, tank's, tanks') labels were smudged and partially illegible.

7. If (address's, addresses, addresses') are difficult to find, drivers will get clearly written directions.

8. Obscured house (numbers, number's, numbers') cause (drivers, driver's drivers') to lose time finding addresses.

9. All (drivers, driver's drivers') routes are posted each morning.

10. Representatives from the insurance (companys, companies, company's) will answer your questions about home medical services.

EXERCISE 1—ANSWERS

1. suppliers, problems
2. truck's
3. deliveries
4. patients
5. memoranda, positions
6. tanks'
7. addresses
8. numbers, drivers
9. drivers'
10. companies

EXERCISE 2

Directions: Add capital letters where needed. Answers follow and refer you to specific rules.

1. the french delegation visited chicago, illinois, and stopped to shop at bloomingdale's.

2. please plan to arrive at 1412 wilmont street by 9:00 est if you want to meet senator johnston.

3. as ernest explained, "working late on the north side of town is okay from march through october, but the drive along riverview expressway is treacherous in winter."

4. since he hails from the west, professor stuart wears boots and hats reminiscent of john wayne movies.

5. a book called *jobs for everyone* gives good tips on how to make the most of one's skills.

6. carlos mailed the check on saturday at the city post office, but by wednesday it still had not reached st. louis, missouri.

7. when my uncle harry met your uncle, they traded world war ii stories about the south pacific.

8. at the corner of main and division streets stands a magazine store that always has copies of *usa today*.

9. are some of your chinese friends buddhists?

10. on new year's day we always eat cabbage since our polish family is superstitious.

EXERCISE 2—ANSWERS

1. The (first word in sentence), French (nationality), Chicago, Illinois (geographic names), Bloomingdale's (business)

2. Please (first word in sentence), Wilmont Street (geographic name), EST (abbreviation of proper name: Eastern Standard Time), Senator Johnston (title of person)

3. As (first word in sentence), Ernest (proper name), Working (first word in quoted sentence), March, October, (months), Riverview Expressway (geographic name)

4. Since (first word in sentence), West (geographic region), Professor Stuart (title of person), John Wayne (proper name)

5. A (first word in sentence), *Jobs for Everyone* (book title)

6. Carlos (proper name and first word in sentence), Saturday, Wednesday (days of week), St. Louis, Missouri (geographic name)

7. When (first word in sentence), Uncle Harry (title), World War II (proper name), South Pacific (geographic area)

8. At (first word in sentence), Main, Division (geographic names), *USA Today* (title of newspaper)

9. Are (first word in sentence), Chinese (nationality), Buddhists (religious reference)

10. On (first word in sentence), New Year's Day (holiday), Polish (nationality)

GED PRACTICE

Directions: Read the passage below. Then apply the rules for correct noun usage to choose the answers to the questions that follow. Note that this practice exercise is set up the way the multiple-choice portion of the GED exam is presented.

Transplanting Techniques for Summer Annuals

A

(1) *My Mother always started seedlings on a South windowsill, usually beginning in early spring, perhaps the middle of march.* (2) *Living in the midwest in Southern Indiana meant guarding against frost until late spring, maybe even early May.* (3) *So, depending on where you live, you may start your transplanting as early as the last week of March or the first week of April.* (4) *And depending on whether you start seedlings on your windowsill or buy them from the Nursery, you may need to take different precautions when you transplant.*

B

(5) *To obtain the best survival rate for flowering annual's, follow these general guidelines for transplanting delicate seedlings into your outdoor summer garden.* (6) *First, keep the seedlings watered regularly until you're ready to transplant.* (7) *Place seedlings outdoors in sunlight appropriate for the plants habitat.* (8) *If nights' are still cool, you should "harden" the seedlings by leaving them out during the day but bringing them in at night until temperatures are well above freezing.* (9) *Next, work the garden soil, adding compost, sand, and/or fertilizer to prepare the soil most suitable to the plants needs.* (10) *Transplant the seedlings' into the prepared soil, setting roots at the same depth as they were in the seedlings packets.* (11) *Press soil lightly in place around the base of the plant.* (12) *Water well.*

1. Sentence 1: <u>My Mother</u> always started seedlings on a South windowsill, usually beginning in early spring, perhaps the middle of march.

   Which correction represents the best noun usage for the underlined portion of the sentence? If you think the original is the best usage, choose option (1).

   (1) My Mother
   (2) My mother
   (3) my Mother
   (4) my mother

2. Sentence 1: My Mother always started seedlings on <u>a South windowsill</u>, usually beginning in early spring, perhaps the middle of march.

   Which correction represents the best noun usage for the underlined portion of the sentence? If you think the original is the best usage, choose option (1).

   (1) a South windowsill
   (2) a south windowsill
   (3) a Southern windowsill
   (4) a South Windowsill

3. Sentence 1: My Mother always started seedlings on a South windowsill, usually beginning <u>in early spring</u>, perhaps the middle of march.

   Which correction represents the best noun usage for the underlined portion of the sentence? If you think the original is the best usage, choose option (1).

   (1)   in early spring
   (2)   in Early spring
   (3)   in early Spring
   (4)   in Early Spring

4. Sentence 1: My Mother always started seedlings on a South windowsill, usually beginning in early spring, perhaps <u>the middle of march.</u>

   Which correction represents the best noun usage for the underlined portion of the sentence? If you think the original is the best usage, choose option (1).

   (1)   the middle of march
   (2)   the Middle of march
   (3)   the Middle of March
   (4)   the middle of March

5. Sentence 2: Living <u>in the midwest in Southern Indiana</u> meant guarding against frost until late spring, maybe even early May.

   Which correction represents the best noun usage for the underlined portion of the sentence? If you think the original is the best usage, choose option (1).

   (1)   in the midwest in Southern Indiana
   (2)   in the midwest in southern Indiana
   (3)   in the Midwest in Southern Indiana
   (4)   in the Midwest in southern Indiana

6. Sentence 2: Living in the midwest in Southern Indiana meant guarding against frost <u>until late spring, maybe even early May.</u>

   Which correction represents the best noun usage for the underlined portion of the sentence? If you think the original is the best usage, choose option (1).

   (1)   until late spring, maybe even early May
   (2)   until late Spring, maybe even early May
   (3)   until late Spring, maybe even Early May
   (4)   until Late Spring, maybe even Early May

7. Sentence 3: So, depending on where you live, you may start your transplanting as early as the <u>last week of March or the first week of April.</u>

   Which correction represents the best noun usage for the underlined portion of the sentence? If you think the original is the best usage, choose option (1).

   (1)   last week of March of the first week of April
   (2)   last Week of March or the first Week of April
   (3)   last week of march or the first week of april
   (4)   Last Week of March of the First Week of April

8. Sentence 4: And depending on whether you start seedlings on your windowsill or buy them <u>from the Nursery</u>, you may need to take different precautions when you transplant.

   Which correction represents the best noun usage for the underlined portion of the sentence? If you think the original is the best usage, choose option (1).

   (1) from the Nursery
   (2) from the nursery
   (3) from The Nursery

9. Sentence 5: To obtain the best survival rate <u>for flowering annual's, follow these general guidelines</u> for transplanting delicate seedlings into your outdoor summer garden.

   Which correction represents the best noun usage for the underlined portion of the sentence? If you think the original is the best usage, choose option (1).

   (1) for flowering annual's, follow these general guidelines
   (2) for flowering annuals', follow these general guidelines
   (3) for flowering annual's, follow these general guidelines
   (4) for flowering annuals, follow these general guidelines
   (5) for flowering annual's, follow these general guideline's

10. Sentence 6: First, <u>keep the seedlings watered</u> regularly until you're ready to transplant.

    Which correction represents the best noun usage for the underlined portion of the sentence? If you think the original is the best usage, choose option (1).

    (1) keep the seedlings watered
    (2) keep the seedling's watered
    (3) keep the seedlings' watered

11. Sentence 7: Place seedlings outdoors in sunlight appropriate for <u>the plants habitat</u>.

    Which correction represents the best noun usage for the underlined portion of the sentence? If you think the original is the best usage, choose option (1).

    (1) the plants habitat
    (2) the plants' habitat
    (3) the plant's habitat

12. Sentence 8: <u>If nights' are still cool</u>, you should "harden" the seedlings by leaving them out during the day but bringing them in at night until temperatures are well above freezing.

    Which correction represents the best noun usage for the underlined portion of the sentence? If you think the original is the best usage, choose option (1).

    (1) If nights' are still cool
    (2) If night's are still cool
    (3) If nights are still cool

13. Sentence 8: If nights' are still cool, you should <u>"harden" the seedlings</u> by leaving them out during the day but bringing them in at night <u>until temperatures</u> are well above freezing.

    Which correction represents the best noun usage for the underlined portion of the sentence? If you think the original is the best usage, choose option (1).

    (1) "harden" the seedlings . . . until temperatures
    (2) "harden" the seedlings' . . . until temperatures
    (3) "harden" the seedlings . . . until temperatures'
    (4) "harden" the seedling's . . . until temperature's
    (5) "harden" the seedlings' . . . until temperature's

14. Sentence 9: Next, work the garden soil, adding compost, sand, and/or fertilizer to prepare the soil most suitable to <u>the plants needs</u>.

Which correction represents the best noun usage for the underlined portion of the sentence? If you think the original is the best usage, choose option (1).

(1) the plants needs
(2) the plant's needs
(3) the plants' needs

15. Sentence 10: <u>Transplant the seedlings'</u> into the prepared soil, setting roots at the same depth as they were in the seedlings packets.

Which correction represents the best noun usage for the underlined portion of the sentence? If you think the original is the best usage, choose option (1).

(1) Transplant the seedlings'
(2) Transplant the seedlings
(3) Transplant the seedling's

16. Sentence 10: Transplant the seedlings' into the prepared soil, <u>setting roots</u> at the same depth as they were in the seedlings packets.

Which correction represents the best noun usage for the underlined portion of the sentence? If you think the original is the best usage, choose option (1).

(1) setting roots
(2) setting roots'
(3) setting root's

17. Sentence 10: Transplant the seedlings' into the prepared soil, setting roots at the same depth as they were <u>in the seedlings packets</u>.

Which correction represents the best noun usage for the underlined portion of the sentence? If you think the original is the best usage, choose option (1).

(1) in the seedlings packets
(2) in the seedling's packets
(3) in the seedlings' packets
(4) in the seedlings' packet's

18. Sentence 11: Press soil lightly in place around the <u>base of the plant</u>.

Which correction represents the best noun usage for the underlined portion of the sentence? If you think the original is the best usage, choose option (1).

(1) base of the plant
(2) base's of the plant
(3) bases' of the plant
(4) bases's of the plant

GED PRACTICE—ANSWERS

1. (2) The word *mother* is not capitalized unless it's a title (the pronoun *my* shows it's not a title).

2. (2) *South* is not capitalized unless it refers to a geographical region or is part of a proper name, like *South Carolina.*

3. (1) Do not capitalize names of seasons.

4. (4) Capitalize the names of months.

5. (4) Capitalize geographical regions, but do not capitalize directions.

6. (1) Capitalize names of months, but do not capitalize names of seasons.

7. (1) Capitalize names of months.

8. (2) Do not capitalize common nouns.

9. (4) The word *annuals* is plural. It does not show ownership and therefore needs no apostrophe.

10. (1) The word *seedlings* is plural. It does not show ownership and therefore needs no apostrophe.

11. (2) The word *plants* is plural and shows possession of *habitat*; thus, you need an apostrophe after the –*s.*

12. (3) The word *nights* is plural. It does not show ownership and therefore needs no apostrophe.

13. (1) Both *seedlings* and *temperatures* are simple plurals showing no ownership.

14. (3) The word *plants* is both plural and possessive, so the apostrophe goes after the –*s.*

15. (2) *Seedlings* is a simple plural showing no ownership.

16. (1) *Roots* is a simple plural showing no ownership.

17. (3) *Seedlings* is plural and shows ownership of *packets*, so the apostrophe goes after the –*s.*

18. (1) No apostrophe is needed for the singular word *base.*

Using Pronouns Correctly

Pronouns, as we told you in Chapter 1, are simply noun substitutes. However, these noun substitutes can be a source of frustration only because you may not be sure which pronoun to use. Should you say "between you and I" or "between you and me"? Should you say "Us voters are registered" or "We voters are registered"? Should you say "Among those who played are George, Bill, and me" or ". . . George, Bill, and I"? Ten easy rules should solve all these problems for you.

RULE 1: SUBJECT PRONOUNS

The pronoun-subject of a sentence must be one of these pronouns:

I, you, he, she, it, we, or *they*

Usually a writer has no difficulty with this rule unless confused by compound parts.

Example: Barbara and (he/him) went to the new shopping mall.

To Test: Use the pronoun alone. Cross out the plural parts:

. . .*he* went to the new shopping mall.

Example: My sister and (her/she) planned to watch the late show.

. . . *she* planned to watch the late show.

When you write, you'll want to maintain the same pronouns throughout your essay. Avoid switching, for instance, from *we* to *you* or from *I* to *they.* (We'll talk more about consistent point of view in Chapter 19.)

RULE 2: PRONOUNS AS PREDICATE WORDS

If the pronoun is a predicate word, it must be in the same form as the subject. In other words, after a linking verb, you must use one of the following pronouns:

I, you, he, she, it, we, or *they*

Examples: It *was I* who called last night.

(I was.)

The man you need to see *is he* in the other room.
(He is.)

The people whom we met *were George and he.*

(George and he were.)

RULE 3: OBJECT PRONOUNS

If a pronoun is an object (direct object, indirect object, object of a preposition), use one of these pronouns:

me, you, him, her, it, us, or *them*

If you have trouble remembering which pronouns are used as objects, say the pronoun with *to*:

to me, to you, to him, to us, to them

To Test: Cross out the compound parts.

Example 1: The newspaper named Jose and (he/him) as the award recipients.

The newspaper named . . . *him* as the award recipients.

(*Him* is a direct object.)

Example 2: The carnival man sold (I/me) and (she/her) three tickets.

The carnival man sold *me* . . . three tickets.

(*Me* is an indirect object.)

The carnival man sold . . . *her* three tickets.

(*Her* is an indirect object.)

Example 3: The Bumbler of the Year Award was given to (he/him) and (I/me).

The Bumbler of the Year Award was given to *him* . . .

(*Him* is an object of the preposition *to*.)

The Bumbler of the Year Award was given to . . . *me*.

(*Me* is an object of the preposition *to*.)

HINT

As in Rule 1, you will probably have no trouble until you meet compound parts.

RULE 4: PRONOUNS WITH NOUNS

When a noun immediately follows a pronoun, cross out the noun to make finding the correct pronoun easier.

Example 1: (We/Us) beekeepers are a rather small group.

We . . . are a rather small group.

Example 2: The policeman helped (we/us) motorists through the heavily traveled intersection.

The policeman helped *us* . . . through the heavily traveled intersection.

Example 3: It was (we/us) taxpayers who needed help.

It was *we* . . . who needed help.

(Remember the linking verb here! That is Rule 2.)

RULE 5: PRONOUNS IN COMPARISON

When there is a pronoun in a comparison, complete the comparison to help you find the correct pronoun. (You can complete the comparison by adding a verb.)

Example 1: He is taller than (I/me).

He is taller than *I* [am].

Example 2: Jeremy works harder than (he/him).

Jeremy works harder than *he* [does].

Example 3: This young lady is as clever as (he/him).

This young lady is as clever as *he* [is].

RULE 6: PRONOUNS USED AS APPOSITIVES

When a pronoun is used as an appositive, it is in the same form as the word to which it refers. An appositive is a noun that renames another noun preceding it and is set off with commas: *My boss, Mr. Ratherwood, collects Indian relics. Mr. Ratherwood,* the appositive, renames *boss.* If the appositive refers to a subject, you will use the subject form. If the appositive refers to an object, you will use the object form. If the appositive refers to a predicate word, use the subject form.

> **NOTE**
>
> An appositive is a noun that renames another noun preceding it and is set off with commas.

Example 1: The two elected to the County Council, Gerry and (he/him), spoke to us.

Gerry and (he/him) is the appositive and refers to the subject, *two.* Since the appositive refers to a subject, you will use the subject form, *he.*

Example 2: The chairman introduced the evening's two speakers, Dorothea and (I/me).

Dorothea and (I/me) is the appositive and refers to the object *speakers.* Since the appositive refers to an object, you will use the object form, *me.*

To make the decision easier, try these two steps:

Step 1: Cross out the word or words to which the appositive refers.

Step 2: Read without any compound parts.

Application 1

Step 1: The two elected to the County Council, Gerry and (he/him), spoke to us.

. . . Gerry and (he/him), spoke to us.

Step 2: . . . (he/him) spoke to us.

Solution: He spoke to us.

Application 2

Step 1: Martin worked at the sawmill with his two friends, Billy Joe and (he/him).

Martin worked at the sawmill with . . . Billy Joe and (he/him).

Step 2: Martin worked at the sawmill with . . . (he/him).

Solution: Martin worked at the sawmill with *him.*

Application 3

Step 1: Two neighbors were professional photographers, Mrs. Martin and (he/him).

Two neighbors were . . . Mrs. Martin and (he/him).

Step 2: Two neighbors were . . . (he/him).

Solution: Two neighbors were *he* (and Mrs. Martin). (Remember to use the subject form after the linking verb! That is Rule 2 again!)

RULE 7: COMPOUND PRONOUNS

Do not use a compound pronoun unless the word it refers to is in the same sentence. The following are compound pronouns:

myself	herself	yourselves
yourself	itself	themselves
himself	ourselves	

Example 1: Incorrect: Those who bid on the barnwood picture frames were Mr. Lewis, Miss Qualls, and myself.

Correct: Those who bid on the barnwood picture frames were Mr. Lewis, Miss Qualls, and *I.*

Example 2: Incorrect: Himself was selected leader.

Correct: Jerome himself was selected leader.

(Now *himself* refers to *Jerome.*)

Example 3: Incorrect: Himself bought the antique pocket watch.

Correct: He bought the antique pocket watch *himself.*

(*Himself* refers to *he.*)

Example 4: Correct: Mother baked the whole-wheat breads for *herself.*

(*Herself* refers to *Mother.*)

RULE 8: WHO/WHOM

Use the pronouns *who* and *whom* the same way you would use *he* and *him. Who* is like *he* and *whom* is like *him.* (The *m*'s make remembering easy!)

Use these three steps to determine correct use of *who* or *whom*:

Step 1: Cross out everything up to *who* or *whom.*

Step 2: Reword the sentence as necessary.

Step 3: Substitute *he* or *him* for *who* or *whom.*

Application 1

Step 1: We didn't know (who/whom) could operate the new calculator.

. . . (who/whom) could operate the new calculator.

Step 2: (no rewording necessary)

Step 3: *He* could operate the new calculator.

Solution: We didn't know *who* could operate the new calculator.

Application 2

Step 1: I'm not sure (who/whom) you could ask for the money.

　　. . . (who/whom) you could ask for the money.

Step 2: You could ask (who/whom) for the money.

Step 3: You could ask *him* for the money.

Solution: I'm not sure *whom* you could ask for the money.

RULE 9: AGREEMENT

Pronouns must agree with the words to which they refer in both number and gender. In other words:

- If the pronoun refers to a singular word, the pronoun must be singular.
- If the pronoun refers to a plural word, the pronoun must be plural.
- If the pronoun refers to a masculine word, the pronoun must be masculine (*he, him, his*).
- If the pronoun refers to a feminine word, the pronoun must be feminine (*she, her, hers*).
- If the pronoun refers to a neuter word, it must be neuter (*it, its, their, theirs, they, them*).

(Obviously, the pronouns *I, we, you,* and *they* in all their forms can be either masculine or feminine.)

Study these comparisons:

Singular Nouns	Singular Pronouns
The telephone repair *person*	files *her* job report at the end of each day.
No *employee*	shares *his* computer password with anyone else.
Every cell phone *user*	should avoid using *his or her* phone while driving.

Plural Nouns	Plural pronouns
All cell phone *users*	should avoid using *their* phones while driving.
Three assistant *managers*	submitted *their* letters of resignation.
Both dry cleaning *companies*	have placed *their* discount coupons in today's newspaper.

Compare the following examples:

Example 1: Each of the workers was at *his* station.

　　　　　(Did you remember to watch out for that first prepositional phrase? All the other words are singular; the masculine *his* refers to *each.* Since we do not know whether *each* is masculine or feminine—or a combination—we usually use the masculine form. To avoid sexist writing, however, you can also say: *Each of the workers was at his or her station.*)

Example 2: *Neither* of the men brought *his* lunch.

　　　　　(*Neither* is singular [refer to Chapter 3, Problem 2], so the pronoun that refers to it is also singular: *his.*)

Four pronouns can cause peculiar problems in agreement:

　　this, that, these, those

This and *that* are singular and refer to singular words: *this* sort of apple, *that* kind of apple. But *these* and *those* are plural and refer to plural words: *those* kinds of apple*s*, *these* sorts of apple*s*. Never use *them* the way you would use *these* and *those: these* apples, not *them* apples.

RULE 10: APOSTROPHES WITH CONTRACTIONS

Use an apostrophe with a pronoun only if you are writing a contraction.

Pronouns have possessive forms. Compare the following pronouns and their possessive forms. Note that *none* of the possessive forms use an apostrophe to show ownership.

WARNING

Possessive forms of pronouns do not use an apostrophe to show ownership.

Pronoun	Possessive Forms
I	*my* book; the book is *mine*
we	*our* yearly bonus; the bonus is *ours*
you	*your* insurance forms; these forms are *yours*
he	*his* overtime pay
she	*her* weekly wage; the wage is *hers*
it	*its* taxable amount
they	*their* refund; the refund is *theirs*

Example 1: This is *your* computer station; that one is *his*.

(*Your* and *his* are possessive forms of the pronouns *you* and *he*; use no apostrophes.)

Example 2: *My* office cubicle has *its* wall surface covered with photographs of *our* family.

(*My* is the possessive form of the pronoun *I*; *its* is the possessive form of *it*; and *our* is the possessive form of *we*. Use no apostrophes.)

If the pronoun is part of a contraction, however, you use an apostrophe to show that letters have been omitted. Study this word list:

Pronoun	Pronoun and Verb	Contraction
I	I am	I'm
I	I will	I'll
I	I have	I've
I	I would	I'd
we	we are	we're
we	we will	we'll
we	we have	we've
we	we would	we'd
you	you are	you're
you	you will	you'll
you	you have	you've
you	you would	you'd
he	he is	he's
he	he will	he'll
he	he has	he's
he	he would	he'd
she	she is	she's
she	she will	she'll
she	she has	she's
she	she would	she'd
it	it is	it's
it	it has	it's
they	they are	they're
they	they will	they'll
they	they have	they've
they	they would	they'd

The six pronouns that cause the most confusion are the following:

your, you're
its, it's
their, they're

In each case, the pronoun *without* the apostrophe shows ownership and the pronoun *with* the apostrophe is a contraction.

If you use an apostrophe with a pronoun, always check to see if you can read it as a pronoun with its verb. For example, you must be able to read *it's* as *it is* or as *it has*. If you can't read it as a pronoun with its verb, you have a possessive form. Use no apostrophes with possessive forms. (For more about using apostrophes in contractions, see Chapter 13, Part III.)

Study the following examples:

Example 1: If you miss *your* bus, *you're* going to miss your appointment.

(*Your* is a possessive form; you cannot say *you are bus*. On the other hand, *you're* is a contraction; you can say *you are going to miss*. Use the apostrophe to show the omission of the letter *a*.)

Example 2: The clock has *its* new battery, so we can safely say *it's* five o'clock.

(*Its* is a possessive form; you cannot say *the clock has it is new battery*. Thus, use no apostrophe. On the other hand, *it's* is a contraction; you can say *it is five o'clock*. Use the apostrophe to show the omission of the letter *i*.)

Example 3: *They're* going to make an announcement to the media about *their* plant expansion.

(*They're* is a contraction; you can say *they are going to make*. Use the apostrophe to show the omission of the letter *a*. On the other hand, *their* shows ownership and needs no apostrophe. You cannot say *about they are plant expansion*.)

These ten rules should help you answer correctly any GED exam questions about pronoun usage.

PRACTICE
EXERCISE

Directions: Apply these rules now in practice. When you finish, check your answers with those that follow these sentences. Rule numbers are included so that you can review if you find you still have a problem.

1. Everyone stood at (his/their) seat when the conductor came into the concert hall.
2. Kenneth is braver than (I/me).
3. (We/Us) secretaries must be able to work with numerous kinds of complicated equipment.
4. (These/Them) apples keep well through winter.
5. The award was given jointly by my brother and (I/me).
6. The two automobile drivers, Mr. Johnson and (he/him), appeared in traffic court yesterday morning.
7. The Boy Scouts try to help (whoever/whomever) is in need.
8. (Its/It's) certain that the test will be timed.
9. All of the accountants were ready with (his/their) annual projections.
10. Charles bought my sister and (I/me) some medicinal plants for our greenhouse.
11. Organic gardeners object to (your/you're) using non-organic fertilizers and insecticides.
12. The agricultural agent thought (that/those) kind of shrub would be insect resistant.
13. Race car drivers must keep (his/their) bodies in excellent condition.
14. (Their/They're) the men wearing insulated jackets.
15. (This/These) kind of fabric print is called a *calico* print.
16. Mathilda and (she/her) taught us how to prepare homemade hominy.
17. The best model-ship builder in this community is (he/him) in the red plaid shirt.
18. The chirping crickets lulled (he/him) and (I/me) to sleep.
19. (He/Himself) collected moths as a hobby.
20. Patricia said that each child at the day-care center had to pick up (his/their) own toys.
21. The nominees for president and vice-president will probably be Mrs. Gallmeister and (I/me) respectively.
22. Shoveling snow in subzero weather delighted neither (he/him) nor (I/me).
23. United Parcel Service delivered a package addressed to (we/us) women in the family.
24. Several workers earn more money than (he/him).
25. The nighthawk objected to (your/you're) being near (its/it's) eggs, which were lying in the gravel of the courtyard.
26. Someone left (her/their) jacket lying on the bench.
27. If (your/you're) counting on sunny weather for the picnic, I'll tell you that (its/it's) supposed to rain.
28. Dad bought a new compact car for (him/himself).

29. The naturalist and (she/her) led our group along a fascinating nature trail.

30. The motorcycle riders selected two riders they themselves thought excellent, Robert and (he/him).

31. Did everybody get all the cake and ice cream (he/they) wanted?

32. The best bread baker in Vanderburgh County was (she/her).

33. The man (who/whom) they selected to be the speaker was pleased to accept the invitation.

34. Each of the members cast (his/their) ballots for the four officers.

35. The winner will be (he or she/him or her) who has the best attendance record.

EXERCISE—ANSWERS

1. his (Rule 9): *Everyone* is singular.

2. I [am] (Rule 5)

3. We (Rule 4)

4. These (Rule 9)

5. me (Rule 3): *By* is a preposition and needs an object.

6. he (Rule 6): *He* renames part of the subject, *drivers*.

7. whoever (Rule 8): Think "*he* is in need."

8. It's (Rule 10)

9. their (Rule 9)

10. me (Rule 3): Charles bought *me* plants.

11. your (Rule 10)

12. that (Rule 9)

13. their (Rule 9)

14. They're (Rule 10)

15. This (Rule 9)

16. she (Rule 1): Think "she taught."

17. he (Rule 2): The linking verb *is* requires the same form as the subject.

18. him and me (Rule 3)

19. He (Rule 7)

20. his (Rule 9): *Each child* is singular and so requires a singular pronoun.

21. I (Rule 2): The linking verb *will be* requires the same form as the subject.

22. him nor me (Rule 3)

23. us (Rule 4)

24. he [did] (Rule 5)

25. your, its (Rule 10)

26. her (Rule 9): *Someone* is singular and so requires a singular pronoun.

27. you're, it's (Rule 10)

28. himself (Rule 7)

29. she (Rule 1)

30. him (Rule 6): Think "the riders selected *him*."

31. he (Rule 9): *Everybody* is singular and so requires a singular pronoun.

32. she (Rule 2): Here is another linking verb!

33. whom (Rule 8): Think "they selected *him*."

34. his (Rule 9): *Each* is singular and so requires a singular pronoun. Do not let the prepositional phrase *of the members* interfere.

35. he or she (Rule 2): It is another linking verb!

GED PRACTICE

Directions: The following passage includes errors in subject-verb agreement, noun usage, and pronoun usage. Choose the letter representing the best usage and then compare your answers with those that follow. Problem numbers from Chapter 3 and rules from Chapters 4 and 5 will help you review items you miss. Notice that this practice segment is patterned after the GED format. It should help you prepare for the way you'll be tested.

THE FISHERMEN TEAM
A

(1) *Two crappie fishermen, F. J. Botz and Alan Goodson, have entered the Kingston fishing tournament where their hoping to land big dollars for theirselves.* (2) *Since each pair of fishermen work as a team, Botz hopes to have his own boat ready for he and Goodson to launch on tournament day.* (3) *Although Goodson usually catches more fish than him, Botz prefers his long-time partner to anyone else.* (4) "In a tournament situation," Botz explained, "he and I support each other. (5) If he catches the first fish, I cheer him on, and whomever catches the most pounds gets a free dinner from the other." (6) "There is," as Goodson added, however, "also free-dinner rewards for friendly weekend competition between Botz and I."*

B

(7) *So far, the men agree, the free dinners from tournament's or from weekend fishing is about equal, and each holds they're own in a nearly equal pound-for-pound contest.* (8) *As a result, the two men believe each have a chance at some tournament prizes; but together, its these teams that should give real competition to the others.* (9) *If Goodson lands the slab crappie he usually does, the biggest prize may go to himself.* (10) *According to Roger Yates, tournament chairman, "The final decision, of course, will not be by we tournament judges.* (11) *The Weights and Measures people from the state will give the final say when he reads the official scales.* (12) *The scales' readings themselves tell the final story."*

1. Sentence 1: Two crappie fishermen, <u>F. J. Botz and Alan Goodson, have entered</u> the Kingston fishing tournament where their hoping to land big dollars for theirselves.

    Which of the following represents the best way to write the underlined portion of the sentence? If you think the original is the best way, choose option (1).

    (1)   F. J. Botz and Alan Goodson, have entered
    (2)   F. J. Botz and Alan Goodson, has entered
    (3)   F. J. Botz and Alan Goodson, has both entered

2. Sentence 1: Two crappie fishermen, F. J. Botz and Alan Goodson, have entered the Kingston fishing tournament <u>where their hoping to land big dollars for theirselves.</u>

    Which of the following represents the best way to write the underlined portion of the sentence? If you think the original is the best way, choose option (1).

    (1)   where their hoping to land big dollars for theirselves
    (2)   where there hoping to land big dollars for theirselves
    (3)   where they're hoping to land big dollars for theirselves
    (4)   where their hoping to land big dollars for themselves
    (5)   where they're hoping to land big dollars for themselves

3. Sentence 2: <u>Since each pair of fishermen work as a team</u>, Botz hopes to have his own boat ready for he and Goodson to launch on tournament day.

    Which of the following represents the best way to write the underlined portion of the sentence? If you think the original is the best way, choose option (1).

    (1)   Since each pair of fishermen work as a team
    (2)   Since each pair of fishermen works as a team
    (3)   Since each pairs of fishermen work as a team
    (4)   Since each pair of fishermen's work as a team

4. Sentence 2: Since each pair of fishermen work as a team, Botz hopes to have his own boat ready <u>for he and Goodson</u> to launch on tournament day.

    Which of the following represents the best way to write the underlined portion of the sentence? If you think the original is the best way, choose option (1).

    (1)   for he and Goodson
    (2)   for him and Goodson
    (3)   for Goodson and he
    (4)   for Goodson and him

5. Sentence 3: Although Goodson usually catches more fish than him, Botz prefers his long-time partner to anyone else.

    Which correction should be made to this sentence?

    (1)   Change <u>than him</u> to <u>than he.</u>
    (2)   Change <u>Goodson usually catches</u> to <u>Goodson usually catch.</u>
    (3)   Change <u>to anyone else</u> to <u>to anyone.</u>
    (4)   No correction is necessary.

6. Sentence 4: "In a tournament situation," Botz explained, "he and I support each other."

   Which correction should be made to this sentence?

   (1) Change he and I to him and me.
   (2) Change he and I to him and I.
   (3) Change he and I to he and me.
   (4) No correction is necessary.

7. Sentence 5: "If he catches the first fish, I cheer him on, and whomever catches the most pounds gets a free dinner from the other."

   Which correction should be made to this sentence?

   (1) Change whomever catches to whomever catch.
   (2) Change whomever catches to whoever catch.
   (3) Change whomever catches to whoever catches.
   (4) No correction is necessary.

8. Sentence 6: "There is," as Goodson added, however, "also free-dinner rewards for friendly weekend competition between Botz and I."

   Which of the following represents the best way to write the underlined portion of the sentence? If you think the original is the best way, choose option (1).

   (1) There is
   (2) Theres
   (3) There are
   (4) They're

9. Sentence 6: "There is," as Goodson added, however, "also free-dinner rewards for friendly weekend competition between Botz and I."

   Which of the following represents the best way to write the underlined portion of the sentence? If you think the original is the best way, choose option (1).

   (1) rewards for friendly weekend competition between Botz and I
   (2) reward's for friendly weekend competition between Botz and I
   (3) rewards' for friendly competition between Botz and I
   (4) rewards for friendly competition between Botz and me

10. Sentence 7: So far, the men agree, the free dinners from tournament's or from weekend fishing is about equal, and each holds they're own in a nearly equal pound-for-pound contest.

    Which of the following represents the best way to write the underlined portion of the sentence? If you think the original is the best way, choose option (1).

    (1) from tournament's
    (2) from tournaments'
    (3) from tournaments
    (4) from tournaments's

11. Sentence 7: So far, the men agree, the free dinners from tournament's or <u>from weekend fishing is</u> about equal, and each holds they're own in a nearly equal pound-for-pound contest.

Which of the following represents the best way to write the underlined portion of the sentence? If you think the original is the best way, choose option (1).

(1) from weekend fishing is
(2) from weekend fishing are
(3) from weekend fishing's is
(4) from weekend's fishing are

12. Sentence 7: So far, the men agree, the free dinners from tournament's or from weekend fishing is about equal, and <u>each holds they're own</u> in a nearly equal pound-for-pound contest.

Which of the following represents the best way to write the underlined portion of the sentence? If you think the original is the best way, choose option (1).

(1) each holds they're own
(2) each holds there own
(3) each hold their own
(4) each holds his own

13. Sentence 8: As a result, <u>the two men believe each have</u> a chance at some tournament prizes; but together, its these kind of teams that should give real competition to the others.

Which of the following represents the best way to write the underlined portion of the sentence? If you think the original is the best way, choose option (1).

(1) the two men believe each have
(2) the two men believe he has
(3) the two men believe each has
(4) the two men believes each has

14. Sentence 8: As a result, the two men believe each have a chance at some tournament prizes; but together, its <u>these kind of teams</u> that should give real competition to the others.

Which of the following represents the best way to write the underlined portion of the sentence? If you think the original is the best way, choose option (1).

(1) these kind of teams
(2) these kinds of team
(3) this kinds of teams
(4) these kinds of teams

15. Sentence 9: If Goodson lands the slab crappie he usually does, the biggest prize may go to himself.

Which correction should be made to this sentence?

(1) Change <u>may go to himself</u> to <u>might go to himself</u>.
(2) Change <u>may go to himself</u> to <u>may go to hisself</u>.
(3) Change <u>may go to himself</u> to <u>may go to him</u>.
(4) No correction is necessary.

16. Sentence 10: According to Roger Yates, tournament chairman, "The final decision, of course, will not be by we tournament judges."

    Which correction should be made to this sentence?

    (1) Change by we tournament judges to by we tournament judge's.
    (2) Change by we tournament judges to by we tournament judges'.
    (3) Change by we tournament judges to by us tournament judges.
    (4) No correction is necessary.

17. Sentence 11: The Weights and Measures people from the state will give the final say when he reads the official scale.

    Which correction should be made to this sentence?

    (1) Change when he reads to when he or she reads.
    (2) Change when he reads to when they read.
    (3) Change when he reads to when he read.
    (4) No correction is necessary

18. Sentence 12: The scales' readings themselves tell the final story."

    Which correction should be made to this sentence?

    (1) Change themselves to theirselves.
    (2) Change tell to tells.
    (3) Change scales to scale's.
    (4) No correction is necessary.

GED PRACTICE—ANSWERS

1. (1) fishermen *have* [correct] (Chapter 3, Problem 1)
2. (5) they're [for *they are*] hoping (Chapter 5, Rule 10) ; for *themselves* (Chapter 5, Rule 7)
3. (2) pair *works* (Chapter 3, Problem 1, Situation A)
4. (4) for *Goodson and him* (Chapter 5, Rule 3)
5. (1) more than *he* [does] (Chapter 5, Rule 5)
6. (4) [correct] (Chapter 5, Rule 1)
7. (3) *whoever* catches (Chapter 5, Rule 8)
8. (3) There *are* rewards (Chapter 3, Problem 1, Situation B)
9. (4) between Botz and *me* (Chapter 5, Rule 3)
10. (2) tournaments [plural, not possessive] (Chapter 5, Rule 10)
11. (2) dinners *are* (Chapter 3, Problem 1, Situation A)
12. (4) each holds *his* own (Chapter 5, Rule 9)
13. (3) each *has* (Chapter 3, Problem 2, Group A)
14. (4) these *kinds* (Chapter 5, Rule 9)
15. (3) prize may go to *him* (Chapter 5, Rule 7)
16. (3) by *us* judges (Chapter 5, Rule 4)
17. (2) when *they read* (Chapter 5, Rule 9)
18. (4) [correct] (Chapter 5, Rule 7)

Using Adjectives and Adverbs Correctly

Usage errors can occur when choosing between an adjective and an adverb form. Should you say, "I don't feel good" or "I don't feel well"? "I feel bad" or "I feel badly"? To help solve adjective and adverb usage problems, remember two rules from Chapter 1:

1. Adjectives must modify *nouns*.

2. Adverbs must modify *verbs, adjectives,* or other *adverbs.*

Nine rules will help solve other adjective and adverb problems:

RULE 1: ADVERBS AND ACTION VERBS

Use adverbs to modify action verbs.

> Example: Harold drives his new car *carefully*.
>
> > (*Carefully*, an adverb, modifies the action verb *drives*.)

RULE 2: ADVERBS WITH ADJECTIVES

Use adverbs to modify adjectives.

> Example: We thought the test was *really* (not *real*) difficult.
>
> > (*Really*, an adverb, modifies the adjective *difficult*.)

RULE 3: ADJECTIVES WITH LINKING VERBS

Use an adjective after a linking verb. (Remember, substitute some form of *to be* to test for a linking verb.)

> Example 1: The owner of the automobile appeared angry.
>
> > (*Appeared* is a linking verb: *The owner of the automobile is angry.* So we need the adjective *angry.*)
>
> Example 2: The owner of the car appeared *suddenly*.
>
> > (Now *appeared* is an action verb. You cannot say, *The owner of the car is suddenly.* So, since *appeared* is an action verb, you must use the adverb *suddenly*. See Rule 1.)

ROAD MAP

- *Adverbs and Action Verbs*
- *Adverbs and Adjectives*
- *Adjectives with Linking Verbs*
- *Bad/Badly*
- *Good/Well*
- *Fewer/Less*
- *Comparatives and Superlatives*
- *Double Negatives*
- *Illogical Comparisons*
- *Practice*
- *GED Practice*

RULE 4: BAD/BADLY

Bad is an adjective; *badly* is an adverb. Use the adjective, *bad*, after the linking verb.

Example 1: He feels *bad*.

    (*Feels* is a linking verb and so requires the adjective *bad*.)

Example 2: The repairman did a *bad* job on the car.

    (*Bad* functions as an adjective to modify the noun *job*.)

Example 3: The inexperienced actor performed *badly* even in the small role.

    (*Badly* functions as an adverb to modify the verb *performed*.)

RULE 5: GOOD/WELL

Good is an adjective; *well* can be an adjective *or* an adverb.

When *well* is an adjective, it means

    a. in good health.
    b. of good appearance.
    c. satisfactory.

NOTE: Usually, *well* as an adjective is used after a linking verb.

Example 1: Charlie did a *good* job welding the lawnmower handle back in place.

    (*Good* is an adjective modifying the noun *job*.)

Example 2: Mother looks *well* in that dress.

    (*Well* here is an adjective meaning "of good appearance" after a linking verb, *looks*.)

Example 3: He did the job *well*.

    (*Well* is now used as an adverb modifying the action verb *did*.)

Example 4: All is *well*.

    (*Well* is an adjective meaning "satisfactory" after the linking verb *is*.)

Example 5: I don't feel *well*.

    (*Well* is an adjective meaning "in good health" after the linking verb *don't feel*.)

HINT

Anytime you use *fewer* or *less*, be sure to say fewer or less *than what*.

Incorrect:
The oak tree has fewer leaves.

Correct:
The oak tree has fewer leaves *than the maple tree*.

RULE 6: FEWER/LESS

Use *fewer* to refer to countable things and *less* to refer to amounts.

Example 1: The recipe calls for *less* sugar than vinegar.

    (You cannot count sugar: one sugar, two sugars.)

Example 2: My recipe calls for *fewer* cups of sugar than yours does.

    (You *can* counts cups of sugar: one cup of sugar, two cups of sugar.)

Example 3: Bob has *less* money than Gino.

    (You *cannot* count money: one money, two monies.)

Example 4: Bob has *fewer* dollar bills than Gino.

    (You *can* count dollar bills: one dollar bill, two dollar bills.)

RULE 7: COMPARATIVES AND SUPERLATIVES

Distinguish between the comparative and the superlative forms.

Part A

If you are discussing *two* things, use the comparative form of the adjective or adverb. (The comparative form ends in *–er* or uses the word *more*.)

>   Example 1: Paul is the *older* one of the two brothers.

>   Example 2: Tex is the *more handsome* of the two actors.

Part B

If you are discussing more than two, use the superlative form. (The superlative form ends in *–est* or uses the word *most*.)

>   Example 1: Aunt Mary is the *tallest* one of the three sisters.

>   Example 2: Katherine is the *most energetic* of the group.

RULE 8: DOUBLE NEGATIVES

Avoid double negatives.

>   Example 1: Incorrect: We *didn't* do *no* homework.

>   Correct: We didn't do any homework.

>   Example 2: Incorrect: *There aren't hardly* any good building sites left there anymore.

>   Correct: There are hardly any good building sites left there anymore.

RULE 9: ILLOGICAL COMPARISONS

Avoid illogical comparisons.

>   Example: Illogical: Quincy is taller than any student in his class. (But since Quincy is, obviously, in his own class, you are saying that he is taller than himself!)

>   Better: Quincy is taller than any *other* student in his class.

These nine rules should help you answer correctly any GED exam questions that deal with adjective or adverb usage. The following practice will help you determine if you understand the rules.

PRACTICE
EXERCISE

Directions: Check yourself on the exercise below. If you miss an item, be sure to go back to the rule and study the examples for further clarification. Rule numbers are given with the answers following these sentences.

1. The medicated lotion was (good/well) for bee stings.
2. Marjorie felt (bad/badly) about having embarrassed her dear friend.
3. The mongrel appeared (happy/happily) lying there on the velvet cushion.
4. When in training, our neighbor runs four miles a day (regular/regularly).
5. Lately, our winters have been (real/really) cold.
6. The leg was broken (bad/badly).
7. Compared with my brother, I am the (taller/tallest) one.
8. I have little patience, but she has even (fewer/less).
9. The caterers (didn't hardly have/hardly had) enough food for everyone.
10. Clovis won more awards than (anyone/anyone else) in his sales district.
11. The vice-president of the group is the (more/most) assertive of the officers.
12. There are (fewer/less) cars in the parking lot now than there were at noon.
13. After being sick yesterday, Father says he is feeling (good/well) today.
14. The situation appeared (bad/badly).
15. The holiday was a (delightful/delightfully) beautiful day.
16. The colors in the five-piece outfit went together (good/well).
17. There are three of us girls in the family, and Sue Ellen is the (older/oldest) one of my sisters.
18. The child behaved (bad/badly).
19. The job was done (good/well).
20. Marilyn looks (good/well) with her hair cut short.

EXERCISE—ANSWERS

1. good (Rule 5)

2. bad (Rule 4): *Felt* is a linking verb.

3. happy (Rule 3): *Appeared* is a linking verb.

4. regularly (Rule 1)

5. really (Rule 2): *Really*, the adverb, is required to modify the predicate adjective *cold*.

6. badly (Rule 4): *Badly* modifies the action verb *was broken*.

7. taller (Rule 7)

8. less (Rule 6)

9. hardly had (Rule 8)

10. anyone else (Rule 9)

11. most (Rule 7)

12. fewer (Rule 6)

13. well (Rule 5): The adjective *well* is used here to mean "in good health."

14. bad (Rule 4): *Appeared* is a linking verb.

15. delightfully (Rule 2)

16. well (Rule 5): *Well* is used as an adverb to modify the action verb *went*.

17. older (Rule 7): Bet you goofed! If there are three of us, then I have only two sisters.

18. badly (Rule 4): *Badly* modifies the action verb *behaved*.

19. well (Rule 5): The adverb modifies the action verb *was done*.

20. well (Rule 5): The adjective means "of good appearance."

GED PRACTICE

Directions: The following passage includes a mixture of errors: subject-verb agreement, noun usage, pronoun usage, and adjective-adverb usage. Apply your understanding to choose the letter of the correct usage. Then check your answers below. Rule numbers will help you review problem areas. Note that this practice format is similar to what you will find on the GED test.

TELLING TIME
A

(1) *Today's children, for whom science makes life good, need read only digital clocks.* (2) *He can turn easily to a digital clock on the bedside table, check the digital time on the DVD player, and find digital time on the computer and television screens.* (3) *In my opinion, that's a real sad situation.* (4) *Not only do the young generation have a different sense of time, but they also lose the urgency of time.* (5) *If you have a five o'clock appointment, its more pressing to say its "five minutes till five" than it is to say it's "four fifty-five."* (6) *To say that he has five minutes to get to an appointment makes more sense to me.*

B

(7) *Of course, my critics will say that reading "eight forty-five" takes less words than reading "fifteen minutes until nine."* (8) *On the other hand, every child should know what us adults mean by "quarter 'til nine."* (9) *How can these children understand "quarter past" or "half hour" by merely reading digital numbers?* (10) *Neither the children nor I are able to talk about matters as simple as bedtime or dinner hour without confusion!* (11) *Even if mathematics is the child's best subject, the digital clock will never help them understand our traditional-clock vocabulary.*

1. Sentence 1: Today's children, for whom science makes life good, need read only digital clocks.

    What correction should be made to the sentence?

    (1) Change Today's to Todays'.
    (2) Change whom to who.
    (3) Change good to well.
    (4) No correction is necessary.

2. Sentence 1: Today's children, for whom science makes life good, need read only digital clocks.

    What correction should be made to the sentence?

    (1) Change makes life good to make life good.
    (2) Change makes life good to makes life well.
    (3) Change makes life good to make life well.
    (4) No correction is necessary.

3. Sentence 2: He can turn easily to a digital clock on the bedside table, check the digital time on the DVD play, and find digital time on the computer and television screens.

    What correction should be made to the sentence?

    (1) Change he can to she can.
    (2) Change he can to they can.
    (3) Change easily to easy.
    (4) No correction is necessary.

4. Sentence 3: In my opinion, that's a real sad situation.

    What correction should be made to the underlined portion of the sentence?

    (1) Change my opinion to our opinion.
    (2) Change my opinion to his opinion.
    (3) Change my opinion to my opinions.
    (4) No correction is necessary to the underlined portion.

5. Sentence 3: In my opinion, that's a real sad situation.

    What correction should be made to the underlined portion of the sentence?

    (1) Change that's to thats'.
    (2) Change that's to thats.
    (3) Change that's to that.
    (4) No correction is necessary to the underlined portion.

6. Sentence 3: In my opinion, that's a real sad situation.

    What correction should be made to the underlined portion of the sentence?

    (1) Change a real sad to a really sad.
    (2) Change a real sad to a real sadly.
    (3) Change a real sad to a really sadly.
    (4) No correction is necessary to the underlined portion.

7. Sentence 4: Not only do the young generation have a different sense of time, but they also lose the urgency of time.

    What correction should be made to the sentence?

    (1) Change only do the young generation have to only do the young generation has.
    (2) Change only do the young generation have to only does the young generation have.
    (3) Change only do the young generation have to only does the younger generation have.
    (4) No correction is necessary.

8. Sentence 5: If you have a five o'clock appointment, its more pressing to say its "five minutes till five" than it is to say it's "four fifty-five."

    What correction should be made to the underlined portion of the sentence?

    (1) Change its more pressing to it's more pressing.
    (2) Change its more pressing to it's most pressing.
    (3) Change its more pressing to its most pressing.
    (4) No correction is necessary to the underlined portion.

9. Sentence 5: If you have a five o'clock appointment, its more pressing <u>to say its</u> "five minutes till five" than it is to say it's "four fifty-five."

   What correction should be made to the underlined portion of the sentence?

   (1) Change to read <u>to say it's.</u>
   (2) Change to read <u>just to say its.</u>
   (3) Change to read <u>saying its.</u>
   (4) No correction is necessary to the underlined portion.

10. In Sentence 6: To say that he has five minutes to get to an appointment makes more sense to me.

    What correction should be made to the sentence?

    (1) Change <u>more sense to me</u> to <u>more sense to them.</u>
    (2) Change <u>more sense to me</u> to <u>more sense to me than the digital way.</u>
    (3) Change <u>more sense to me</u> to <u>more sense to me than to them.</u>
    (4) No correction is necessary.

11. Sentence 7: Of course, <u>my critics</u> will say that reading "eight forty-five" takes less words than reading "fifteen minutes until nine."

    What correction should be made to the underlined portion of the sentence?

    (1) Change <u>my critics</u> to <u>your critics.</u>
    (2) Change <u>my critics</u> to <u>our critics.</u>
    (3) Change <u>my critics</u> to <u>their critics.</u>
    (4) No correction is necessary to the underlined portion.

12. In Sentence 7: Of course, my critics will say that reading "eight forty-five" <u>takes less words than reading</u> "fifteen minutes until nine."

    What correction should be made to the underlined portion of the sentence?

    (1) Change the underlined portion to read <u>take less words than reading</u>
    (2) Change the underlined portion to read <u>take fewer word than reading</u>
    (3) Change the underlined portion to read <u>takes fewer words than reading</u>
    (4) No correction is necessary to the underlined portion.

13. Sentence 8: On the other hand, every child should know what us adults mean by "quarter 'til nine."

    What correction should be made to the sentence?

    (1) Change <u>what us adults mean</u> to <u>what us adults means.</u>
    (2) Change <u>what us adults mean</u> to <u>what we adults means.</u>
    (3) Change <u>what us adults mean</u> to <u>what we adults mean.</u>
    (4) No correction is necessary.

14. Sentence 9: How can these children understand "quarter past" or "half hour" by merely reading digital numbers?

    What correction should be made to the sentence?

    (1) Change <u>these children</u> to <u>this child.</u>
    (2) Change <u>these children</u> to <u>them children.</u>
    (3) Change <u>these children</u> to <u>that child.</u>
    (4) No correction is necessary.

15. Sentence 10: Neither the children nor I are able to talk about matters as simple as bedtime or dinner hour without confusion!

What correction should be made to the sentence?

(1) Change children nor I are to children nor me are.
(2) Change children nor I are to children nor I am.
(3) Change children nor I are to children nor me is.
(4) No correction is necessary.

16. Sentence 11: Even if mathematics is the child's best subject, the digital clock will never help them understand our traditional-clock vocabulary.

What correction should be made to the underlined portion of the sentence?

(1) Change the underlined portion to read if mathematics are the child's best subject.
(2) Change the underlined portion to read if mathematics is the childs' best subject.
(3) Change the underlined portion to read if mathematics are the childs' best subject.
(4) No correction is necessary to the underlined portion.

17. Sentence 11: Even if mathematics is the child's best subject, the digital clock will never help them understand our traditional-clock vocabulary.

What correction should be made to the underlined portion of the sentence?

(1) Change help them to help him.
(2) Change help them to help us.
(3) Change help them to help you.
(4) No correction is necessary to the underlined portion.

18. Sentence 11: Even if mathematics is the child's best subject, the digital clock will never help them understand our traditional-clock vocabulary.

What correction should be made to the underlined portion of the sentence?

(1) Change our to your.
(2) Change our to their.
(3) Change our to our's.
(4) No correction is necessary to the underlined portion.

GED PRACTICE—ANSWERS

1. (4) correct (Chapter 5, Rule 10)

2. (4) correct (Chapter 6, Rule 5)

3. (2) *they* refers to *children* (Chapter 5, Rule 9)

4. (4) correct (Chapter 5, Rule 9)

5. (4) correct (Chapter 5, Rule 10)

6. (1) *really* sad (Chapter 6, Rule 2)

7. (3) *younger* (Chapter 6, Rule 7); generation *does have* (Chapter 3, Problem 1, Situation B)

8. (1) think *it is more pressing* (Chapter 5, Rule 10)

9. (1) think *it is "five minutes..."* (Chapter 5, Rule 10)

10. (2) complete the comparison (Chapter 6, Rule 9)

11. (4) correct (Chapter 5, Rule 9)

12. (3) *fewer* words (Chapter 6, Rule 6)

13. (3) *we* adults (Chapter 5, Rule 4)

14. (4) correct (Chapter 5, Rule 9)

15. (2) children nor I *am* (Chapter 3, Problem 3, Situation C)

16. (4) correct (Chapter 3, Problem 5, Situation B)

17. (1) never help *him*—or *her*—[referring to *child's*] (Chapter 5, Rule 9)

18. (4) correct (Chapter 5, Rule 9)

Using Verbs Correctly

Usage problems can occur when you're using verbs. This chapter looks at four kinds of problems with verbs.

- First, because verbs show time, they have what we call "tense." So if you use the wrong tense, you'll confuse the reader's understanding of what happened when.

- Second, some verbs show greater strength than others. So your writing improves if you use the strongest verbs.

- Third, because verbs have something called "voice," you'll learn how to improve your writing by using active rather than passive voice.

- Fourth, some verbs have irregular parts, so you'll see how to use the correct verb form.

Four rules for good verb usage follow.

RULE 1: CONSISTENT VERB TENSE

Use consistent verb tense.

When we first talked about identifying verbs, we said that the verb is the word that changes time. You will remember examples like the following:

Example: Today our Internet access *is* speedy.

Yesterday our Internet access *was* speedy.

Tomorrow our Internet access *will be* speedy.

Certain verb endings and some key words help readers understand time. Here are some of them:

Kind of Clue	Clue Endings and Words	Examples
Clues of Yesterday Verbs:	*-ed* endings on regular verbs	investiga*ted*, sig*ned*, whistl*ed*
	have, has, had	*has* investigated, *have* signed, *had* whistled
Clues of Today Verbs:	*-s* endings on singular verbs	investigate*s*, sign*s*, whistle*s*
	no ending on plural verbs	investigate, sign, whistle
Clues of Ongoing Action Verbs:	*-ing* endings with *is*, *am*, or *are*	*is* investiga*ting*, *am* sign*ing*, *are* whistl*ing*
Clues of Tomorrow Verbs:	*will*	*will* investigate, *will* sign, *will* whistle
	will with *have* and *-ed* ending	*will have* investiga*ted*, *will have* sig*ned*, *will have* whistl*ed*

ROAD MAP

- *Consistent Verb Tense*
- *Action, not Linking Verbs*
- *Active, not Passive Voice*
- *Irregular Verbs*
- *Practice*
- *GED Practice*

Now let's apply the clues so you can see how a sentence changes with time. Compare the following sentences.

Much Earlier than Today	Before this month, he *had worked* regularly on weekends. Before marrying, she *had finished* school.
Before Yesterday	He *has worked* steadily for five years. Since you saw her last, she *has finished* school.
Yesterday	He *worked* late last night. She *finished* school in June.
Today	Most days he *works* laying bricks. She *finishes* classes at 4:00 p.m.
Ongoing	He *is working* overtime all this week. She *is finishing* school in order to get a better job.
Tomorrow	He *will work* all year without a vacation. She *will finish* school in another year.
After Tomorrow	By next month, he *will have worked* a full year for the company. By next year, she *will have finished* school.

Why do you need to know about all of the clue words and endings? Because when you're writing, you must maintain consistent time throughout your essay. Here are two hints about how to do that:

1. Maintain the same tense throughout your essay. That means if you start writing with "today" verbs, you'll want to continue throughout the essay to use "today" verbs.

2. When you must show the passing of time or a change in time, be sure to use "yesterday," "today," and "tomorrow" verbs logically.

Example: Use of e-mail in the workplace *has become* a matter of ethics. Whether employees *use* e-mail for inner-office memos or for communication with vendors and customers, they *should remember* old-fashioned courtesies. And like it or not, employers *can* eavesdrop on e-mail communications. Thus employees *should* always *use* courteous and business-like language whether communicating by e-mail or snail-mail.

Note that the verbs above follow this pattern:

has become	before yesterday
use	today
should remember	today
can	today
should use	today

Thus, all verbs are "today" words except the first. The "before yesterday" verb *has become* tells about something that happened earlier to cause today's situation. Thus, it's a logical change in time.

By way of comparison, the following example uses illogical tenses.

Illogical Example: Use of e-mail in the workplace *will become* a matter of ethics. Whether employees *have used* e-mail for inner-office memos or for communication with vendors and customers, they *will remember* old-fashioned courtesies. And like it or not, employers *are eavesdropping* on e-mail communications. Thus employees *have* always *used* courteous and business-like language whether communicating by e-mail or snail-mail.

Perhaps some of the verbs above didn't "sound" right to you. That's good. That means you already have a sense of correct verb usage. Whether or not you thought the verbs sounded wrong, here's why the verb tenses in the passage above are illogical:

will become	tomorrow
have used	before yesterday
will remember	tomorrow
are eavesdropping	ongoing
have used	before yesterday

Notice that unlike the earlier passage, this paragraph does not maintain consistent verb time, or tense. (For more about consistent verb tense, see Chapter 19.)

RULE 2: ACTION, NOT LINKING VERBS

Use action verbs rather than linking verbs.

You will remember that we talked about the differences between action verbs and linking verbs in Chapter 1. (See Chapter 1, Part 2, Section C, if you need to review.)

For almost all writing, you should use action verbs rather than linking verbs. Compare these pairs of sentences. The first sentence in each pair uses a linking verb; the second uses an action verb.

Example 1: The painting *is* above the office manager's desk. (linking verb)

The painting *hangs* above the office manager's desk. (action verb)

Example 2: The CEO's assistant *was* here yesterday. (linking verb)

The CEO's assistant *visited* here yesterday. (action verb)

Example 3: We *are* all full-time employees. (linking verb)

We all *work* as full-time employees. (action verb)

NOTE

Whenever possible, use action verbs rather than linking verbs.

RULE 3: ACTIVE, NOT PASSIVE VOICE

In most instances, use active voice rather than passive voice.

Active voice verbs are those whose subjects do the acting. Passive voice verbs are those whose subjects are acted upon. You can identify passive voice by its two characteristics:

1. has *is, am, are, was, were, be, been,* or *being* as the first word in the verb phrase

2. has a "by" phrase, either stated or implied

Compare the following pairs of verbs:

Active Voice	Passive Voice
Ted *rode* his Harley to work every day.	The Harley *was ridden* by Ted to work every day.
Jarrod *took* the minutes of the meeting.	The minutes of the meeting *were taken* by Jarrod.
Nanette *sent* invitations to the retirement party.	Invitations to the retirement party *were sent* by Nanette.

Obviously, passive voice has a purpose or it wouldn't exist. So when should you use passive voice? Use it in only two situations:

Situation 1: Use passive voice when you don't know who took action.

Example: Juanita's home office was ransacked and her computer stolen.
(*Was ransacked* and *[was] stolen* are passive voice verbs. The "by" phrase is implied—"by someone unknown." Thus, since the person who did the ransacking and stealing are unknown, passive voice is appropriate.)

Situation 2: Use passive voice when you want to protect the name of the person who took action.

Example: The anonymous $1,000 cash gift *was delivered* by a courier.
(*Was delivered* is a passive voice verb. Since the person who took the action prefers to remain anonymous, passive voice is appropriate.)

RULE 4: IRREGULAR VERBS

Use the correct form of irregular verbs.

A regular verb, like *walk*, *walked, have/has walked*, simply adds *–ed* to form past and perfect verb tenses. Irregular verbs, however, change form in some other way.

Thus, irregular verbs often create problems. Your dictionary will solve most of these problems, but here is a list of common irregular verbs that you should know:

begin	began	have/has begun
bite	bit	have/has bitten
blow	blew	have/has blown
break	broke	have/has broken
catch	caught	have/has caught
choose	chose	have/has chosen
come	came	have/has come
do	did	have/has done
draw	drew	have/has drawn
drink	drank	have/has drunk
drive	drove	have/has driven
eat	ate	have/has eaten
fall	fell	have/has fallen
fly	flew	have/has flown
freeze	froze	have/has frozen
get	got	have/has got or gotten
give	gave	have/has given
go	went	have/has gone
grow	grew	have/has grown
know	knew	have/has known
lose	lost	have/has lost
ride	rode	have/has ridden
ring	rang	have/has rung
run	ran	have/has run
say	said	have/has said
see	saw	have/has seen
shake	shook	have/has shaken
speak	spoke	have/has spoken
steal	stole	have/has stolen
take	took	have/has taken
tear	tore	have/has torn
throw	threw	have/has thrown
wear	wore	have/has worn
write	wrote	have/has written

Three pairs of verbs, however, create special problems because the verbs in each pair look so much alike:

Present	Past	Participle (Use with *has*, *have,* or *had*)	Progressive
sit	sat	sat	sitting
set	set	set	setting
rise	rose	risen	rising
raise	raised	raised	raising
lie	lay	lain	lying
lay	laid	laid	laying

SPECIAL PROBLEM—VERBS

Pair 1: Sit/Set

Sit means "to rest," *as in a chair.*

Set means "to put or place."

Examples: The team members will *sit* together.
The team members will *set* their goals.

NOTE: *Sit* will not take a direct object. *Set must* have a direct object, either stated or implied. So anytime you use the word *set*, there must be an answer to the question, "Set *who* or *what*?"

Pair 2: Rise/Raise

Rise, like *sit*, will not take a direct object.

Raise, like *set*, must have a direct object.

Example 1: The window *rises* mysteriously.
(no direct object)

Example 2: Please *raise* the windows!
Ask, "Raise *who* or *what*?" Answer: *windows*

Example 3: The bread dough *rose* almost double in an hour.
(no direct object)

Example 4: That truck farmer *raises* especially beautiful produce.
Ask, "Raises *who* or *what*?" Answer: *produce.*

Pair 3: Lie/Lay

Lie means to rest or recline, and, like *rise* and *sit*, will not take a direct object.

Lay means to put or place, and, like *raise* and *set*, it *must* have a direct object.

What makes these two verbs so confusing is that *lay* in the present is the same as *lie* in the past:

lie	lay	lying
lay	laid	laying

NOTE: To help you select the correct word, test by substituting "rest or recline" for the forms of *lie* and "put or place" for the forms of *lay*.

Example 1: (Lie/Lay) the baby in her crib.
Substitute: Put or place the baby in her crib.
Solution: *Lay* the baby in her crib.

Example 2: (Laying/Lying) in the sun can cause unfortunate side effects.
Substitute: Resting or reclining in the sun can cause unfortunate side effects.
Solution: *Lying* in the sun can cause unfortunate side effects.

SUMMARY

s(i)t
r(i)se } have *no* direct objects
l(i)e

(Think of *i* as representing *i*ndependent: not dependent on a direct object for existence!)

set
raise } *must* have direct objects
lay

PRACTICE
EXERCISE

Directions: Check your understanding of irregular verbs by choosing the correct verb form for each of the following sentences. When you finish, check your answers with those that follow these sentences.

1. When I finish raking the lawn, I plan to (lay/lie) down for a nap.

2. Have you (wrote/written) a reply to Mr. Robinson's letter?

3. Grandpa always (knew/know) how to mend wicker furniture.

4. The temperature and our tempers were both (raising/rising).

5. "He can't read the letter to you on the phone," she explained; "he's just (throwed/thrown) it away."

6. The gardener was (sitting/setting) tomato plants in three one-hundred-foot rows.

7. Last night's low temperatures may have (froze/frozen) the tender plants.

8. The family pet, a dog of mixed descent, (lay/laid) in front of the television set.

9. (Lying/Laying) flat on his back, the football player appeared to be injured.

10. The group did exercises in a (sitting/setting) position since one of the members had (fell/fallen).

11. The doctor's report (raised/rose) the family's hopes.

12. Has the patient (drank/drunk) all of his medicine?

13. Those old newspapers have (blew/blown) around the alley for three weeks now.

14. Citizens watched in helpless frustration as the flood waters (teared/tore) the buildings apart.

15. Has the City Council (chose/chosen) to vote for new floodwalls for our fair city?

16. Has the baby (broke/broken) this plate?

17. The big Persian cat, (laying/lying) in the open window, dozed peacefully.

18. Before the speaker made his unpopular announcement, he (drawed/drew) himself up tall.

19. The fund-raising campaign has (began/begun).

20. The toys along the edge of the driveway were (tore/torn) from abuse.

EXERCISE—ANSWERS

1. lie (no direct object; substitute *rest*)
2. [have] written
3. knew
4. rising (no direct object)
5. [he's = he has] thrown
6. setting (direct object: plants)
7. [have] frozen
8. lay (no direct object; substitute *rested*)
9. Lying (no direct object; substitute *reclining*)
10. sitting (no direct object), [had] fallen
11. raised (direct object: hopes)
12. [has] drunk
13. [have] blown
14. tore
15. [has] chosen
16. [has] broken
17. lying (no direct object; substitute *resting*)
18. drew
19. [has] begun
20. [were] torn

GED PRACTICE

Directions: Now apply your understanding to the following passages. Choose the correct usage from the choices below. Then compare your answers with the answers that follow.

CAT NAPPING
A

(1) At 6:15 p.m. when I come in from work, Jennifer, the cat, was laying curled on the couch asleep. (2) As usual I set in my chair to read the day's mail and glanced at the paper. (3) Shortly, however, for no apparent reason I felt compelled to put down my paper and look again at Jennifer. (4) While I watched her, the paper had fell to the floor, and the thought crost my mind that she was too quiet for too long. (5) I freezed, holding my breath, watching her carefully.

B

(6) I raised from my chair, had fell over the newspaper, and walked toward her. (7) I study her carefully, noting how her tail was brought over her nose and showed not a hair stirring. (8) I watched her side, trying to distinguish the slightest rise or fall of her rib cage, but I could see nothing. (9) Her name was called. (10) A whisker moved; an eyelid raised; one paw begun to stretch out; but her tail done stayed carefully curled across her nose. (11) Ah, that I could have took such cat naps!

1. Sentence 1: At 6:15 p.m. <u>when I come in</u> from work, Jennifer, the cat, was laying curled on the couch asleep.

    What correction should be made to the underlined portion of the sentence?

    (1)   Change <u>when I come in</u> to <u>when I have come in.</u>
    (2)   Change <u>when I come in</u> to <u>when I came in.</u>
    (3)   Change <u>when I come in</u> to <u>whenever I come in.</u>
    (4)   No correction is necessary to the underlined portion.

2. Sentence 1: At 6:15 p.m. when I come in from work, Jennifer, the cat, <u>was laying curled</u> on the couch asleep.

    What correction should be made to the underlined portion of the sentence?

    (1)   Change <u>was laying curled</u> to <u>were laying curled.</u>
    (2)   Change <u>was laying curled</u> to <u>were lying curled.</u>
    (3)   Change <u>way laying curled</u> to <u>was lying curled.</u>
    (4)   No correction is necessary to the underlined portion.

3. Sentence 2: As usual <u>I set in my chair</u> to read the day's mail and glanced at the paper.

    What correction should be made to the underlined portion of the sentence?

    (1)   Change <u>I set in my chair</u> to <u>I sit in my chair.</u>
    (2)   Change <u>I set in my chair</u> to <u>I am sitting in my chair.</u>
    (3)   Change <u>I set in my chair</u> to <u>I sat in my chair.</u>
    (4)   No correction is necessary to the underlined portion.

4. Sentence 2: As usual I set in my chair to read the day's mail and <u>glanced at the paper</u>.

   What correction should be made to the underlined portion of the sentence?

   (1) Change <u>glanced at the paper</u> to <u>glance at the paper</u>.
   (2) Change <u>glanced at the paper</u> to <u>glances at the paper</u>.
   (3) Change <u>glanced at the paper</u> to <u>glancing at the paper</u>.
   (4) No correction is necessary to the underlined portion.

5. Sentence 3: Shortly, however, for no apparent reason <u>I felt compelled</u> to put down my paper and look again at Jennifer.

   What correction should be made to the underlined portion of the sentence?

   (1) Change <u>I felt compelled</u> to <u>I have felt compelled</u>.
   (2) Change <u>I felt compelled</u> to <u>I was feeling compelled</u>.
   (3) Change <u>I felt compelled</u> to <u>I had felt compelled</u>.
   (4) No correction is necessary to the underlined portion.

6. Sentence 3: Shortly, however, for no apparent reason I felt compelled to put down my paper and <u>look again</u> at Jennifer.

   What correction should be made to the underlined portion of the sentence?

   (1) Change <u>look again</u> to <u>looked again</u>.
   (2) Change <u>look again</u> to <u>looks again</u>.
   (3) Change <u>look again</u> to <u>am looking again</u>.
   (4) No correction is necessary to the underlined portion.

7. Sentence 4: While I watched her, the <u>paper had fell</u> to the floor, and the thought crost my mind that she was too quiet for too long.

   What correction should be made to the underlined portion of the sentence?

   (1) Change <u>paper had fell</u> to <u>paper fell</u>.
   (2) Change <u>paper had fell</u> to <u>paper had fallen</u>.
   (3) Change <u>paper had fell</u> to <u>paper falls</u>.
   (4) No correction is necessary to the underlined portion.

8. Sentence 4: While I watched her, the paper had fell to the floor, and <u>the thought crost my mind</u> that she was too quiet for too long.

   What correction should be made to the underlined portion of the sentence?

   (1) Change <u>the thought crost my mind</u> to <u>the thought crosses my mind</u>.
   (2) Change <u>the thought crost my mind</u> to <u>the thought crossed my mind</u>.
   (3) Change <u>the thought crost my mind</u> to <u>the thought had crossed my mind</u>.
   (4) No correction is necessary to the underlined portion.

9. Sentence 5: I freezed, holding my breath, watching her carefully.

   What correction should be made to the sentence?

   (1) Change the sentence to read <u>I freezed, held my breath, watched her carefully</u>.
   (2) Change the sentence to read <u>I froze, hold my breath, watched her carefully</u>.
   (3) Change the sentence to read <u>I froze, holding my breath, watching her carefully</u>.
   (4) No correction is necessary.

10. Sentence 6: I <u>raised from my chair</u>, had fell over the newspaper, and walked toward her.

    What correction should be made to the underlined portion of the sentence?

    (1) Change <u>raised from my chair</u> to <u>rose from my chair.</u>
    (2) Change <u>raised from my chair</u> to <u>had raised from my chair.</u>
    (3) Change <u>raised from my chair</u> to <u>was raising from my chair.</u>
    (4) No correction is necessary to the underlined portion.

11. Sentence 6: I raised from my chair, <u>had fell over</u> the newspaper, and walked toward her.

    What correction should be made to the underlined portion of the sentence?

    (1) Change <u>had fell over</u> to <u>had fallen over.</u>
    (2) Change <u>had fell over</u> to <u>fell over.</u>
    (3) Change <u>had fell over</u> to <u>falling over.</u>
    (4) No correction is necessary to the underlined portion.

12. Sentence 7: I <u>study</u> her carefully, noting how her tail was brought over her nose and showed not a hair stirring.

    What correction should be made to the underlined portion of the sentence?

    (1) Change <u>study</u> to <u>had studied.</u>
    (2) Change <u>study</u> to <u>studied.</u>
    (3) Change <u>study</u> to <u>am studying.</u>
    (4) No correction is necessary to the underlined portion.

13. Sentence 7: I study her carefully, noting how <u>her tail was brought over</u> her nose and showed not a hair stirring.

    What correction should be made to the underlined portion of the sentence?

    (1) Change <u>her tail was brought over</u> to <u>her tail was brung over.</u>
    (2) Change <u>her tail was brought over</u> to <u>her tail has been brought over.</u>
    (3) Change <u>her tail was brought over</u> to <u>she had brought her tail over.</u>
    (4) No correction is necessary to the underlined portion.

14. Sentence 8: <u>I watched</u> her side, trying to distinguish the slightest rise or fall of her rib cage, but I could see nothing.

    What correction should be made to the underlined portion of the sentence?

    (1) Change <u>I watched</u> to <u>I had watched.</u>
    (2) Change <u>I watched</u> to <u>I am watching.</u>
    (3) Change <u>I watched</u> to <u>I have been watching.</u>
    (4) No correction is necessary to the underlined portion.

15. Sentence 8: I watched her side, trying to distinguish the slightest <u>rise or fall</u> of her rib cage, but I could see nothing.

    What correction should be made to the underlined portion of the sentence?

    (1) Change <u>rise or fall</u> to <u>raise or fall.</u>
    (2) Change <u>rise or fall</u> to <u>rising or fall.</u>
    (3) Change <u>rise or fall</u> to <u>rise or fallen.</u>
    (4) No correction is necessary to the underlined portion.

16. Sentence 8: I watched her side, trying to distinguish the slightest rise or fall of her rib cage, but <u>I could see nothing</u>.

    What correction should be made to the underlined portion of the sentence?

    (1)   Change <u>I could see nothing</u> to <u>I couldn't seen nothing</u>.
    (2)   Change <u>I could see nothing</u> to <u>I can see nothing</u>.
    (3)   Change <u>I could see nothing</u> to <u>I can't see nothing</u>.
    (4)   No correction is necessary to the underlined portion.

17. Sentence 9: Her name was called.

    What correction should be made to the sentence?

    (1)   Change <u>Her name was called</u> to <u>Her name called</u>.
    (2)   Change <u>Her name was called</u> to <u>I called her name</u>.
    (3)   Change <u>Her name was called</u> to <u>I was calling her name</u>.
    (4)   No correction is necessary.

18. Sentence 10: A whisker moved; an eyelid raised; one <u>paw begun to stretch out</u>; but her tail done stayed carefully curled across her nose.

    What correction should be made to the underlined portion of the sentence?

    (1)   Change <u>paw begun to stretch out</u> to <u>paw began to stretch out</u>.
    (2)   Change <u>paw begun to stretch out</u> to <u>paw had begun to stretch out</u>.
    (3)   Change <u>paw begun to stretch out</u> to <u>paw was begun to stretch out</u>.
    (4)   No correction is necessary to the underlined portion.

19. Sentence 10: A whisker moved; an eyelid raised; one paw begun to stretch out; but her <u>tail done stayed carefully curled</u> across her nose.

    What correction should be made to the underlined portion of the sentence?

    (1)   Change <u>tail done stayed carefully curled</u> to <u>tail stayed carefully curled</u>.
    (2)   Change <u>tail done stayed carefully curled</u> to <u>she had kept her tail carefully curled</u>.
    (3)   Change <u>tail done stayed carefully curled</u> to <u>tail does stay carefully curled</u>.
    (4)   No correction is necessary to the underlined portion.

20. Sentence 11: Ah, that I could have took such cat naps!

    What correction should be made to the sentence?

    (1)   Change <u>could have took</u> to <u>should have took</u>.
    (2)   Change <u>could have took</u> to <u>could have taken</u>.
    (3)   Change <u>could have took</u> to <u>could take</u>.
    (4)   No correction is necessary.

GED PRACTICE—ANSWERS

Note that this piece is written in simple past tense, so you will use "yesterday" verbs throughout.

1. (2) (past tense)
2. (3) (no direct object)
3. (3) (no direct object)
4. (1) (to read and [to] glance)
5. (4) (past tense)
6. (4) (to put . . . and [to] look)
7. (1) (past tense)
8. (2) (past tense)
9. (3) (past tense)
10. (1) (no direct object, past tense)
11. (2) (past tense)
12. (2) (past tense)
13. (3) (active voice)
14. (4) (past tense)
15. (4) (no direct object)
16. (4) (past tense)
17. (2) (active voice)
18. (1) (past tense)
19. (1) (past tense)
20. (3) (past tense)

Using Prepositions and Conjunctions Correctly

Only a few rules apply to using prepositions and conjunctions correctly, so let's get right to them.

PART 1: PREPOSITIONS

You'll probably face two common problems with prepositions, grammar situations that many people find troubling. First, prepositions are always followed by pronouns in the objective case. Second, prepositions and their objects and modifiers (called prepositional phrases) often cause people to make errors in subject-verb agreement. So that we can deal with the specifics here, you may want to review three matters we've discussed earlier:

1. A preposition is "any place a rat can run." And a preposition and its object, called a prepositional phrase, function as a single word, either as an adjective or adverb (See Chapter 1, Part 5).

2. A prepositional phrase does not function as part of a sentence. Rather, it is a modifier (See Chapter 2, Step 1).

3. A prepositional phrase does not affect the subject's agreement with its verb (See Chapter 3, Problem 1).

Here are the rules for using prepositions correctly:

RULE 1: OBJECTS WITH PREPOSITIONS

After a preposition, use the objective form of a pronoun. Objective pronouns are as follows:

>   *me, us, you, him, her, it, them*

Thus, you will use one of these words after a preposition. Study the following examples:

between you and me	We'll keep this information just *between you and me*.
between us	We'll divide the bonus check *between us*.
between you and us	These family matters are really just *between you and us*.
between them	The couple's child sat *between them*.
among us	Someone passed the cooler of drinks *among us*.
after you and me	He came in the office door *after you and me*.
after them	I expect we'll be next *after them*.
about him and me	The article in today's paper was *about him and me*.
beyond them	The explanation was *beyond them*.
without her or them	Unfortunately, the tour boat left *without her or them*.

ROAD MAP

- *Prepositions*
  - *Objects with Prepositions*
  - *Prepositional Phrases in Subject-Verb Agreement*
- *Conjunctions*
  - *To Join Two Sentences*
  - *To Join Two Groups of Words*
  - *To Join Groups of Words in a Series*
- *GED Practice*

RULE 2: PREPOSITIONAL PHRASES IN SUBJECT-VERB AGREEMENT

Never let a prepositional phrase interfere with subject-verb agreement.

You already know from the work you did in Chapter 3 that the subject of a sentence agrees with its verb. Often, however, when a prepositional phrase comes between the subject and its verb, some people are confused about which verb to use. Compare the following examples:

Example 2:   The box of dishes has been delivered.

(*Of dishes* is a prepositional phrase. The subject *box* agrees with its verb *has been delivered*.)

Example 2:   The same message from Tom, you, and me is certain to get Roger's attention.

(*From Tom, you and me* is a prepositional phrase. The subject *message* agrees with its verb *is*.)

PART 2: CONJUNCTIONS

We have talked only briefly about conjunctions, and only one kind of conjunction: the coordinating conjunctions *and, or, nor, but,* and *so.* (See Chapter 1, Part 6.) Although we'll talk about some other kinds of conjunctions later, let's focus on using coordinating conjunctions correctly.

RULE 1: TO JOIN TWO SENTENCES

When a coordinating conjunction joins two sentences together, use a comma in front of the conjunction.

WARNING

Avoid joining more than two sentences with a conjunction.

Example 1:   Some agricultural communities have turned to sunflower seed production, and many farmers have found that crop a good alternative to tobacco.
(The comma and conjunction *and* join two complete sentences, either of which could stand alone.)

Example 2:   The company's business plan sounded terrific, but the plan turned out to be far too optimistic.
(The comma and conjunction *but* join two complete sentences, either of which could stand alone.)

Warning 1:   Make sure you don't use conjunctions to string together a whole group of sentences. Generally, avoid joining more than two sentences with a conjunction.

Warning 2:   Use a conjunction to join two sentences only if they are closely related.

Poor Writing: The new insurance plan provides good family benefits, and now the annual deductible is $100 instead of $200 per person, and employees will pay only 1 percent of the premium, and we'll still have better benefits than before.

Better Writing: The insurance plan provides good family benefits. In fact, the new annual deductible is $100 instead of $200 per person. Employees will pay only 1 percent of the premium, and we'll still have better benefits than before.

(The first two sentences are not closely enough related to join with a conjunction and comma. The second two are related and work well with the comma and conjunction *and* joining them.)

Warning 3:   Never join two sentences without a comma and conjunction. The result is a serious error called a "run-on sentence."

Incorrect: Employees will pay only 1 percent of the premium we'll still have better benefits than before.

(Two sentences are run together.)

Correct: Employees will pay only 1 percent of the premium, and we'll still have better benefits than before.

(Two sentences are joined with a comma and conjunction.)

RULE 2: TO JOIN TWO GROUPS OF WORDS

When a coordinating conjunction joins two groups of words that are not complete sentences, use no comma.

Example 1:   Some agricultural communities have turned to sunflower seed and safflower seed production as an alternative to tobacco crops.

(The conjunction *and* joins two objects, *seed* and *seed*. It does not join two sentences. Use no comma.)

Example 2:   The company's business plan sounded terrific and seemed to make a great deal of sense.

(The conjunction *and* joins two verbs, *sounded* and *seemed*. Use no comma.)

RULE 3: TO JOIN GROUPS OF WORDS IN A SERIES

When a coordinating conjunction joins three or more groups of words in a series, use commas to mark the groups.

Example 1:   Refreshments included cookies, pretzels, and colas.

(The conjunction *and* joins three nouns, *cookies, pretzels,* and *colas*. Commas set off the three.)

Example 2:   During lunch hours, several of us walk for general exercise, do aerobics for heart exercise, or do stretching for mental acuity.

(The conjunction *or* joins three verb phrases: *walk . . . , do . . . ,* and *do. . . .* Commas set of the three groups of words.)

Example 3:   During lunch hours, several of us walk for general exercise or do aerobics for heart exercise or do stretching for mental acuity.

(The conjunction *or* appears between each group of words. Use no commas.)

NOTE

Do not use a comma if a conjunction appears between each group of words.

GED PRACTICE

Directions: Read the following passage. Choose the correct usage from the choices below. Then check your answers with those that follow.

LETTERS OF COMPLAINT

A

(1) A letter of complaint can bring quick results or it can go unnoticed for weeks on someone's desk. (2) What you say, and how you say it will make a difference. (3) Just between you and I, here's the best plan if your complaint is about a product: (4) First, give the reader all the identifying details, like model number serial number date of purchase and any warranty information, especially if you purchased an extended warranty. (5) Next, explain the problem and give enough detail so that he or she will understand the problem, for only then is your reader able to offer a satisfactory solution. (6) If you find yourself struggling with how to explain the problem, try explaining the problem to a friend. (7) See what questions he asks then revise your explanation accordingly.

B

(8) You'll use a different plan, however, if your complaint is about service, or a lack thereof. (9) First, clarify in your letter what service you've tried to get from the company, how you tried to get it, and what their response has been. (10) Next, document the dates of phone calls be sure to give the names of the people with whom you spoke. (11) Finally, be specific about what you want. (12) Do you want a serviceman to come to your home? (13) Do you want your bill adjusted, do you have questions you want answered?

C

(14) In most cases, your letters of complaint is going to get a response. (15) If it doesn't, however, you may be dealing with a disreputable company. (16) In that case, check with the Better Business Bureau in the city where the company is located when all else fails, the folks there may be able to help you.

1. Sentence 1: A letter of complaint can bring quick results or it can go unnoticed for weeks on someone's desk.

   What correction should be made to the sentence?

   (1) Insert a comma after <u>results</u>.
   (2) Insert a comma after <u>or</u>.
   (3) Insert a comma after <u>results</u> and remove the word <u>or</u>.
   (4) No correction is necessary.

2. Sentence 2: What you say, and how you say it will make a difference.

   What correction should be made to the sentence?

   (1) Insert a comma after <u>and</u>.
   (2) Insert a comma after <u>say</u> and remove the word <u>and</u>.
   (3) Omit the comma after <u>say</u>.
   (4) No correction is necessary.

3. Sentence 3: <u>Just between you and I</u>, here's the best plan if your complaint is about a product:

What correction should be made to the underlined portion of the sentence?

(1) Change it to read <u>Just among you and I.</u>
(2) Change it to read <u>Just between you and me.</u>
(3) Change it to read <u>Just among you and me.</u>
(4) No correction is necessary to the underlined portion.

4. Sentence 4: First, give the reader all the identifying details, <u>like model number serial number date of purchase and any warranty information</u>, especially if you purchased an extended warranty.

What correction should be made to the underlined portion of the sentence?

(1) Change it to read <u>like model number serial number, date of purchase, and any warranty.</u>
(2) Change it to read <u>like model number, serial number, date of purchase and any warranty.</u>
(3) Change it to read <u>like model number, serial number, date of purchase, and any warranty.</u>
(4) No correction is necessary to the underlined portion.

5. Sentence 5: Next, <u>explain the problem and give enough detail</u> so that he or she will understand the problem, for only then is your reader able to offer a satisfactory solution.

What correction should be made to the underlined portion of the sentence?

(1) Insert a comma after <u>problem</u>.
(2) Insert a comma after <u>and</u>.
(3) Omit the word <u>and</u>.
(4) No correction is necessary to the underlined portion.

6. Sentence 5: Next, explain the problem and give enough detail so that he or she will understand the <u>problem, for only then</u> is your reader able to offer a satisfactory solution.

What correction should be made to the underlined portion of the sentence?

(1) Omit the comma after <u>problem</u>.
(2) Move the comma from after <u>problem</u> to after <u>for</u>.
(3) Omit the word <u>for</u>.
(4) No correction is necessary to the underlined portion.

7. Sentence 7: See what questions he asks then revise your explanation accordingly.

What correction should be made to the sentence?

(1) Insert a comma after <u>asks</u>.
(2) Insert a comma after <u>asks</u> and add the word <u>and</u> after the comma.
(3) Add the word <u>and</u> after the word <u>asks</u> and follow it by a comma.
(4) No correction is necessary.

8. Sentence 8: You'll use a different plan, however, if your complaint is about service, or a lack thereof.

   What correction should be made to the sentence?

   (1) Omit the comma after service.
   (2) Move the comma from after service to after or.
   (3) Omit the word or.
   (4) No correction is necessary.

9. Sentence 9: First, clarify in your letter what service you've tried to get from the company, how you tried to get it, and what their response has been.

   What correction should be made to the underlined portion of the sentence?

   (1) Omit the comma after it.
   (2) Move the comma from after it to after and.
   (3) Omit the comma and the word and.
   (4) No correction is necessary to the underlined portion.

10. Sentence 10: Next, document the dates of phone calls be sure to give the names of the people with whom you spoke.

    What correction should be made to the underlined portion of the sentence?

    (1) Insert a comma after calls.
    (2) Insert a comma after calls and add the word and after the comma.
    (3) Add the word and after calls and insert a comma after and.
    (4) No correction is necessary.

11. Sentence 13: Do you want your bill adjusted, do you have questions you want answered?

    What correction should be made to the sentence?

    (1) Insert the word or after the comma.
    (2) Insert the word or in front of the comma.
    (3) Insert a question mark after the word adjusted and begin the word Do with a capital letter.
    (4) No correction is necessary.

12. Sentence 14: In most cases, your letters of complaint is going to get a response.

    What correction should be made to the underlined portion of the sentence?

    (1) Change it to read your letter of complaint is going.
    (2) Change it to read your letters of complaint are going.
    (3) Change it to read your letter of complaint, are going.
    (4) No correction is necessary.

13. Sentence 16: In that case, check with the Better Business Bureau in the city where the company is located when all else fails, the folks there may be able to help you.

    What correction should be made to the underlined portion of the sentence?

    (1) Change it to read is located, when all else.
    (2) Change it to read is located. When all else.
    (3) Change it to read is located, and when all else.
    (4) No correction is necessary.

GED PRACTICE—ANSWERS

1. (1) A comma and a conjunction join two sentences.
2. (3) There is no comma with a conjunction that does not join two complete sentences.
3. (2) *Me* is in the objective case and follows the preposition *between*.
4. (3) Separate with commas each of the objects of the preposition *like*.
5. (4) There is no comma with a conjunction that does not join two complete sentences.
6. (4) Use a comma in front of a conjunction that joins two complete sentences.
7. (2) Use a comma in front of a conjunction that joins two complete sentences.
8. (1) There is no comma with a conjunction that does not joint two complete sentences.
9. (4) The commas separate the series of three clauses, the final two of which are joined by the conjunction *and*.
10. (2) Join two sentences with a comma and conjunction.
11. (3) Starting a new sentence makes the three questions parallel.
12. (1) Use the singular noun *letter* to be consistent throughout the paragraphs. *Is* agrees with *letter*. Don't let the prepositional phrase *of complaint* cause confusion.
13. (2) Avoid stringing sentences together.

Commonly Confused Words

This chapter on usage helps you understand words that are commonly confused. Be sure you know how to use them correctly before you tackle the GED test.

accept, except

> *Accept* means "to receive." It is always a verb. Example: He *accepted* the gift.
>
> *Except* is most often a preposition. Example: I ate everything *except* the pie.
>
> *Except* is sometimes a verb. Then it means "to leave out or omit." Example: The judge *excepted* the man from jury duty.

affect, effect

> *Affect* is always a verb. It means "to influence" or "to bring about a change." Example: Will the weather *affect* your plans?
>
> *Effect* is usually a noun. It means "result." Example: What *effect* will the pay raise have on you?
>
> *Effect* can also be a verb. Then it means "to bring about" or "to accomplish." Example: The negotiator *effected* a compromise between the company and union officials.

all ready, already

> *All ready* means "everything is ready." Example: The fabric, pattern, scissors, and pins are *all ready* for the seamstress.
>
> *Already* is an adverb. It means "by or before a given time." Example: We were *already* late for dinner when we had the flat tire.

amount, number

> *Amount* is used to refer to things we cannot count. Example: The *amount* of sugar he uses is unhealthy. (We cannot count sugar: 1 sugar, 2 sugars, etc.)
>
> *Number* is used to talk about things we can count. Example: The number of cups of sugar in the recipe surprised me. (We can count cups of sugar: 1 cup, 2 cups, etc.)

between, among

> *Between* is used to refer to two items. Example: Divide this pie *between* the two of you.
>
> *Among* is used to refer to more than two items. Example: Can you choose from *among* the three dresses?

borrow, lend

> *Borrow* means "to take or receive something" with the understanding that it will be returned. Example: He asked to *borrow* my lawn mower.
>
> *Lend* means "to allow someone to use something" of yours. Example: Yes, I will *lend* him my lawn mower.

ROAD MAP

- *Practice*

bring, take

Bring means "to carry or lead to where the speaker is." Example: Tiffanie will *bring* potato salad to our carry-in supper.

Take means "to carry or lead away from where the speaker is." Example: Tiffanie will *take* potato salad to the neighbor's carry-in supper.

capital, the Capitol

Capital refers to wealth. Example: I don't have the *capital* to finance a new car.

Capital also refers to the seat of state government. Example: Frankfort is the *capital* of Kentucky.

Capitol (always with an uppercase C) refers to the building in Washington, D.C., where the U.S. Congress meets. Example: While in our nation's capital, we toured the *Capitol*.

desert, desert, dessert

Desert (pronounced de sert') is a verb. It means "to leave." Example: How strange that the cat *deserted* her kittens.

Desert (pronounced des' ert) is a noun. It refers to dry, sandy regions. Example: The Mojave *Desert* has a mysterious beauty all its own.

Dessert refers to something sweet eaten at the end of a meal. Example: Apple pie is Dad's favorite *dessert*.

different from

Say *different from*, not *different than*. Example: This paint surface is *different from* that one.

farther, further

Farther refers to physical distance. Example: How much *farther* is it to the next rest area?

Further means "in addition." Example: I needed *further* explanation in order to understand the problem.

fewer, less

Fewer, like *number*, refers to things we can count. Example: Use *fewer* cups of sugar when you make this recipe. (We can count cups: 1 cup, 2 cups, etc.)

Less, like *amount*, refers to things we cannot count. Example: Use *less* sugar than the recipe calls for. (We cannot count sugar: 1 sugar, 2 sugars, etc.)

had of, off of

Omit *of*. Examples: I *had* gone home by then. He fell *off* the bicycle.

hear, here

Hear is one of the five senses. (Note the word *ear* in *hear*.) Example: Fred can *hear* water dripping somewhere.

Here refers to a place. (Note that its opposite, *there*, has the word *here* in it.) Example: Put the book *here* on the table.

imply, infer

Imply means "to suggest a meaning" when you make a statement. Example: Did you *imply* that you don't like my dress?

Infer means "to draw meaning out of" what someone else says. Example: She *inferred* that I didn't like her dress, but she was wrong.

its, it's

Its is a possessive pronoun. Example: The dog lost its collar.

It's is a contraction for it is. The apostrophe shows the omission of the second i. Example: It's (It is) really cold today.

learn, teach

Learn means "to gain knowledge." Example: Ned learned how to ski last year.

Teach means "to give knowledge." Example: Carlton taught Ned to ski last year.

lend, loan

Lend is a verb. (See borrow, lend.) Example: He lent me his lawn mower. (Do not say, "He loaned me his lawn mower.")

Loan is a noun. Example: The lawn mower was only a loan.

let, leave

Let means "to allow." Example: Please let me help you.

Leave means "to go away." Example: I'll leave in five minutes.

like, as

Like is a preposition and is followed by a noun. Example: He looks just like his brother.

As is an introductory word that is followed by a noun and a verb. Example: Gerald runs as I do.

loose, lose

Loose means "not tight." Example: The steering is loose in the old truck.

Lose means "to not know the whereabouts" of something. Example: I'm afraid I will lose this expensive ring.

of, have

Use have, not of, with could. Example: I could have called earlier.

principal, principle

Principal can be a noun or an adjective. As an adjective it means "main." Example: Protecting pedestrians is the principal reason for the law. As a noun it means "the main person in a school" or "a sum of money." Example: Mrs. Caston is the principal at Hinton High School. We invested a principal of $1000 in a savings certificate.

Principle is a noun and means "underlying rule." Example: We studied the principles of economics.

stationary, stationery

Stationary means "not moving." Example: He rides a stationary bicycle for exercise in the winter.

Stationery means "writing materials," especially paper. Example: I received a letter on the President's personal stationery.

their, there, they're

Their is a possessive pronoun. It shows ownership. Example: The men left their jackets in the car.

There is the opposite of here and refers to a place. (Notice that the word there is made up of the word here plus a t.) Example: Put your cola there on the coaster.

They're is a contraction for they are, and the apostrophe shows the missing a. Example: I'm sure they're (they are) home.

to, too, two

To is used with a noun or with a verb. Examples: Walter went *to* the races. (*to* followed by a noun) Do you want *to* eat lunch at 11:30? (*to* followed by a verb)

Too means "also" or "excessively." Examples: I'm driving. Are you driving *too*? That print is *too* small to read without my glasses.

Two means 2. Example: He reserved a table for *two*.

way, ways

Way is singular. Examples: San Francisco is a long *way* from New York. Your *way* is better than mine.

Ways is plural. Example: There are three *ways* to reach the industrial center.

weather, whether

Weather refers to climate. Example: This rainy *weather* should make the plants grow.

Whether shows a choice. Example: I don't know *whether* to apply for a different job or not.

whose, who's

Whose is a possessive pronoun. Example: *Whose* coat is this?

Who's is a contraction for *who is*. The apostrophe shows the omission of the *i*. Example: *Who's* (Who is) going with me in my car?

your, you're

Your is a possessive pronoun. Example: Don't forget *your* tickets!

You're is a contraction for *you are*, and the apostrophe shows the missing *a*. Example: I hope *you're* (you are) staying for lunch.

PRACTICE
EXERCISE

Directions: Check each of the twenty underlined words below and decide if each is used correctly. Change those that are not used correctly. Then check your answers on the following page.

GUIDES IN THE SKY
A

Just (1) *among the* (2) *two of us, I'm old enough to remember the days when airline flight attendants* (3) *had of been called "stewardesses."* (4) *Different from now, in those earlier years they were all female, all of a certain youth and appearance. By the late 60s, however, it was* (5) *all ready apparent that change was under way.*

B

Now, (6) *accept for some rare instances, the* (7) *amount of male flight attendants continues to grow.* (8) *Further,* (9) *less flight attendants are model-perfect. Instead,* (10) *they're representatives of a broad cultural, age, and physical range. The* (11) *effect of this change on travelers seems obvious.* (12) *Weather* (13) *you're a frequent flier or not, you'll surely agree* (14) *to the* (15) *principal behind the change. Airlines have certainly* (16) *gone a ways to* (17) *infer that they,* (18) *too, recognize the diversity of* (19) *their clients—clients* (20) *who's dollars pay the bills.*

EXERCISE—ANSWERS

1. between
2. (correct)
3. were called
4. (correct)
5. already
6. except
7. number
8. (correct)
9. fewer
10. (correct)
11. (correct)
12. Whether
13. (correct)
14. (correct)
15. principle
16. tried
17. imply
18. (correct)
19. (correct)
20. whose

GED Practice, Chapters 1–9

Directions: The following practice covers material you have studied so far. It's set up in a format similar to that you'll find on the GED test. Read the five paragraphs, and then choose the correct answer from the numbered items below. Finally, check your answers against those given below, and review items that cause you difficulty.

ROAD MAP

- *GED Practice*

FINE FLYING

A

(1) *Whether its for business or pleasure, air travel can be painfully stressful.* (2) *There are frequently long check-in lines, delayed departures, missing connections, and canceled flights.* (3) *So how will the savvy traveler relax and avoid the hassles?* (4) *There is three principals to smooth your way.*

B

(5) *First, travel light so that you'll carry all your luggage aboard.* (6) *If you're out for a week, one roll-aboard bag was sufficiently.* (7) *Them airline-approved bags fit either under the seat or in the overhead compartment.* (8) *Thus, with no luggage to check, they can avoid check-in lines and be guaranteed your luggage arrives when you do.*

C

(9) *Second, asked you're travel agent for a paper ticket rather than an electronic one, and make sure she assigns seats for each leg of your flight.* (10) *This way, you can avoid check-in lines and went straight to you're gate.* (11) *More importantly, however, when you miss your connection or your flight are canceled, you have a ticket in hand to take too another airline's ticket agent.* (12) *You'll avoid more long lines and reach your destination faster, two.*

D

(13) *Third, built a cushion into your travel plans.* (14) *If you have a 10:00 a.m. business appointment on Thursday, plan your flight for Wednesday afternoon or evening.* (15) *Frazzled nerves from a hectic flight connection is no help for your business mind.* (16) *If your cruise ship will depart at noon on Friday, plan your flight for the day before.* (17) *The ship won't wait and the airline won't hire a helicopter to take you two your ship at sea, so your out of luck.*

E

(18) *With wise planning, suggested in the three precautions above, weather you're traveling for business or pleasure, you'll have less hassles and smoother flying than before.*

1. Sentence 1: Whether its for business or pleasure, air travel can be painfully stressful.

    What correction should be made to this sentence?

    (1)   Insert an apostrophe in it's.
    (2)   Change Whether to Weather.
    (3)   Change Whether to Weather and insert an apostrophe in it's.
    (4)   No correction is necessary.

2. Sentence 2: There are frequently long check-in lines, delayed departures, missing connections, and canceled flights.

    What correction should be made to the underlined portion of this sentence?

    (1)   Change it to There is.
    (2)   Change it to Their is.
    (3)   Change it to Their are.
    (4)   No correction is necessary to the underlined portion.

3. Sentence 2: There are frequently long check-in lines, delayed departures, missing connections, and canceled flights.

    What correction should be made to the underlined portion of this sentence?

    (1)   Change it to missed connections.
    (2)   Change it to miss connections.
    (3)   Change it to misses connections.
    (4)   No correction is necessary to the underlined portion.

4. Sentence 3: So how will the savvy traveler relax and avoid the hassles?

    What correction should be made to this sentence?

    (1)   Change how will to how would.
    (2)   Change how will to how does.
    (3)   Change how will to how had.
    (4)   No correction is necessary.

5. Sentence 4: There is three principals to smooth your way.

    What correction should be made to the underlined portion of this sentence?

    (1)   Rewrite it as There are.
    (2)   Rewrite it as Their are.
    (3)   Rewrite it as They're.
    (4)   No correction is necessary.

6. Sentence 4: There is three principals to smooth your way.

    What correction should be made to the underlined portion of this sentence?

    (1)   Change principals to principles.
    (2)   Change principals to principals'.
    (3)   Change principals to principal's.
    (4)   No correction is necessary to the underlined portion.

7. Sentence 5: First, travel light <u>so that you'll</u> carry all your luggage aboard.

What correction should be made to the underlined portion of this sentence?

(1)   Rewrite it as <u>so that you would.</u>
(2)   Rewrite it as <u>so that you can.</u>
(3)   Rewrite it as <u>so that you should.</u>
(4)   No correction is necessary to the underlined portion.

8. Sentence 5: First, travel light so that you'll <u>carry all your luggage</u> aboard.

What correction should be made to the underlined portion of this sentence?

(1)   Rewrite it as <u>carry all you're luggage.</u>
(2)   Rewrite it as <u>carry all you luggage.</u>
(3)   Rewrite it as <u>carry all your luggages.</u>
(4)   No correction is necessary to the underlined portion.

9. Sentence 6: <u>If you're out</u> for a week, one roll-aboard bag was sufficiently.

What correction should be made to the underlined portion of this sentence?

(1)   Rewrite it as <u>If youre out.</u>
(2)   Rewrite it as <u>If your out.</u>
(3)   Rewrite it as <u>If you out.</u>
(4)   No correction is necessary to the underlined portion.

10. Sentence 6: If you're out for a week, <u>one roll-aboard bag was</u> sufficiently.

What correction should be made to the underlined portion of this sentence?

(1)   Rewrite it as <u>one roll-aboard bag will be.</u>
(2)   Rewrite it as <u>one roll-aboard bag should be.</u>
(3)   Rewrite it as <u>one roll-aboard has been.</u>
(4)   No correction is necessary to the underlined portion.

11. Sentence 6: If you're out for a week, one roll-aboard bag was <u>sufficiently</u>.

What correction should be made to the underlined portion of this sentence?

(1)   Change <u>sufficiently</u> to <u>more sufficient.</u>
(2)   Insert <u>mostly</u> in front of <u>sufficiently.</u>
(3)   Change <u>sufficiently</u> to <u>sufficient.</u>
(4)   No correction is necessary to the underlined portion.

12. Sentence 7: Them airline-approved bags fit either under the seat or in the overhead compartment.

What correction should be made to this sentence?

(1)   Insert the word <u>there</u> after <u>Them.</u>
(2)   Change <u>Them</u> to <u>These.</u>
(3)   Change <u>Them</u> to <u>These here.</u>
(4)   No correction is necessary.

13. Sentence 8: Thus, with no luggage to check, they can avoid check-in lines and be guaranteed your luggage arrives when you do.

    What correction should be made to this sentence?

    (1) Change they can avoid to he can avoid.
    (2) Change they can avoid to you can avoid.
    (3) Change they can avoid to we can avoid.
    (4) No correction is necessary.

14. Sentence 9: Second, asked you're travel agent for a paper ticket rather than an electronic one, and make sure she assigns seats for each leg of your flight.

    What correction should be made to the underlined portion of this sentence?

    (1) Rewrite it as Second, askt.
    (2) Rewrite it as Second, asks.
    (3) Rewrite it as Second, ask.
    (4) No correction is necessary to the underlined portion.

15. Sentence 9: Second, asked you're travel agent for a paper ticket rather than an electronic one, and make sure she assigns seats for each leg of your flight.

    What correction should be made to the underlined portion of this sentence?

    (1) Rewrite it as your travel agent.
    (2) Rewrite it as yours travel agent.
    (3) Rewrite it as you travel agent.
    (4) No correction is necessary to the underlined portion.

16. Sentence 10: This way, you can avoid check-in lines and went straight to you're gate.

    What correction should be made to this sentence?

    (1) Rewrite it to read went straight to you're gate.
    (2) Rewrite it to read go straight to you're gate.
    (3) Rewrite it to read go straight to your gate.
    (4) No correction is necessary.

17. Sentence 11: More importantly, however, when you miss your connection or your flight are canceled, you have a ticket in hand to take too another airline's ticket agent.

    What correction should be made to the underlined portion of this sentence?

    (1) Rewrite it as your connection or your flight is canceled.
    (2) Rewrite it as you're connection or you're flight are canceled.
    (3) Rewrite it as you're connection or you're flight is canceled.
    (4) No correction is necessary to the underlined portion.

18. Sentence 11: More importantly, however, when you miss your connection or your flight are canceled, you have a ticket in hand to take too another airline's ticket agent.

    What correction should be made to the underlined portion of this sentence?

    (1) Rewrite it as take two another.
    (2) Rewrite it as take to another.
    (3) Rewrite it as takes too another.
    (4) No correction is necessary to the underlined portion.

19. Sentence 11: More importantly, however, when you miss your connection or your flight are canceled, you have a ticket in hand to take too <u>another airline's ticket agent.</u>

What correction should be made to the underlined portion of this sentence?

(1) Rewrite it as <u>another airlines' ticket agent.</u>
(2) Rewrite it as <u>another airlines ticket agent.</u>
(3) Rewrite it as <u>another airline ticket agent.</u>
(4) No correction is necessary to the underlined portion.

20. Sentence 12: <u>You'll avoid</u> more long lines and reach your destination faster, two.

What correction should be made to the underlined portion of this sentence?

(1) Change <u>You'll</u> to <u>You'd.</u>
(2) Change <u>You'll</u> to <u>You.</u>
(3) Change <u>You'll</u> to <u>You would.</u>
(4) No correction is necessary to the underlined portion.

21. Sentence 12: You'll avoid more long lines and <u>reach your destination faster, two.</u>

What correction should be made to the underlined portion of this sentence?

(1) Rewrite it as <u>reach</u> your destination faster, to.
(2) Rewrite it as <u>reach you're destination faster, two.</u>
(3) Rewrite it as <u>reach your destination faster, too.</u>
(4) No correction is necessary to the underlined portion.

22. Sentence 13: Third, built a cushion into your travel plans.

What correction should be made to this sentence?

(1) Change <u>built</u> to <u>build.</u>
(2) Change <u>built</u> to <u>building.</u>
(3) Change <u>built</u> to <u>have built.</u>
(4) No correction is necessary.

23. Sentence 14: If you have a 10:00 a.m. business appointment on Thursday, plan your flight for Wednesday afternoon or evening.

What correction should be made to this sentence?

(1) Change <u>have</u> to <u>had.</u>
(2) Change <u>have</u> to <u>have had.</u>
(3) Change <u>you have</u> to <u>you're having.</u>
(4) No correction is necessary.

24. Sentence 15: Frazzled nerves from a hectic flight connection is no help for your business mind.

What correction should be made to this sentence?

(1) Change <u>is</u> to <u>are.</u>
(2) Change <u>flight connection is</u> to <u>flight connections is.</u>
(3) Change <u>flight connection is</u> to <u>flight connection aren't.</u>
(4) No correction is necessary.

25. Sentence 16: <u>If your cruise ship</u> will depart at noon on Friday, plan your flight for the day before.

    What correction should be made to the underlined portion of this sentence?

    (1)   Change <u>your</u> to <u>you're</u>.
    (2)   Change <u>your</u> to <u>you</u>.
    (3)   Capitalize the words <u>Cruise Ship</u>.
    (4)   No correction is necessary to the underlined portion.

26. Sentence 16: If your cruise <u>ship will depart</u> at noon on Friday, plan your flight for the day before.

    What correction should be made to the underlined portion of this sentence?

    (1)   Change <u>will depart</u> to <u>has departed</u>.
    (2)   Change <u>will depart</u> to <u>departs</u>.
    (3)   Capitalize the word <u>Ship</u>.
    (4)   No correction is necessary to the underlined portion.

27. Sentence 17: <u>The ship won't wait</u> and the airline won't hire a helicopter to take you two your ship at sea, so your out of luck.

    What correction should be made to the underlined portion of this sentence?

    (1)   Omit the apostrophe from <u>won't</u>.
    (2)   Capitalize the word <u>Ship</u>.
    (3)   Capitalize the word <u>Ship</u> and omit the apostrophe from <u>won't</u>.
    (4)   No correction is necessary to the underlined portion.

28. Sentence 17: The ship won't <u>wait and the airline</u> won't hire a helicopter to take you two your ship at sea, so your out of luck.

    What correction should be made to the underlined portion of this sentence?

    (1)   Insert a comma after <u>wait</u>.
    (2)   Omit the word <u>and</u> after <u>wait</u>.
    (3)   Insert a comma after the word <u>wait</u> and omit the word <u>and</u>
    (4)   No correction is necessary to the underlined portion.

29. Sentence 17: The ship won't wait and the airline won't hire a helicopter to <u>take you two your ship</u> at sea, so your out of luck.

    What correction should be made to the underlined portion of this sentence?

    (1)   Rewrite it as <u>take you too your ship</u>.
    (2)   Rewrite it as <u>take you two you're ship</u>.
    (3)   Rewrite it as <u>take you to your ship</u>.
    (4)   No correction is necessary to the underlined portion.

30. Sentence 17: The ship won't wait and the airline won't hire a helicopter to take you two your ship <u>at sea, so</u> your out of luck.

    What correction should be made to the underlined portion of this sentence?

    (1)   Omit the comma.
    (2)   Omit the comma and add the word <u>and</u> after <u>sea</u>.
    (3)   Insert a period after the word <u>sea</u> and capitalize the word <u>So</u>.
    (4)   No correction is necessary to the underlined portion.

31. Sentence 17: The ship won't wait and the airline won't hire a helicopter to take you two your ship at sea, so <u>your out of luck</u>.

What correction should be made to the underlined portion of this sentence?

(1) Rewrite it as <u>your are out of luck</u>.
(2) Rewrite it as <u>you're out of luck</u>.
(3) Rewrite it as <u>your' out of luck</u>.
(4) No correction is necessary to the underlined portion.

32. Sentence 18: With wise planning, suggested in the three precautions <u>above, weather</u> you're traveling for business or pleasure, you'll have less hassles and smoother flying than before.

What correction should be made to the underlined portion of this sentence?

(1) Rewrite it as <u>above, whether</u>.
(2) Rewrite it as <u>above, weather or not</u>.
(3) Rewrite it as <u>above, if or weather</u>.
(4) No correction is necessary to the underlined portion.

33. Sentence 18: With wise planning, suggested in the three precautions above, weather <u>you're traveling for business or pleasure</u>, you'll have less hassles and smoother flying than before.

What correction should be made to the underlined portion of this sentence?

(1) Change <u>you're</u> to <u>your</u>.
(2) Change <u>you're</u> to <u>your</u> and capitalize the word <u>Business</u>.
(3) Capitalize the word <u>Business</u>.
(4) No correction is necessary to the underlined portion.

34. Sentence 18: With wise planning, suggested in the three precautions above, weather you're traveling for business or pleasure, <u>you'll have less hassles</u> and smoother flying than before.

What correction should be made to the underlined portion of this sentence?

(1) Change <u>less</u> to <u>fewer</u>.
(2) Change <u>you'll</u> to <u>you</u>
(3) Change <u>you'll</u> to <u>you</u> and change <u>less</u> to <u>fewer</u>.
(4) No correction is necessary to the underlined portion.

35. Sentence 18: With wise planning, suggested in the three precautions above, weather you're traveling for business or pleasure, you'll have less hassles <u>and smoother flying</u> than before.

What correction should be made to the underlined portion of this sentence?

(1) Change <u>smoother</u> to <u>smooth</u>.
(2) Change <u>smoother</u> to <u>smoothest</u>.
(3) Change <u>smoother</u> to <u>more smooth</u>.
(4) No correction is necessary to the underlined portion.

GED PRACTICE—ANSWERS

1. (1) The apostrophe in *it's* means *it is*. See Chapter 5, Rule 10.
2. (4) The plural verb *are* agrees with the compound subject *lines, departures, connections,* and *flights*. See Chapter 3, Problem 1, Situation B.
3. (1) The word *missed* should be in the same form as the other verb-like words, *delayed* and *canceled*. See Chapter 7, Rule 1.
4. (2) Maintain the same tense throughout an essay. See Chapter 7, Rule 1.
5. (1) The plural verb *are* agrees with its plural subject *principles*. See Chapter 3, Problem 1, Situation B.
6. (1) *Principles* refers to rules. See Chapter 9.
7. (2) Maintain the same verb tense throughout an essay. See Chapter 7, Rule 1.
8. (4) Maintain the same verb tense. See Chapter 7, Rule 1.
9. (4) *You're* is a contraction meaning *you are*. See Chapter 5, Rule 10.
10. (2) Maintain present verb tense. See Chapter 7, Rule 1.
11. (3) *Sufficient* is an adjective that modifies the noun *bag*. See Chapter 6, Rule 3.
12. (2) The pronoun *these* is plural to agree with *bags*. See Chapter 5, Rule 9.
13. (2) Maintain the same point of view throughout an essay (second person in this case). See Chapter 5, Rule 1, Hint 2.
14. (3) *Ask* is a regular verb. See Chapter 7, Rule 4.
15. (1) Use the possessive *your*. See Chapter 5, Rule 10.
16. (3) Use consistent tense (present tense in this case). See Chapter 7, Rule 1. Also use the possessive form of the pronoun, not a contraction. See Chapter 5, Rule 10.
17. (1) *Your* is the possessive pronoun. See Chapter 5, Rule 10. The singular verb *is* agrees with the singular subject *connection or flight*. See Chapter 3, Problem 3.
18. (2) *To* is the preposition. See Chapter 9.
19. (4) *Airline's* is singular possessive. See Chapter 4, Part II.
20. (4) *You'll* is the contraction meaning *you will*. See Chapter 5, Rule 10.
21. (3) *Too* means "also." See Chapter 9.
22. (1) Use present tense to be consistent with other verbs in the essay. See Chapter 7, Rule 1. *Build* is an irregular verb. See Chapter 7, Rule 4.
23. (4) Present tense is accurate. See Chapter 7, Rule 1.
24. (1) *Are* is a plural verb to agree with the plural subject *nerves*. See Chapter 3, Problem 1.
25. (4) The possessive pronoun *your* is correct. See Chapter 5, Rule 10. Do not capitalize common nouns. See Chapter 4, Part III, Rule 2.
26. (2) Maintain present tense throughout the essay. See Chapter 7, Rule 1.
27. (4) The contraction *won't* means *will not* and is consistent with other verbs. See Chapter 7, Rule 1. Do not capitalize common nouns. See Chapter 4, Part III, Rule 2.
28. (1) Use a comma and conjunction to join two sentences. See Chapter 8, Part II, Rule 1.
29. (3) *To* is a preposition; it's object is *ship*. See Chapter 9.
30. (3) Avoid stringing multiple sentences together with commas or with commas and conjunctions. See Chapter 8, Part II, Rule 1, Warning 1.
31. (2) *You're* is a contraction meaning *you are*. See Chapter 5, Rule 10.
32. (1) *Whether* refers to making a choice. See Chapter 9.
33. (4) *You're* is a contraction meaning *you are*. See Chapter 5, Rule 10. Do not capitalize common nouns. See Chapter 4, Part III, Rule 2.
34. (1) Use *fewer* with anything you can count. See Chapter 6, Rule 6.
35. (4) *Smoother* is the comparative form of the adjective. See Chapter 6, Rule 7.

Verbal Phrases

You can get through life quite comfortably without knowing anything about phrases, particularly verbal phrases. In fact, verbals function as nouns, adjectives, or adverbs; so, in essence, you already know about them from Chapter 1. Why, then, spend any time talking about them? For the purposes of the GED, there are two main reasons: First, understanding some of the basics about phrases will make understanding punctuation much easier. Second, knowing how to use phrases will improve your ability to vary sentence structure. (There were three phrases in that last sentence, by the way!)

You've already learned about prepositional phrases (see Chapter 1, Part 5, and Chapter 8, Part 1, to review). And you've already learned about verb phrases (see Chapter 1, Part 2, and Chapter 7 to review). Now you're ready to learn about verbal phrases.

So, what are verbals? Verbals are words that look like verbs but are not used as verbs. Verbals can be used as nouns, adjectives, or adverbs; so they can function in the following ways:

> subjects
> direct objects
> objects of prepositions
> predicate words
> appositives
> noun modifiers
> verb modifiers
> adjective modifiers
> adverb modifiers

We will talk about the characteristics and functions of the three kinds of verbals:

> infinitives
> gerunds
> participles

ROAD MAP

- *Infinitives*
- *Gerunds*
- *Participles*
- *Practice*
- *GED Practice*

PART 1: INFINITIVES

A. Characteristics

An infinitive has the following characteristics to help you recognize it:

1. Basic appearance: An infinitive is made up of *to* plus a verb.

   Example 1: *To advance* is his goal. (*To* plus the verb *advance* make the infinitive.)

   Example 2: He wanted *to work* late. (*To* and the verb *work* make the infinitive.)

2. Infinitive phrase: Verbals, like verbs, take both adverb modifiers and direct objects. The infinitive and its objects and/or modifiers form the infinitive phrase. (Remember that objects answer *who?* or *what?* after the verbal; adverb modifiers tell *how, when, where,* or *to what extent.*)

Example: He wanted *to drive the borrowed car carefully.* (*To* and the verb *drive* make the infinitive. If you ask, "To drive *who* or *what?*" you get *car* as your answer. That, of course, is the object of the infinitive *to drive.* *Carefully* tells *how* about the infinitive *to drive,* so it is an adverb modifier. The entire infinitive phrase, then, is *to drive the borrowed car carefully.*

To put it simply:

$$\text{to} + \text{verb} + \left\{ \begin{array}{c} \text{object(s)} \\ \text{and/or} \\ \text{modifier(s)} \end{array} \right\} = \text{infinitive phrases}$$

Now consider this additional example:

Example: To instruct his young relatives in the routines of square dancing was the fiddler's only desire.

Infinitive: *to instruct* (*to* + the verb *instruct*)

Object: *relatives* (Instruct *who* or *what*?)

Modifiers: *young* (adjective modifying the object *relatives*); *in the routines* (prepositional phrase that modifies *instruct*); and *of square dancing* (prepositional phrase that modifies *routines*)

The entire infinitive phrase, then, is *to instruct his young relatives in the routines of square dancing.*

Warning: Remember that not every *to* will introduce an infinitive.

to + noun = prepositional phrase
to + verb = infinitive

Example 1: He walked to the convention hall early. (*To the convention hall* is *to* plus the noun *hall* and so is a prepositional phrase, not an infinitive.)

Example 2: He walked to keep trim. (*To keep trim* is *to* plus the verb *keep* and therefore an infinitive.

B. Function

An infinitive or infinitive phrase functions as a noun or as an adjective or as an adverb. Think of the whole phrase as one word. You can then use the sentence attack plan to determine which part of the sentence it is. (See Chapter 2.) If the infinitive does not fit in the sentence attack plan, then you know you have a modifier.

Consider now the specific functions of an infinitive:

1. Noun: Since an infinitive functions as a noun, it can function in most of the ways a noun can function:

    a. As subject

        Example: *To become educated* was their primary ambition. (*To become educated* is the subject of *was.*)

b.   As predicate word

Example: The program's purpose was *to entertain*. (*To entertain* follows the linking verb *was* and renames the subject *purpose*.)

c.   As an appositive

Example: While in college, Marlene had only one goal: *to get as thorough an education as possible*. (Remember that an appositive renames a noun. *To get as thorough an education as possible* renames *goal*.)

d.   As direct object

Example: The City Councilman wanted *to expand the Park Board budget*.

(*To expand the Park Board budget* answers *what*? after the action verb *wanted*.)

2.   Adjective: As an adjective, an infinitive modifies a noun:

Example: This is the class *to take*! (*To take* modifies the noun *class*.)

3.   Adverb: Like other adverbs, infinitives can modify verbs, adjectives, and other adverbs:

a.   As verb modifier

Example: Martha has gone *to visit her sister in New Orleans*. (*To visit her sister in New Orleans* answers the adverb question *where*? about the action verb *gone*.)

b.   As adjective modifier

Example: You were lucky *to pass the course*. (*To pass the course* explains *how* about the predicate adjective *lucky*.)

c.   As adverb modifier

Example: The doctor operated too late *to save the accident victim*. (*To save the accident victim* explains *to what extent* about the adverb *late*.)

D. Process

Use the following steps to identify the function of the infinitive phrase:

Step 1: Identify the phrase.

Step 2: Think of the phrase as one word.

Step 3: Use the sentence attack plan to determine the functions of subject, direct object, and predicate word.

Step 4: If the phrase does not fit in the sentence attack plan, you will know the phrase is a modifier.

Example 1: The incumbent hoped to win the election.

Step 1: The incumbent hoped *to win the election*.

Step 2: Think: The incumbent hoped *towintheelection*.

Step 3: a. Find the verb; *hoped*

b. *Hoped* is an action verb.

c. Ask: *who* or *what* hoped?

Answer: *incumbent* (subject)

d. Ask: incumbent hoped *who* or *what?*

Answer: towintheelection

(The infinitive phrase is the direct object.)

Example 2: The man to see about gardening problems is the county agent.

Step 1: The man *to see about gardening problems* is the county agent.

Step 2: Think: The man *toseeaboutgardeningproblems* is the county agent.

Step 3: a. Find the verb: *is*

b. *Is* is a linking verb.

c. Ask: *who* or *what is?*

Answer: *man* (subject)

d. Ask: man is *who* or *what?*

Answer: *agent* (predicate noun)

Step 4: The infinitive did not fit in the sentence attack plan, so it must be a modifier. *To see about gardening problems* answers *which one* about the noun *man,* so the infinitive phrase functions as an adjective.

E. Usage

As you begin consciously using infinitive phrases to increase sentence variety, keep in mind that the *to* and the verb form should not be separated:

Example: Incorrect: He planned *to* not *go* on a vacation this year.

Correct: He planned not *to go* on a vacation this year.

The separation of *to* from the verb form is called a *split infinitive.* Effective writers try to avoid split infinitives.

WARNING

Never split an infinitive!

PART 2: GERUNDS

A. Characteristics

A gerund has the following characteristics:

1. Basic appearance: A gerund ends in *-ing*.

   Example 1: *Swimming* at Hartke Pool is his favorite pastime.

   Example 2: *Running* weekend marathons in the city keeps him in good physical shape.

   Example 3: He considered *running* for office.

   Example 4: After *eating* the cake and ice cream, I felt stuffed.

2. Gerund phrases: Gerunds, like infinitives, can take objects and modifiers. All of these together make up the gerund phrase:

   –*ing* word
   +
   objects(s)   } = gerund phrase
   +
   modifier(s)

   Example 1: *Swimming at Hartke Pool* is his favorite pastime.

   (*At Hartke Pool* modifies *swimming* by explaining *where.* So the entire gerund phrase is the gerund plus its modifier: *swimming at Hartke Pool.*)

Example 2:   *Running weekend marathons in the city* keeps him in good physical shape.

(*Marathons* answers *what?* about *running,* so it is the object of the gerund. *Weekend* describes *which* about *marathons.* *In the city,* a prepositional phrase, functions as an adverb to tell *where* about *marathons.* The gerund and its object and modifiers, then, make up the entire gerund phrase: *running weekend marathons in the city.*)

Example 3:   He considered *running for office.*

(*For office* tells *how*? about *running,* so the gerund phrase is *running for office.*)

Example 4:   After *eating the cake and ice cream,* I felt stuffed.

(*Cake and ice cream* answer *what?* after *eating.* *Cake and ice cream* are the compound objects of the gerund *eating.* They and the gerund make up the complete gerund phrase: *eating the cake and ice cream.*)

Warning: Not all *-ing* words are gerunds. With that warning in mind, think about *function.*

B. Function

A gerund or a gerund phrase functions as a noun. (Remember, think of the phrase as a single word.)

1.   As subject

Example: *Playing flag football* was not his idea of fun.
(*Playing flag football* is the subject of *was.*)

2.   As predicate word

Example: Aunt Mary's hobby is *crocheting doilies.*

(*Crocheting doilies* answers *what?* after the linking verb *is* and renames the subject *hobby.*)

3.   As direct object

Example: Most people enjoy *listening to music.*

(*Listening to music* answers *what*? after the action verb *enjoy.*)

4.   As object of the preposition

Example: The attorney won the case by *proving the witness a liar.*

(*By* is a preposition, and *proving the witness* a liar answers *by what?*

The whole prepositional phrase functions to tell *how?* about the verb *won.*)

5.   As appositive

Example: His job, *collecting data for the Environmental Protection Agency,* required painstaking effort.

(Remember, an appositive, which renames another noun, is usually set off with commas. This gerund phrase, which functions as an appositive, renames the noun *job.*)

WARNING

Not all *-ing* words are gerunds.

REMEMBER

Function tells all. To be gerunds, *-ing* words must function as *nouns*.

Now let us reconsider the warning above: Not all *-ing* words are gerunds. Which of the following *-ing* words are gerunds?

1. Robert is *swimming* forty laps a day, now.

2. The small child, *walking* alone, became lost.

3. *Sobbing,* the old woman sank to her knees.

4. Woolen garments are *rising* in price.

5. The puppy was *chewing* on my shoes for two days.

None of these *-ing* words are gerunds. Why? None of them function as *nouns*. Look at the following explanations:

1. *Is swimming* is the verb.

2. *Walking* functions as an adjective.

3. *Sobbing* functions as an adjective.

4. *Are rising* is the verb.

5. *Was chewing* is the verb.

PART 3: PARTICIPLES

A. Characteristics

Participles have the following characteristics to help you recognize them:

1. Basic appearance: Because there are two kinds of participles, they have two different forms:

   a. Past participles usually end in *-ed* (the form of the verb you would use with the helping words *have* or *has:* have *walked,* have *taken,* have *sung.*)

   Example: The picture frame, *mottled* with old paint, needed refinishing.

HINT

A participle functions as an adjective; a gerund functions as a noun. Because they look alike, participles and gerunds are distinguished only by function.

   b. Present participles end in *-ing.* (So they *look* like gerunds. They do *not,* however, function as gerunds do.)

   Example 1: The picture *hanging* above the sofa depicts a pastoral scene.

   > (a present participle functioning as an adjective to modify the noun *picture*)

   Example 2: Warren likes *walking* for daily exercise.

   > (a gerund functioning as a noun, the object of the verb *likes*)

2. Participial phrases: Just like infinitives and gerunds, participles can have objects and modifiers.

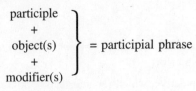

$$\left. \begin{array}{c} \text{participle} \\ + \\ \text{object(s)} \\ + \\ \text{modifier(s)} \end{array} \right\} = \text{participial phrase}$$

a. As present participial phrase

Example 1: *Walking home from work,* John tripped on the sidewalk.

(*Home* tells *where* about *walking;* and *from work,* a prepositional phrase, modifies *walking.* The whole phrase, then, is the participle plus its modifiers: *walking home from work.*)

Example 2: *Humming a haunting melody,* my coworker helped relieve my stress.

(*Melody* answers *what?* about *humming,* so it is the object of the participle. *Haunting* tells *what kind* about *melody.* So the whole participial phrase is *humming a haunting melody.*)

b. As past participial phrase

Example: *Beaten by the wind,* the tomato plants looked wilted.

(*By the wind* tells *how* about *beaten;* then the whole participial phrase is made of the participle and its modifier: *beaten by the wind.*)

B. Function

Participles always function as adjectives. They modify nouns. As adjectives, participles may serve in the following ways:

1. Noun modifier

Example 1: *Walking down the road,* we saw a fox terrier.

(The participle modifies the subject *we.*)

Example 2: We saw a fox terrier *walking down the road.*

(The participle modifies the object *terrier.*)

2. Predicate word

Example 1: The supervisor was *mistaken.*

(*Mistaken* follows the linking verb *was* and describes the subject *supervisor.*)

Example 2: The defendant seemed *unconcerned about the attorney's questioning.*

(The participial phrase follows the linking verb *seemed* and describes the subject *defendant.*)

NOTE

When a participial phrase appears at the beginning of a sentence, follow the phrase with a comma.

C. Usage

When the participial phrase appears at the beginning of a sentence, the phrase is followed by a comma. The phrase will modify the noun immediately after the comma.

Example: *Watching the sunrise from inside their tent,* the two campers reveled in their enjoyment of the peace and quiet.

(The participial phrase, followed by a comma, modifies *campers,* the first noun after the comma.)

Warning: Since the participial phrase *must* modify the first noun after the comma, be sure to avoid ridiculous sentences:

Example 1: Ridiculous: Arriving late at the bus stop, the bus went off without me.

(The *bus* did not arrive late!)

Better: Arriving late at the bus stop, I missed the bus.

(The participial phrase must modify the noun after the comma: *I.*)

Example 2: Ridiculous: Having forgotten to wind it, the clock stopped at midnight.

(The *clock* did not forget to wind itself!)

Better: Having forgotten to wind the clock, I found it had stopped at midnight.

Example 3: Ridiculous: Walking home from the graveyard, an old abandoned house seemed especially eerie.

(A *house* walking??)

Better: Walking home from the graveyard, Robert thought the old abandoned house seemed especially eerie.

PRACTICE
EXERCISE

Directions: Look at the following sentences and find the verbals. Identify the kind of verbal (infinitive, gerund, or participle) and its function (subject, modifier of noun, predicate word, etc.). Answers follow the sentences. Hint: *Some sentences have more than one verbal.*

1. Startled, he stood quietly, breathing rapidly.
2. An excellent form of exercise is jogging at a steady, even pace for a mile or so.
3. To find the old cemetery, we followed the nearly invisible trail; but, suffering from the heat, we gave up.
4. To eat moderately seemed advisable.
5. Washing a car is sometimes tedious to do.
6. The old man's hobby was playing in a German folk band.
7. After the heavy snows ceased, I no longer wished to be confined to the house.
8. The try-outs, conducted by the orchestra director and her assistant, were held once each year.
9. Sustained by chocolate, I shall win all battles except those with the waistline.
10. Having refused his phone call, Evelyn had little chance of accepting his apology.

EXERCISE—ANSWERS

1. *Startled* is a participle and functions as an adjective to modify the noun *he*. *Breathing rapidly* is a participial phrase and functions to modify the noun *he*. (Remember, participles can modify only *nouns*, not verbs.)
2. *Jogging at a steady, even pace for a mile or so* is a gerund phrase and is the predicate word after the linking verb *is*.
3. *To find the old cemetery* is an infinitive phrase and functions as an adverb to modify the verb *followed*. *Suffering from the heat* is a participial phrase and functions as an adjective to modify the noun *we*.
4. *To eat moderately* is an infinitive phrase and is the subject of the sentence.
5. *Washing a car* is a gerund phrase and is the subject of the sentence. *To do* is an infinitive and functions as an adverb to modify the adjective *tedious*.
6. *Playing in a German folk band* is a gerund phrase and is the predicate word after the linking verb *was*.
7. *To be confined to the house* is an infinitive phrase; and, in a noun function, it is the direct object of the verb *wished*.
8. *Conducted by the orchestra director and her assistant* is a participial phrase and functions as an adjective to modify the noun *try-outs*.
9. *Sustained by chocolate* is a participial phrase and functions as an adjective to modify the noun *I*.
10. *Having refused his phone call* is a participial phrase and functions as an adjective to modify the noun *Evelyn*. *Accepting his apology* is a gerund phrase; and, acting as a noun, it is the object of the preposition *of*.

GED PRACTICE

Directions: The following practice is similar in format to the GED exam. Read the paragraphs. Then, select the best answer from the choices given. Next, check your answers against those that follow, paying particular attention to explanations accompanying any items you missed. Finally, review the portions of this material on phrases that have caused you difficulty.

ELEVATOR MUSIC

A

(1) We hear it everywhere—in elevators, in restaurants, airport terminals, in offices. (2) Non-musical music annoys me, white noise that's supposed to mask conversations, relieve stress, and help us avoid silence. (3) In fact in today's society silence apparently is no longer golden. (4) For instance, when making a business call we often find ourselves put on hold and fed mindless music. (5) Or finding ourselves waiting for that important business appointment, we're bombarded by annoying music in the waiting room that destroys our concentration on the upcoming task.

B

(6) I'm in favor to eliminate the so-called elevator music. (7) Let's return to golden silence. (8) At home we can choose real music like jazz, country, rock, or classical. (9) In our homes and cars without imposing our preferences on others we can play our favorite CDs. (10) In the workplace, the waiting room, on the phone, or elevator, however, let's have relief! (11) From the otherwise non-stop assault on our ears we need a break. (12) If, on the other hand, some of us can't cope with silence, those folks can clamp on headphones, leaving the rest of us in blessed silence.

1. Sentence 1: We hear it everywhere—in elevators, in restaurants, airport terminals, in offices.

   What correction should be made to this sentence?

   (1) Add the word <u>in</u> in front of <u>airport terminals.</u>
   (2) Omit the comma after <u>terminals.</u>
   (3) Omit the word <u>in</u> in front of <u>offices.</u>
   (4) No correction is necessary.

2. Sentence 2: <u>Non-musical music annoys me, white noise that's supposed</u> to mask conversations, relieve stress, and help us avoid silence.

   What correction should be made to the underlined portion of this sentence?

   (1) Reword it to read <u>It's annoying non-musical music, white noise that's supposed.</u>
   (2) Reword it to read <u>Annoying non-musical music, white noise that's supposed.</u>
   (3) Reword it to read <u>I'm annoyed by non-musical music white noise that's supposed.</u>
   (4) No correction is necessary to the underlined portion.

3. Sentence 3: In fact in today's society silence apparently is no longer golden.

What correction should be made to this sentence?

(1) Insert a comma after society.
(2) Insert a comma after fact and after society.
(3) Insert a comma after fact.
(4) No correction is necessary.

4. Sentence 4: For instance, when making a business call we often find ourselves put on hold and fed mindless music.

What correction should be made to this sentence?

(1) Rewrite it to read when making a business call, you often find yourself.
(2) Rewrite it to read when making a business call, we often find ourselves.
(3) Rewrite it to read when you're making a business call, you often find yourself.
(4) No correction is necessary.

5. Sentence 5: Or finding ourselves waiting for that important business appointment, we're bombarded by annoying music in the waiting room that destroys our concentration on the upcoming task.

What correction should be made to the underlined portion of this sentence?

(1) Reword it to read we're bombarded by annoying music that destroys our concentration on the upcoming task in the waiting room
(2) Reword it to read we're bombarded in the waiting room by annoying music that destroys our concentration on the upcoming task
(3) Reword it to read we're in the waiting room bombarded by annoying music that destroys our concentration on the upcoming task
(4) No correction is necessary to the underlined portion.

6. Sentence 6: I'm in favor to eliminate the so-called elevator music.

What correction should be made to this sentence?

(1) Change to eliminate to of eliminating.
(2) Change in favor to favorable.
(3) Change in favor to favorable and change eliminate to eliminating.
(4) No correction is necessary.

7. Sentence 8: At home we can choose real music like jazz, country, rock, or classical.

What correction should be made to this sentence?

(1) Change like to as.
(2) Insert a comma after music.
(3) Insert a comma after music and omit the word like.
(4) No correction is necessary.

8. Sentence 9: In our homes and cars without imposing our preferences on others we can play our favorite CDs.

   How can this sentence best be rewritten?

   (1) Reword it to read In our homes and cars we can play our favorite CDs without imposing our preferences on others.
   (2) Reword it to read In our homes and cars, we can play our favorite CDs without imposing our preferences on others.
   (3) Reword it to read Without imposing our preferences on others, in our homes and cars we can play our favorite CDs.
   (4) No rewriting is necessary.

9. Sentence 10: In the workplace, the waiting room, on the phone, or elevator, however, let's have relief!

   What correction should be made to the underlined portion of this sentence?

   (1) Rewrite it as In the workplace, in the waiting room, on.
   (2) Rewrite it as In the workplace in the waiting room on.
   (3) Rewrite it as In the workplace, or in the waiting room on.
   (4) No correction is necessary to the underlined portion.

10. Sentence 10: In the workplace, the waiting room, on the phone, or elevator, however, let's have relief!

   What correction should be made to the underlined portion of this sentence?

   (1) Rewrite it as on the phone or in the elevator, however.
   (2) Rewrite it as on the phone, or the elevator, however.
   (3) Rewrite it as on the phone, or in the elevator, however.
   (4) No correction is necessary to the underlined portion.

11. Sentence 11: From the otherwise non-stop assault on our ears we need a break.

   How can this sentence best be rewritten?

   (1) Rewrite it to read We need a break from the assault on our ears that is otherwise non-stop.
   (2) Rewrite it to read We need a break from the otherwise non-stop assault on our ears.
   (3) Rewrite it to read We need a break, from the otherwise non-stop assault on our ears.
   (4) No rewriting is necessary.

12. Sentence 12: If, on the other hand, some of us can't cope with silence, those folks can clamp on headphones, leaving the rest of us in blessed silence.

   What correction should be made to the underlined portion of this sentence?

   (1) Rewrite it as can clamp on headphones, and leaving the rest.
   (2) Rewrite it as can clamp on headphones, leave the rest.
   (3) Rewrite it as can clamp on headphones and leaving the rest.
   (4) No correction is necessary to the underlined portion.

GED PRACTICE—ANSWERS

1. (1) The three prepositional phrases should be written the same way; thus, since *in elevators* and *in offices* include the preposition, so should *in airport terminals*.

2. (1) The appositive phrase *white noise that's supposed to mask conversations...* must appear immediately after the noun it renames, in this case *non-musical music*. Note that choice (2) would result in an incomplete sentence and that choice (3) omits the necessary comma to set off appositives.

3. (1) The comma after *society* avoids confusion and sets off the two introductory prepositional phrases.

4. (2) The comma after *call* marks the end of the introductory phrase. Since the remainder of the paragraphs are written from first person plural point of view [using *we*], it would be bad usage to change to *you*.

5. (2) *Bombarded* modifies *we* and so needs to be close to the word. Likewise, *in the waiting room* tells where about *bombarded* and so needs to be close to the word. *By annoying music* tells how about *bombarded*.

6. (1) The word *favor* is usually followed by the preposition *of*.

7. (2) The comma after *music* clarifies what follows; the preposition *like* creates a prepositional phrase and makes clear the writer's intent to name kinds of music.

8. (2) The introductory prepositional phrase is followed by a comma to eliminate confusion. Other phrases need to appear closest to the words they modify.

9. (1) Each part in the series of prepositional phrases needs to be written in the same way with commas separating each item in the series.

10. (3) Each part in the series of prepositional phrases needs to be written in the same way, with commas separating each item in the series.

11. (2) No commas separate the verb from its modifiers. *On our ears* modifies *assault* and so must follow it.

12. (4) The participle *leaving* needs no coordinating conjunction in front of it.

Clauses

There are two kinds of clauses:

1. Independent clauses (sometimes called main clauses) have subjects and verbs and can stand alone as sentences. That's where the name "independent" comes in. We'll talk more about independent clauses—especially when they stand alone as sentences—in Chapter 15, Basic Sentence Structures.

2. Dependent clauses (sometimes called subordinate clauses) have subjects and verbs but cannot stand alone. That's what this chapter is about. Consider these examples of dependent clauses:

>. . . after the *snow began.* . . .

>. . . *that stands* in the front yard. . . .

>. . . that I *told* you about. . . .

Notice that clauses are different from phrases that you studied in the last chapter. Clauses *must* have subjects and verbs; phrases do not have subjects and verbs.

You will learn more about how independent and dependent clauses work together in Chapter 15, Basic Sentence Structures.

There are three kinds of dependent clauses that we will be studying in this chapter:

1. noun clause

2. adjective clause

3. adverb clause

PART 1: NOUN CLAUSE

A. Characteristics:

1. The noun clause will have a subject and a verb and will usually start with one of these words:

>who   which
>whose what
>whom   that

(*Ever* can be added to most of these words, too: *whoever, whatever.*)

Example 1: That man is *who came to the door.*

>(Subject, *who*; verb, *came*)

Example 2: No one knew *whose book was left behind.*

>(Subject, *book*; verb, *was left*)

Example 3: I talked with *whomever the company sent to settle my claim.*

>(Subject, *company*; verb, *sent*)

ROAD MAP

- *Noun Clause*
- *Adjective Clause*
- *Adverb Clause*
- *Practice*
- *GED Practice*

Example 4: *Which party is guilty* is the question.

(Subject, *party*; verb, *is*)

Example 5: There is no excuse for *what happened*.

(Subject, *what*; verb, *happened*)

Example 6: Brad explained that *Jim's work was done exceptionally well.*

(Subject, *work*; verb, *was done*)

2. Sometimes the first word in the noun clause is the subject of the verb of the clause.

Example: . . . who came to the door. . . .

(*Who* is the subject of the verb *came.*)

3. The clause may have an object and/or modifiers.

Example 1: . . . who came *to the door.* . . .

(*To the door*, a prepositional phrase, tells *where* about *came*, so the phrase is an adverb modifier.)

Example 2: *Whoever designed the building* took credit for its striking appearance.

(*Building* answers *what*? after the action verb *designed*, so it is the direct object of *designed.*)

4. Sometimes the first word in the noun clause is the object of the verb or a predicate word.

Example 1: *What he saw* startled him.

(*He* is the subject of the action verb *saw; what* is the direct object of *saw.*)

Example 2: No one knew *who she was.*

(*Who* is the predicate word after the linking verb *was.*)

B. Function

The noun clause may function many of the same ways a single noun functions:

1. As subject

Example: *Whoever called you yesterday* mispronounced your name.

(The noun clause, when thought of as a single word, answers *who*? in front of the verb.)

2. As predicate word

Example: His faith is *what keeps him alive.*

(The noun clause follows the linking verb *is* and renames *faith*. Notice that the sentence order can be reversed so that the noun clause becomes the subject: *What keeps him alive* is his faith.)

3. As direct object

Example: The witness explained *what he saw.*

(The noun clause answers *what*? after the action verb *explained.*)

4. As object of preposition

Example: Unfortunately, people are sometimes judged by *what they wear.*

(*By* is a preposition, and the noun clause, when thought of as a single word, answers the question *by what*?)

5. As appositive

   Example: My long-range concern, *that you learn grammar*, helps me to keep finding examples!

   (The noun clause renames the noun *concern* and is set off with commas.)

C. Attack plan

Use the following steps to determine the function of the noun clause.

Step 1: Find the clause, beginning with one of the special words (*who, whose, whom, which, what,* or *that*) and ending after all the modifiers and/or objects.

Step 2: Think of the clause as a single word.

Step 3: Use the sentence attack plan (see Chapter 2) to determine how the noun is used. (An appositive will rename, remember, and so will not fit in the sentence attack plan.)

Example: What happens next remains to be seen.

   Step 1: Find the clause: *what happens next* (*What* is the subject of the verb *happens*; *next* tells *when* about *happens*.)

   Step 2: Think of the clause as one word:

   Whathappensnext remains to be seen.

   Step 3: Use the sentence-attack plan:

   a. Find the verb: *remains*

   b. *Remains* is a linking verb. (You can substitute *is*, a form of *to be*.)

   c. *Who* or *what* remains?

   Answer: whathappensnext

So, the noun clause is the *subject* of the sentence.

PART 2: ADJECTIVE CLAUSE

A. Characteristics

The adjective clause will have a subject and a verb and will usually start with one of these words:

   who   whose   whom
   which   that

Sometimes, *when* and *where* can introduce adjective clauses.

Example 1: The athlete *who won the Best Sportsmanship Award* was captain of her basketball team.

   (Subject, *who*; verb, *won*)

Example 2: The sidewalk artist could draw a caricature of any famous person *whom you could name.*

   (Subject, *you*; verb, *could name*)

Example 3: My brother ate all the strawberries *that I picked.*
   (Subject, *I*; verb, *picked*)

B. Function

The adjective clause functions the same way a single adjective functions: it answers *which one*? *what kind*? or *how many*? about a noun.

Example: The flower arrangement *that was judged Best of Show* was made up of dried corn-shuck flowers.

(*That was judged Best of Show* says *which* about *arrangement*; the clause functions as an adjective modifying the noun *arrangement*.)

C. Attack plan

Since the adjective clause and the noun clause can begin with many of the same words, you will need to consider *function* in order to know whether the clause is an adjective or noun clause.

Example: The man *whose jacket is lying on the ground* is playing tennis in the second court.

(*Jacket* is the subject of *is lying*; *on the ground* is a prepositional phrase that tells *where* about *is lying*; *whose* is possessive and modifies *jacket*.)

Sentence attack plan:

Step 1: Cross out *in the second court* (prepositional phrase).

Step 2: *Is playing* is the action verb.

Step 3: *Who* or *what* is playing?

Answer: *man* (subject)

Step 4: Man is playing *who* or *what*?

Answer: *tennis* (direct object)

Step 5: Man is playing tennis *to whom* or *for whom*?

Answer: none

REMEMBER

If you use the sentence attack plan, the *noun clause* will fit into the plan at some point (with the single exception of the appositive). So, if you finish all steps in the sentence attack plan and have found no use for the clause, you can be fairly certain that the clause is a *modifier*.

So what remains is a modifier. Remember that you must think of the clause as if it were one word. *Whosejacketislyingontheground* tells *which* about the noun *boy*; so the clause is an adjective.

1. People sometimes confuse *who*, *which*, and *that*.

a. *Who* (or *whom* or *whose*) refers to people.

Example: He is the politician *who* made all those promises.

b. *Which* refers to things or non-human animals.

Example 1: This tree, *which* stands taller than any others nearby, provides shade for both of our yards.
(*Which* refers to the thing *tree*.)

Example 2: Our neighbor owns an AKC-registered dog, *which* howls during the early morning hours.
(*Which* refers to the non-human animal *dog*.)

c. *That* also refers to things or non-human animals, but it should not be used when the adjective clause is set off with commas.

Example 1: This tree, *which* [*not that*] stands taller than any others nearby, provides shade for both of our yards.

Example 2: Our neighbor owns the dog *that* howls during the early morning hours.

2. Do not use *what* to start an adjective clause.

Incorrect: The car *what* is painted blue is my mother's car.

Correct: The car *that* is painted blue is my mother's car.

Correct: The car, *which* is painted blue, is my mother's.

Be sure the adjective clause is placed next to the word it modifies. See Chapter 13, Part II, Rule 4, for punctuation of nonrestrictive adjective clauses.

PART 3: ADVERB CLAUSE

A. Characteristics

1. The adverb clause will have a subject and a verb and will start with one of these words:

after	because	though
although	before	unless
as	even though	until
as if	if	when
as long as	in order that	whenever
as much as	provided that	where
as soon as	since	wherever
as though	so that	while
	than	

2. Other characteristics of the adverb clause are similar to those of noun clauses.

B. Function

The adverb clause functions just like a single-word adverb: it modifies verbs, adjectives, and other adverbs; and it tells *when, where, why, how, to what extent,* and *under what conditions.*

The following examples show how adverb clauses function.

Example 1: *After he washed the car,* the sky clouded, threatening rain.

　　　　(Subject, *he*; verb, *washed*; tells *when* about the verb *clouded.*)

Example 2: He spent money *as long as he had it.*

　　　　(Subject, *he*; verb, *had*; tells *when* about the verb *spent.*)

Example 3: *If you fail to pay your taxes,* you will be penalized.

　　　　(Subject, *you;* verb, *fail;* tells *under what conditions* about the verb *will be penalized.*)

Example 4: *While the flagman dozed in the afternoon sun,* his assistant directed traffic.

　　　　(Subject, *flagman*; verb, *dozed*; tells *when* about the verb *directed.*)

Warning A: Some adverb clauses have a missing—but implied—verb.

> Example: The assistant instructor worked harder preparing for the class *than I*.
>
> (Adverb clause: *than I* [did])

Recognizing that implied verb will help you get the pronoun correct. For instance, in the sentence above, you wouldn't say *me did*. Understanding that the verb *did* is missing helps you know to correctly say *I*.

Warning B: Some adverb clauses have a missing—but implied—subject.

> Example 1: *While driving to St. Louis*, he decided to travel on roads other than interstate highways.
>
> (Adverb clause: *while* [he was] *driving to St. Louis*)

> Example 2: *When putting up a tent*, she always gets tangled in the ropes.
>
> (Adverb clause: *when* [she is] *putting up a tent*)

Be sure that you do not say something ridiculous—even unintentionally—when there are implied subjects.

> Example: Ridiculous: When putting up a tent, the ropes often get in the way. (Since the subject is implied, the reader may think you intend *ropes* to be the subject! Ropes are not very good at putting up tents!)

> Improved: When putting up a tent, you must keep the ropes untangled.
>
> (Adverb clause: *when* [you are] *putting up a tent*)

Warning C: Do not confuse adverb clauses with prepositional phrases.

> Example 1: *After dinner*, I took a nap.
>
> (*After* plus the noun *dinner* makes a prepositional phrase.)

Compare that with the following:

> Example 2: *After we ate dinner*, I took a nap.
>
> (*After* and a subject and a verb make an adverb clause.)

> Example 3: I have slept *since one o'clock*.
>
> (*Since* and a noun make a prepositional phrase.)

Compare that with the following:

> Example 4: I have slept *since I came home from work*.
>
> (*Since* and a subject and verb make an adverb clause.)

REMEMBER

A clause must have a subject and a verb. A phrase does not. See Chapter 13, Part II, Rule 5, for punctuation of adverb clauses.

PRACTICE
EXERCISE 1

Directions: Work through the following sentences to find all the noun, adjective, and adverb clauses. Identify the function of each clause. Answers are printed after the sentences, but see if you really understand these clauses before you check. And read carefully. Many sentences have more than one dependent clause!

1. His new car, which was a four-cylinder model, gave him good gas mileage.

2. After the airplane engine was overhauled, the mechanic who had done most of the work pronounced the engine in good shape.

3. Honeybees, industrious creatures that they are, usually work themselves to death after six weeks of gathering honey.

4. Because the July heat was oppressive, the two hikers rested whenever they had the opportunity.

5. Whoever discovered that cooking dried corn in lye water makes hominy aided dietetic variety.

6. The dulcimer, which makes mandolin-like music, is not readily available in most music stores.

7. Because rip-rap rock is quite large, whoever works with it will be exhausted after he handles the first ton or so.

8. Whichever tree limbs are to be pruned should be clearly marked so that no one cuts off the wrong ones.

9. Whoever owns those Chinese geese that make such raucous noises must not be able to hear them when they create such a commotion that it awakens the entire neighborhood.

10. As the wind freshened, we anticipated a storm.

EXERCISE 1—ANSWERS

1. *Which was a four-cylinder model* is an adjective clause that tells *which* about the noun *car.*

2. *After the airplane engine was overhauled* is an adverb clause that tells *when* about the verb *pronounced. Who had done most of the work* is an adjective clause that tells *which* about the noun *mechanic.*

3. *That they are* is an adjective clause that tells *what kind* about the noun *creatures. After* begins a prepositional phrase, not an adverb clause.

4. *Because the July heat was oppressive* is an adverb clause that tells *why* about the verb *rested. Whenever they had the opportunity* is an adverb clause that tells *when* about the verb *rested.*

5. *Whoever discovered that cooking dried corn in lye water makes hominy* is a noun clause that is the subject of the sentence. *That cooking dried corn in lye water makes hominy* is also a noun clause that is the object of the verb *discovered.* (So you have a clause within a clause. Fancy!)

6. *Which makes mandolin-like music* is an adjective clause that tells *what kind* about the noun *dulcimer.*

7. *Because rip-rap rock is quite large* is an adverb clause that tells *why* about the verb *will be exhausted*. *Whoever works with it* is a noun clause that is the subject of the main verb *will be exhausted*. *After he handles the first ton or so* is an adverb clause that tells *when* about the verb *will be exhausted*. (Did you find all three?)

8. *Whichever tree limbs are to be pruned* is a noun clause that is the subject of the sentence. *So that no one cuts off the wrong ones* is an adverb clause that tells *why* about the verb *should be marked*.

9. *Whoever owns those Chinese geese that make such raucous noises* is a noun clause that is subject of the sentence. *That make such raucous noises* is an adjective clause that tells *which* about the noun *geese*. (So you have a clause within a clause again!) *When they create such a commotion that it awakens the entire neighborhood* is an adverb clause that tells *when* about the infinitive *to hear*. *That it awakens the entire neighborhood* is an adjective clause within the adverb clause that tells *what kind* about the noun *commotion*. (All three kinds of clauses in one sentence!)

10. *As the wind freshened* is an adverb clause that tells *when* about the verb *anticipated*.

EXERCISE 2

Directions: The selection below includes both phrases and clauses. Identify each verbal phrase as a gerund, infinitive, or participle. Identify each noun, adjective, or adverb clause.

(1) *Painting the kitchen turned out to be a real chore.* (2) *The problems all began when we discovered that the paint was semigloss instead of flat.* (3) *Although the semigloss goes on smoothly, we knew from experience that it would show the defects in the plaster, now crumbling from age.* (4) *We planned to patch the plaster before painting the walls; but with semigloss paint, the patches show.* (5) *Flat paint, on the other hand, tends to camouflage most of whatever shows.* (6) *Since we had painted the ceiling and one wall before we discovered our error, we were faced with a decision.* (7) *Should we buy more paint to repaint what we had already completed and add to both the expense and the work?* (8) *Or should we just finish the job and let the defects show?*

EXERCISE 2—ANSWERS

Sentence 1

> *painting the kitchen* (gerund phrase, subject); *to be . . . chore* (infinitive phrase, adverb modifying verb *turned out*)

Sentence 2

> *when we discovered . . . instead of flat* (adverb clause, modifying verb *began*); *that . . . paint . . . flat* (noun clause, direct object of verb *discovered*)

Sentence 3

> *although . . . goes on smoothly* (adverb clause, modifying verb *knew*); *that . . . would show . . . plaster . . . crumbling from age* (noun clause, direct object of verb *knew*); *now . . . age* (participial phrase, adjective modifying noun *plaster*)

Sentence 4

> *to patch . . . the walls* (infinitive phrase, direct object of verb *planning*); *painting . . . walls* (gerund phrase, object of preposition *before*)

Sentence 5

> *whatever shows* (noun clause, object of preposition *of*)

Sentence 6

> *since we . . . painted . . . our error* (adverb clause, modifying verb *were faced*); *before . . . error* (adverb clause, modifying verb *had painted*)

Sentence 7

> *to repaint . . . already completed* (infinitive phrase, adjective modifying noun *paint*); *what . . . already completed* (noun clause, direct object of *repaint*)

Sentence 8

> (none)

GED PRACTICE

Directions: The following practice, which combines material from Chapters 10 and 11, follows a format similar to that for the GED test. Read the following paragraphs. Then, choose the best alternative from those given. Next, compare your answers with those given below. Finally, review items that have caused you difficulty.

OPTICALLY SPEAKING

A

(1) *Whether people want to really see their favorite Yankees pitcher up close or to carefully check out the bird perched on a distant fence post, good optics fill the bill.* (2) *While some folks hang on to an old pair of binoculars because the optics were great twenty years ago, technology has changed the definition of great optics.*

B

(3) *Consider first the binoculars' "field of view," or how big the picture is looking through the glass.* (4) *When choosing new optics, the field of view should look brighter than do with the naked eye.* (5) *A pair of binoculars what are dim may be less pricey they're also less helpful for the viewer trying to see his targeted object well.* (6) *In addition, for those that wear glasses, optics that have a long eye relief are the only choice.*

C

(7) *Of course, magnification is the primary issue in choosing good optics.* (8) *A ten-power binocular, which magnifies objects ten times, will give a great close-up view.* (9) *On the other hand, anyone that lacks a steady hand will find the object of his attention too shaky to see clearly.* (10) *As a result, many folks settle for eight power, using hand-held optics.* (11) *Of course, using optics mounted on a tripod, the view can be dramatically magnified, even up to sixty times, with clear results.* (12) *So before buying any optics, they should be field tested.*

1. Sentence 1: Whether people <u>want to really see</u> their favorite Yankees pitcher up close or to carefully check out the bird perched on a distant fence post, good optics fill the bill.

   What correction should be made to the underlined portion of this sentence?

   (1) Reword it to read <u>want really to see.</u>
   (2) Reword it to read <u>really want to see.</u>
   (3) Reword it to read <u>want to see really.</u>
   (4) No correction is necessary to the underlined portion.

2. Sentence 1: Whether people want to really see their favorite Yankees pitcher up close or <u>to carefully check out</u> the bird perched on a distant fence post, good optics fill the bill.

   What correction should be made to the underlined portion of this sentence?

   (1) Reword it to read <u>carefully to check out.</u>
   (2) Reword it to read <u>to check out carefully.</u>
   (3) Reword it to read <u>to check carefully out.</u>
   (4) No correction is necessary to the underlined portion.

3. Sentence 2: While some folks hang on to an old pair of binoculars because the optics were great <u>twenty years ago, technology has changed</u> the definition of great optics.

   What correction should be made to the underlined portion of this sentence?

   (1) Reword it to read <u>twenty years ago technology has changed.</u>
   (2) Reword it to read <u>twenty years ago, these folks must recognize that technology has changed.</u>
   (3) Reword it to read <u>twenty years ago. Technology has changed.</u>
   (4) No correction is necessary to the underlined portion.

4. Sentence 3: Consider first the binoculars' "field of view," or <u>how big the picture is looking through the glass.</u>

   What correction should be made to the underlined portion of this sentence?

   (1) Reword it to read <u>how much a person sees through the glass.</u>
   (2) Reword it to read <u>how big the picture is when you are looking through the glass.</u>
   (3) Reword it to read <u>the size of the picture that the optics reveal.</u>
   (4) No correction is necessary to the underlined portion.

5. Sentence 4: <u>When choosing new optics, the field of view should look</u> brighter than do with the naked eye.

   What correction should be made to the underlined portion of this sentence?

   (1) Reword it to read <u>When choosing new optics, their field of view should look.</u>
   (2) Reword it to read <u>When choosing new optics, you should make sure the field of view looks.</u>
   (3) Reword it to read <u>When choosing new optics, a person should make sure the field of view looks.</u>
   (4) No correction is necessary to the underlined portion.

6. Sentence 4: When choosing new optics, the field of view should <u>look brighter than do with the naked eye.</u>

   What correction should be made to the underlined portion of this sentence?

   (1) Reword it to read <u>look brighter than they do with the naked eye.</u>
   (2) Reword it to read <u>look brighter than it does with the naked eye.</u>
   (3) Reword it to read <u>look bright to the naked eye.</u>
   (4) No correction is necessary to the underlined portion.

7. Sentence 5: A pair of <u>binoculars what are dim</u> may be less pricey they're also less helpful for the viewer trying to see his targeted object well.

   What correction should be made to the underlined portion of this sentence?

   (1) Change <u>what</u> to <u>which.</u>
   (2) Change <u>what</u> to <u>that.</u>
   (3) Change <u>what</u> to <u>that's.</u>
   (4) No correction is necessary to the underlined portion.

8. Sentence 5: A pair of binoculars what are dim may be <u>less pricey they're also less helpful</u> for the viewer trying to see his targeted object well.

   What correction should be made to the underlined portion of this sentence?

   (1) Reword it to read <u>less pricey, but they're also less helpful.</u>
   (2) Reword it to read <u>less pricey, they're also less helpful.</u>
   (3) Reword it to read <u>less pricey than others, but they're also less helpful.</u>
   (4) No correction is necessary to the underlined portion.

9. Sentence 5: A pair of binoculars what are dim may be less pricey they're also less helpful <u>for the viewer trying to see his targeted object well.</u>

   What correction should be made to the underlined portion of this sentence?

   (1) Reword it to read <u>for the viewer trying to see well his targeted object.</u>
   (2) Reword it to read <u>for the viewer tries to see his targeted object well.</u>
   (3) Reword it to read <u>for the viewer who tries to see his targeted object well.</u>
   (4) No correction is necessary to the underlined portion.

10. Sentence 6: In addition, for those that wear glasses, optics that have a long eye relief are the only choice.

    What correction should be made to this sentence?

    (1) Change <u>those that</u> to <u>those what.</u>
    (2) Change <u>those that</u> to <u>those which.</u>
    (3) Change <u>those that</u> to <u>those who.</u>
    (4) No correction is necessary.

11. Sentence 8: A ten-power binocular, which magnifies objects ten times, will give a great close-up view.

    What correction should be made to this sentence?

    (1) Omit the comma after <u>binocular.</u>
    (2) Omit the comma after <u>binocular</u> and change <u>which</u> to <u>that.</u>
    (3) Omit the comma after <u>binocular</u> and change <u>which</u> to <u>what.</u>
    (4) No correction is necessary.

12. Sentence 9: On the other hand, anyone that lacks a steady hand will find the object of his attention too shaky to see clearly

What correction should be made to this sentence?

(1) Change that to what.
(2) Change that to which.
(3) Change that to who.
(4) No correction is necessary.

13. Sentence 10: As a result, many folks settle for eight power, using hand-held optics.

How can this sentence best be rewritten?

(1) Rewrite it to read As a result, many folks settle for eight power using hand-held optics.
(2) Rewrite it to read As a result, many folks using hand-held optics settle for eight power.
(3) Rewrite it to read As a result, many folks settle, using hand-help optics, for eight power.
(4) No correction is necessary.

14. Sentence 11: Of course, using optics mounted on a tripod, the view can be dramatically magnified, even up to sixty times, with clear results.

What correction should be made to the underlined portion of this sentence?

(1) Reword it to read on a tripod, your view can be dramatically magnified.
(2) Reword it to read on a tripod, a person's view can be dramatically magnified.
(3) Reword it to read on a tripod, a person can dramatically magnify his view.
(4) No correction is necessary to the underlined portion.

15. Sentence 12: So before buying any optics, they should be field tested.

What correction should be made to the underlined portion of this sentence?

(1) Rewrite it to read any optics they should be field tested.
(2) Rewrite it to read any optics should be field tested.
(3) Rewrite it to read any optics, a person should field test them.
(4) No correction is necessary to the underlined portion.

GED PRACTICE—ANSWERS

1. (2) In an infinitive, do not separate the *to* from its verbal.

2. (1) In an infinitive, do not separate the *to* from its verbal. In addition, maintain similar structures when writing two or more of any grammatical structure. Thus, since in the first part of the sentence we wrote *want really to see*, then here we should say *carefully to check out*.

3. (2) The introductory clause refers to *folks*, so the words immediately after the comma must name *folks*.

4. (3) The appositive phrase must start with a noun, like *size*.

5. (3) The introductory participial phrase modifies the word after the comma, in this case *person*, to remain consistent with the remainder of the paragraphs' third-person [like *people, folks*] point of view.

6. (2) *Does* agrees with the pronoun *it* and completes the comparison.

7. (2) The noun *binoculars* takes the pronoun *that* since it is a restrictive clause.

8. (3) The use of *less* requires something that says "less than what." The comma avoids confusion.

9. (1) *Trying* is the participle, and *well* modifies *to see* and thus should be positioned close to the infinitive.

10. (3) *Who* refers to persons.

11. (4) *Which* begins the restrictive clause

12. (3) *Who* refers to persons.

13. (2) *Using hand-held optics* restricts all users to just those using binoculars; thus use no commas and place the phrase next to the word it modifies.

14. (3) *Using optics mounted on a tripod* must modify the word that follows the comma, not *view* [which is not using optics], but *a person*.

15. (3) *Before buying any optics* must modify the word that follows the comma, not *they*, but *a person*.

Punctuation

Now that you have a command of the fundamentals of grammar and the basic principles of usage, you are ready to punctuate. In an effort to simplify the many rules for using punctuation, this chapter summarizes end marks, condenses the rules for commas to seven, and emphasizes the correct use of apostrophes. These rules will answer the punctuation questions you may confront on the GED multiple-choice questions or address the applications you face while writing your GED essay.

PART 1: END MARKS

A. Period

1. Use a period at the end of a statement.
2. Use a period for an abbreviation.

Most governmental agency and international organization abbreviations are *not* followed with periods.

Examples: Interstate Commerce Commission = ICC

United Nations = UN

B. Exclamation Point

Use an exclamation point at the end of an exclamatory sentence or expression.

Example: What a game!

C. Question Mark

1. Use a question mark to ask a question.

   Example: Where is the nearest gas station?
2. Do not use a question mark after an indirect question.

   Example: I wonder where the nearest gas station is.
3. It is not usually necessary to use a question mark after a polite command.

   Example: Mary, will you please come here.

PART 2: COMMAS

We'll make commas easy. In short, they're used to avoid confusion. But a few simple rules will help you sort out the most important uses for commas.

REMEMBER

If there is no rule to indicate the need for a comma, do not use one. It is just as wrong to use unnecessary commas as it is to leave them out.

RULE 1: COMMAS WITH A SERIES

Use a comma to separate items in a series. A series is made up of three or more items. A series can be made up of nouns, verbs, modifiers, or phrases.

Examples:

- Series of *nouns: Dogs*, trapeze *artists*, and *clowns* all tumbled down the aisle together.
- Series of *verbs:* The old truck *coughed, lurched,* and then *shuddered.*
- Series of *modifiers:* Those hamburgers were *greasy, tasteless,* and *small.*
- Series of *phrases:* We looked *under the rug, behind the pictures,* but not *inside the cabinet.*

(Note that if you omitted the commas in any of these examples, you would confuse your reader. Always think about commas as a way to clarify what you're trying to say.)

Hint: To be safe and to avoid possible confusion, include the comma before joining words like *and, or,* or *nor*: A, B, and C.

Example: John, Tom, and Sue inherited $15,000.

Hint: If each item has a joining word after it, use no commas: A and B and C; A or B or C.

Example 1: We swam and ate and slept for five days.

Example 2: Milk or water or even ink would have tasted good to us.

Hint: Use no comma after the last item.

Example: Maple, oak, and walnut trees provided dense shade.

RULE 2: COMMAS WITH COORDINATE ADJECTIVES

Use a comma to separate coordinate adjectives. Coordinate adjectives are two or more adjectives that equally modify the same noun.

Example: The low, heavy clouds threatened snow. (*Low* and *heavy* both modify clouds.)

To Test: You must be able to substitute *and* for the comma separating coordinate adjectives. Otherwise, you will use no comma.

Example 1: A sleek, shiny new car sat in the driveway.

A sleek [and] shiny new car sat in the driveway.

But not: A sleek [and] shiny [and] new car sat in the driveway.

Example 2: That pink flowering tree is especially pretty in the spring.

(*Pink* modifies *flowering* and *flowering* modifies *tree.* No comma. We cannot say *that pink and flowering tree.*)

Warning A: Use no comma if the word *and, or,* or *nor* actually appears between the two adjectives.

Example: The long and arduous journey left the explorer with many memories, both pleasant and unpleasant.

Warning B: Omit the comma before numbers and before adjectives of size, shape, and age.

Example 1: Three tired hikers napped against the tree trunks. (No comma after *three*; it is a *number*. You also would not say *three and tired hikers*.)

Example 2: The huge old house stood alone on the hill. (No comma after *huge;* it is an adjective of *size*. And *old* is also an adjective of *age*.)

Example 3: A dilapidated two-storied house stood next door. (No comma after *dilapidated* since *two-storied* is an adjective of *shape*.)

RULE 3: COMMAS WITH COMPOUND SENTENCES

Use a comma to separate two complete sentences joined by a conjunction (*and, but, or, nor,* or *for,* and sometimes *yet* and *so*).

Example 1: Joan walked to the shopping center, but she found the stores all closed.

(You will see that we have joined two sentences with the conjunction *but: Joan walked to the shopping center. She found the stores all closed.* As you join the two sentences with *but,* replace the period with a comma so that you put the comma at the end of the first sentence.)

Compare that example with this one:

Example 2: Joan walked to the shopping center and found that the stores were closed.

(Notice that you need no comma here since there are not two complete sentences—the verb is merely compound.)

With this rule, think of a comma plus a conjunction like *and, but, or, nor,* or *for* as being equal to a period. If you could not put in a period instead of the comma and conjunction, you do not have two sentences. Think of the rule this way:

$$, + \left\{ \begin{array}{c} and \\ but \\ or \\ nor \\ for \end{array} \right\} = .$$

Be sure you have a complete sentence both before and after the conjunctions *and, but, or, nor,* or *for* before you put in a comma. Try substituting the period for the comma and conjunction to see if you have two sentences.

Example 1: The calculator needed new batteries, but it seemed to be functioning accurately.

Two complete sentences:

• The calculator needed new batteries.

• It seemed to be functioning accurately.

(Two complete sentences are joined with a comma and a conjunction.)

Example 2: The calculator needed new batteries but seemed to be functioning accurately.

One complete sentence:

• The calculator needed new batteries.

• seemed to be functioning accurately.

(Since the second group of words is not a sentence, we do *not* use a comma and conjunction. We could *not* substitute with a period.)

NOTE

See also Chapter 8, Using Prepositions and Conjunctions for more about joining sentences with conjunctions.

RULE 4: COMMAS WITH NONRESTRICTIVE ELEMENTS

Set off nonrestrictive verbal phrases or adjective clauses with commas.

A. *Set off* implies *two* commas—one before and one after—unless the phrase or clause is at the end of the sentence.

B. *Nonrestrictive* means "not essential" or "not needed to limit the noun."

C. A verbal phrase is a word group that begins with an infinitive or participle (see Chapter 11).

D. An adjective clause is a word group that has a subject and verb and starts with *who, whose, whom, which,* or *that* (see Chapter 12, Part 2).

Example 1: The brick house that was built across the street is for sale, but the brick house that was built next door is already sold.

(The adjective clauses *that was built across the street* and *that was built next door* are restrictive; that is, they are *necessary* to limit the noun they modify: *house.* Notice that if we read the sentence without the clauses, the sentence would not make much sense: The brick house is for sale, but the brick house is already sold. Again, only use commas to avoid confusion.)

Example 2: My sporty red Fiat, which my father gave me, is no longer in operating condition.

(The clause *which my father gave me* is not needed to limit *my sporty red Fiat.* I have only one! So the information in the clause is added information. The commas avoid confusion.)

Think of added information as being a "by the way" idea: *By the way, my father gave me the Fiat.* By setting that information off with commas, you are saying that the "by the way" idea can be dropped out:

My sporty red Fiat,

which [*by the way*] my father gave me,

is no longer in operating condition.

(Think of the commas as arrows showing that the idea can be dropped without affecting the meaning of the noun it modifies, *Fiat.*)

Example 3: Mr. Tzachosky, just getting off the boat, is a military agent. (*Just getting off the boat* is a nonrestrictive—that is, nonessential—participial phrase. It is not needed to limit all Mr. Tzachoskys to just one. There is just one Mr. Tzachosky about whom the reader knows. The commas indicate that *just getting off the boat* is "by the way" information that can be dropped out. The commas avoid confusion.)

RULE 5: COMMAS WITH INTRODUCTORY ELEMENTS

Set off introductory elements with a comma. Obviously, introductory elements appear at the beginning of the sentence! There are three kinds of introductory elements:

A. Introductory single words

Examples: *Yes,* I'm going to the union meeting.

Oh, did you mean that?

Kathy, please open the door.

B. Introductory prepositional phrases of four or more words (see Chapter 8, Part I)

Example 1: *Behind the door of the closet*, we found the lost computer disks.

(Use the comma after this prepositional phrase. It has six words.)

Example 2: Around the corner we ran into old friends.

(No comma is necessary after a prepositional phrase of only three words.)

C. Introductory verbal modifiers (see Chapter 11)

Example 1: *Walking home from work*, he spotted two new species of birds in the neighborhood.

(Introductory participial phrase modifying *he*)

Example 2: *To catch an early bus*, he left home fifteen minutes ahead of schedule.

(Introductory infinitive phrase modifying *he*)

Warning: If you use a comma, be sure the verbal is a *modifier*, not a subject.

Example 1: Walking home from work is his usual form of exercise.

(Use no comma after *work* since *walking home from work* is the subject of the sentence.)

Example 2: To catch an early bus was his daily goal.

(Use no comma after *bus* since *to catch an early bus* is the subject of the sentence.)

D. Introductory adverb clause (see Chapter 12, Part 3)

Example 1: *After we left*, the rain began.

(Subject, *we*; verb, *left*; tells *when* about *began*.)

Example 2: *Because we all had eaten too much*, most of us fell asleep.

(Subject, *we*; verb, *had eaten*; tells *why* about *fell*.)

Example 3: *If you know the answer*, don't tell!

(Subject, *you*; verb, *know*; tells *under what condition* about *tell*.)

Note: Unlike the limit of four words before using a comma after the introductory prepositional phrase (see item B above), there is no limit regarding adverb clauses.

Example: *If you can*, call me about noon.

(Comma after only three words; it is an introductory adverb clause! The comma avoids confusion.)

RULE 6: COMMAS WITH INTERRUPTERS

Use commas to set off interrupters. Interrupters come in the middle of the sentence and interrupt its natural flow. There are three kinds of interrupters.

A. Appositives (An appositive is a noun with its modifiers that renames another noun.)

Example: Thornton Kleug, *a local author of some acclaim*, spoke at the Elks meeting.

(*A local author of some acclaim* is a noun, along with modifiers, that renames *Thornton Kleug*.)

HINT

When an appositive appears at the end of the sentence, you will, of course, have only one comma.

B. Words of direct address (*Direct address* refers to speaking directly to someone.)

Example 1: Will you, *John,* please close the door.

Example 2: May I, *friends and neighbors,* ask your support?

Hint: Compare these examples with Rule 5, Part A. If the noun of direct address comes at the beginning, you may think of it as introductory (requiring only one comma). If the noun of direct address comes in the middle of the sentence—interrupts the sentence—then you need a comma both before and after to set it off. If the noun of direct address comes at the end of the sentence, you will, of course, have only one comma.

C. Parenthetical expressions

The following are typical—but not all—parenthetical expressions:

of course	in fact	moreover
in the meantime	I believe	consequently
on the other hand	I hope	for example
therefore	I think	nevertheless
however	indeed	she said

Example 1: Our practice books, *on the other hand,* are more thorough than the preparation books.

Example 2: That so-called breeze, *as a matter of fact,* is more like a gale.

RULE 7: COMMAS WITH DATES AND STATES

Use commas to set off dates and states.

Example 1:	Date:	January 5, 1935
	Month and year:	January 1935
		(no comma needed)
	Sentence:	January 5, 1935, was the date of her birth.
		(two commas needed)
Example 2:	City and state:	Louisville, Kentucky
	Sentence:	Louisville, Kentucky, is her home.
		(two commas needed)

SUMMARY FOR USING COMMAS

Here's a quick summary of the seven rules for using commas. This tight little summary makes the rules really easy to remember and shows clearly how you use commas to avoid confusion.

Rule 1: Series

Rule 2: Coordinate adjectives

(except size, shape, age, and numbers)

Rule 3: Two sentences with conjunction

_____, and _____.

Rule 4: Nonrestrictive

A. Adjective clause

B. Verbal phrase

Rule 5: Introductory

   A. Single words

   B. Prepositional phrase of four or more words

   C. Verbal modifier

   D. Adverb clause

Rule 6: Interrupters

   A. Appositive

   B. Direct address

   C. Parenthetical expressions

Rule 7: Dates and states

PART 3: APOSTROPHES
RULE 1: TO SHOW POSSESSION

Use the apostrophe to show possession. (See also Chapter 4, Using Nouns, to review possessive nouns. Compare with Chapter 5, Using Pronouns Correctly, to review pronouns that never take an apostrophe to show possession.)

A. Use the following steps to formulate the possessive:

1. Write the word to be made possessive in a prepositional phrase.

   Example 1: That *cats* ears are pointed.

           The ears *of that cat* are pointed.

   Example 2: All the team *members* shoes are wet.

           The shoes of *all the team members* are wet.

   Example 3: He earned two *weeks* pay.

           He earned the pay *of two weeks*.

   Example 4: An *hours* time is all I can spare.

           The time *of an hour* is all I can spare.

2. Add the apostrophe to the object of the preposition and eliminate the other words.

   Examples: . . . *cat'*

        . . . *members'*

        . . . *weeks'*

        . . . *hour'*

3. If the word does not end in an -*s*, add it.

   Examples:

cat'	cat's	—The *cat's* ears are pointed.
members'	(no change)	—All the team *members'* shoes are wet
weeks'	(no change)	—He earned two *weeks'* pay.
hour'	hour's	—An *hour's* time is all I can spare.

B. Some peculiar situations sometimes result when forming possessives.

1. If you add an apostrophe to a *singular* word that ends in *-s* and that is just one syllable, then you *will* add another *-s*.

    Examples:
    - Charles's

        (*Charles* is singular and only one syllable, so you need the extra *-s*.)

    - waitress'

        (*Waitress* is singular but two syllables, so you do *not* add an extra *-s*.)

2. Compound words are usually made plural at the end of the first word and always made possessive at the end of the second.

    Examples: sister-in-law

    two sisters-in-law (plural)

    sister-in-law's car (possessive)

    two sisters-in-law's cars (plural possessive)

3. Sometimes two people are involved in ownership.

    a. If two people own something together, the second word shows the ownership.

        Example: Mother and Dad's house

        (jointly owned)

    b. If two people own something separately, *both* words show ownership.

        Example: Eisenhower's and Kennedy's administrations

        (Each had his own administration.)

RULE 2: TO SHOW OMISSIONS

Use apostrophes to show omissions.

Examples: cannot—can't

crash of 1929—crash of '29

RULE 3: TO SHOW PLURALS

Use apostrophes to show plurals of letters, signs, numbers, and words referred to as words.

Examples: Avoid *you*'s in formal writing

Be sure to cross your *t*'s

PRACTICE
EXERCISE 1

Directions: Add commas where necessary to the following passage. Check your answers with those below and review the rules as necessary.

STORMY AFTERMATH
A

(1) *Soon after the storm hit streets and roads were flooded.* (2) *At the same time high winds made dangerous missiles of ordinary objects.* (3) *Tree limbs downed wires trash cans and other debris created further dangerous driving conditions.* (4) *Together the flooding high winds and debris caused city officials to ask residents to stay off the streets.* (5) *The dangerous conditions continued throughout most of the night but residents gingerly picked their way to work and school the next morning.*

B

(6) *During the next several weeks clean-up crews worked day and night clearing debris repairing utility lines and restoring services.* (7) *Some areas were without power for four days or more and in other areas downed trees blocked access for several days.* (8) *As the weeks wore on however clean-up crews faced another problem.* (9) *They ran out of space in the county landfill to dump the uprooted trees battered building debris and other off fall like splintered utility poles and flood-sodden furniture.* (10) *Most experts speaking optimistically confirm however that the town will soon be back to normal.*

EXERCISE 1—ANSWERS

All of the following rule numbers refer to Part 2, rules for commas.

Sentence 1

hit, (Rule 5, Section D)

Sentence 2

time, (Rule 5, Section B)

Sentence 3

limbs, wires, cans, (Rule 1)

Sentence 4

Together, (Rule 5, Section A); flooding, winds, (Rule 1)

Sentence 5

night, (Rule 3)

Sentence 6

weeks, (Rule 5, Section B); debris, lines, (Rule 1)

Sentence 7

more, (Rule 3)

Sentence 8

on, (Rule 5, Section D); however, (Rule 6, Section C)

Sentence 9

trees, debris, (Rule 1)

Sentence 10

experts, (Rule 4, Section B); optimistically, (Rule 4, Section B); confirm, (Rule 6, Section C); however, (Rule 6, Section C)

EXERCISE 2

Directions: You now know the basics of punctuation! Apply what you have learned in this chapter to complete the following punctuation review. When you have punctuated these sentences as accurately as you can, check your answers with those that follow the sentences. Rule and section numbers are given with the answers so that you can review those items that may still be causing you some difficulty.

1. After we watched the martins diving acrobatics for nearly an hour Delbert the local ornithologist explained how they feed on insects caught in midair.

2. The orchard included Bartlett Golden Delicious and Starking Delicious pear trees.

3. Gentlemen may I ask your support in Barbara and Gerald endeavor in working with our newspaper.

4. My editor-in-chief attitude which was indeed not at all difficult to accept reflected his superior education and extensive experience.

5. Changing flat tires adjusting carburetors and checking the timing were part of his daily work but he resented doing that same work at home for nonpaying relatives.

6. Yes many people believe that Boonville Indiana located in the southern tip of the state was named after Daniel Boone.

7. Ruffled by the wind the tall golden wheat makes a cool and restful summer scene except to the farmer who finds harvesting the wheat and baling the straw hot itchy work.

8. The elevated highway described in the pamphlet provided quick transportation around the city but gaining access to it was a real puzzle.

9. In the left-hand corner of the top drawer you will find my dear a special surprise package for you.

10. Studying horoscopes interests her for a special reason she believes her own life is guided by the sign of Capricorn.

11. Talking in front of his peers gave him practice so talking in front of strangers became easier.

12. Those committee members who worked most diligently at this assignment will be financially rewarded and recognized at the national meeting.

EXERCISE 2—ANSWERS

1. After we watched the martins' diving acrobatics for nearly an hour, Delbert, the local ornithologist, explained how they feed on insects caught in midair.

    > martins' (Part 3, Rule 1)
    > hour, (Part 2, Rule 5, Section D)
    > Delbert, ornithologist, (Part 2, Rule 6, Section A)

2. The orchard included Bartlett, Golden Delicious, and Starking Delicious pear trees.

    > Bartlett, (Part 2, Rule 1)
    > Delicious, (Part 2, Rule 1)

3. Gentlemen, may I ask your support in Barbara and Gerald's endeavor in working with our newspaper.

    > Gentlemen, (Part 2, Rule 5, Section A)
    > Barbara and Gerald's (Part 3, Rule 1, Section B, Item 3a)

    > (A question mark is not necessary because this is a polite request, not a question.)

4. My editor-in-chief's attitude, which was, indeed, not at all difficult to accept, reflected his superior education and extensive experience.

    > editor-in-chief's (Part 3, Rule 1, Section B, Item 2)
    > attitude, (Part 2, Rule 4, Section A)
    > was, indeed, (Part 2 , Rule 6, Section C)
    > accept, (Part 2, Rule 4, Section A)

5. Changing flat tires, adjusting carburetors, and checking the timing were part of his daily work, but he resented doing that same work at home for nonpaying relatives.

    > tires, carburetors, (Part 2, Rule 1)
    > work, (Part 2, Rule 3)

6. Yes, many people believe that Boonville, Indiana, located in the southern tip of the state, was named after Daniel Boone.

    > Yes, (Part 2, Rule 5, Section A)
    > Boonville, (Part 2, Rule 7)
    > Indiana, (Part 2, Rule 7 or Rule 4, Section B)
    > state, (Part 2, Rule 4, Section B)

7. Ruffled by the wind, the tall, golden wheat makes a cool and restful summer scene except to the farmer, who finds harvesting the wheat and baling the straw hot, itchy work.

    > wind, (Part 2, Rule 5, Section C)
    > tall, (Part 2, Rule 2)
    > farmer, (Part 2, Rule 4, Section A)
    > hot, (Part 2, Rule 2)

8. The elevated highway described in the pamphlet provided quick transportation around the city, but gaining access to it was a real puzzle.

    > city, (Part 2, Rule 3)

9. In the left-hand corner of the top drawer, you will find, my dear, a special surprise package for you.

    drawer, (Part 2, Rule 5, Section B)
    find, dear, (Part 2, Rule 6, Section B)

10. Studying horoscopes interests her for a special reason. She believes her own life is guided by the sign of Capricorn.

    reason. (Part I)

11. Talking in front of his peers gave him practice, so talking in front of strangers became easier.

    practice, so (Part II, Rule 3)

12. No further punctuation needed

GED PRACTICE

Directions: The following practice is written in a manner similar to the text you will encounter on the GED test. Read the four paragraphs. Note that there is no punctuation included in any of the paragraphs. Your task is to insert all necessary punctuation. Then check your answers and review any parts that remain confusing for you.

CELL PHONE ETHICS

A

(1) *Youre having a quiet dinner with someone special and in the midst of it all youre interrupted by someones cell phone ringing* (2) *Then comes the robust greeting and one side of an overly loud conversation* (3) *Its usually nothing more than meaningless chatter like where hes dining and what hes eating* (4) *It may be a sign of the times but its also a sign of many peoples rudeness* (5) *Their phone habits demonstrate that they simply have no consideration of others*

B

(6) *This lack of consideration extends to the road both in the city and out on the Interstate* (7) *Cell-phoning drivers who must certainly take their eyes from the road punch in numbers or rummage about to locate a ringing phone* (8) *As a result they weave across lanes off the shoulder or worse yet across the center line* (9) *If cell-phoning drivers want to kill themselves on the road I guess its their business* (10) *Unfortunately too often they take someone else with them* (11) *Maybe thats a lack of consideration for others or maybe its just plain common stupidity*

C

(12) *Granted cell-phone use is riddled with ethical issues* (13) *Cell phones ring during concerts movies church services doctors examinations seminars and classes* (14) *Theyre disruptive annoying and frequently entirely unnecessary* (15) *I once overheard a woman who was doing her grocery shopping chatting on her cell phone about yesterdays tennis game* (16) *I also overheard a person in a public restroom at the mall calling a friend just to say hello* (17) *I couldnt help wondering if the friend would have been pleased to know what the caller was doing at the time*

D

(18) *Apparently the obsession with cell phones causes otherwise sensible reasonable folks to use the gadget even when theres no real reason* (19) *Perhaps its a fear of being disconnected even for those few minutes that it takes to drive to the mall or go to the bathroom* (20) *Maybe its time cell-phone ethics should become a part of a required manners class*

GED PRACTICE—ANSWERS

1. You're having a quiet dinner with someone special, and in the midst of it all, you're interrupted by someone's cell phone ringing.

2. Then comes the robust greeting and one side of an overly loud conversation.

3. It's usually nothing more than meaningless chatter, like where he's dining and what he's eating.

4. It may be a sign of the times, but it's also a sign of many people's rudeness.

5. Their phone habits demonstrate that they simply have no consideration of others.

6. This lack of consideration extends to the road, both in the city and out on the Interstate.

7. Cell-phoning drivers, who must certainly take their eyes from the road, punch in numbers or rummage about to locate a ringing phone.

8. As a result, they weave across lanes, off the shoulder, or, worse yet, across the center line.

9. If cell-phoning drivers want to kill themselves on the road, I guess it's their business.

10. Unfortunately, too often they take someone else with them.

11. Maybe that's a lack of consideration for others, or maybe it's just plain, common stupidity.

12. Granted, cell-phone use is riddled with ethical issues.

13. Cell phones ring during concerts, movies, church services, doctors' examinations, seminars, and classes.

14. They're disruptive, annoying, and frequently entirely unnecessary.

15. I once overheard a woman who was doing her grocery shopping chatting on her cell phone about yesterday's tennis game.

16. I also overheard a person in a public restroom at the mall calling a friend just to say hello.

17. I couldn't help wondering if the friend would have been pleased to know what the caller was doing at the time.

18. Apparently, the obsession with cell phones causes otherwise sensible, reasonable folks to use the gadget even when there's no real reason.

19. Perhaps it's a fear of being disconnected, even for those few minutes that it takes to drive to the mall or go to the bathroom.

20. Maybe it's time cell-phone ethics should become a part of a required manners class.

14

GED Practice, Chapters 1-13

You have studied the fundamentals of the English language: elements of usage, phrases and clauses, and punctuation. What you need to understand now is how those fundamentals will appear on the GED test. You will *not* be asked to identify all of the parts of speech in a sentence or underline the phrases or identify the kinds of clauses. Rather, you will be asked to *apply* what you know about parts of speech, phrases and clauses, and usage to improve sentences or correct errors. You've worked through GED practices with many earlier chapters, but this one may be more difficult because it asks you to recall everything you've studied up to this point. Thus the following sample will further familiarize you with the GED approach and help you know whether you understand how to apply what you've learned so far. The following sample includes directions. Work your way through the sample, and then study the answers that follow. You will find not only the correct answer listed but also an explanation and references to chapters, rules, and parts where you can find details about the application. By studying these responses, you can learn to think your way through the test. The more you understand about the test, the more successful you will be. So practice carefully now! And good luck!

ROAD MAP

- *GED Practice*

SAMPLE PRACTICE TEST

Directions: Choose the *one best answer* to each item. Items 1 to 20 refer to the following paragraphs.

TAXING TAXES

A

(1) *Between the controversies facing tax revenue planners is one over sales tax.* (2) *Some experts think we pay too much sales tax.* (3) *In some states, for instance, the sales tax edges above 10 percent a situation what makes a $50 jacket cost $55.* (4) *Of course at the other extreme, there is a few states that have no sales tax at all.*

B

(5) *Those that oppose the sales tax offer another alternative.* (6) *He believes instead that the value-added tax is more fair than a sales tax.* (7) *A value-added tax are those that tax each step of production.* (8) *For instance, a company that makes aluminum cans pays tax only on the value it's process puts in the cans.* (9) *Here's how it works.* (10) *Perhaps the sheet aluminum is worth $1.00 but the finished aluminum cans are worth $4.00.* (11) *After the process is finished the can maker pays tax only on the $3.00 value added to the product.* (12) *When the Beverage Company fills the $4.00 cans to make them worth $10.00, it pays tax on the $6.00 added value.* (13) *When you and I buy the canned beverage, we pay no tax.* (14) *Except, of course, indirectly through increased prices.*

C

(15) *Will we ever have a value-added tax in the United States.* (16) *Its doubtful.* (17) *Because our nation thrives on interstate commerce any value-added tax plan would have to be national.* (18) *The beverage company cant pay value-added tax in Georgia only to have their colorado customers pay sales tax in they're local store's.* (19) *At present every state sets its own tax rate and a few states have no sales tax at all.* (20) *It seems unlikely then that well ever reach a national agreement for such a tax.*

1. Sentence 1: Between the controversies facing tax revenue planners is one over sales tax.

   What correction should be made to the sentence?

   (1) Replace is with are.
   (2) Change sales to sale's.
   (3) Replace between with among.
   (4) Insert a comma after planners.
   (5) No correction is necessary.

2. Sentence 2: Some experts think we pay too much sales tax.

   What correction should be made to the sentence?

   (1) Replace too much with too many.
   (2) Change sales to sale's.
   (3) Insert a comma after experts.
   (4) Change too to to.
   (5) No correction is necessary.

3. Sentence 3: In some states, for instance, the sales tax edges above 10 percent a situation what makes a $50 jacket cost $55.

   What correction should be made to the sentence?

   (1) Insert a comma after percent.
   (2) Omit the commas before and after for instance.
   (3) Insert a comma after percent and change what to that.
   (4) Omit the comma after instance and insert a comma after percent.
   (5) No change is necessary.

4. Sentence 4: Of course at the other extreme, there is a few states that have no sales tax at all.

   What correction should be made to the sentence?

   (1) Omit the comma after extreme.
   (2) Change is to are.
   (3) Change states to states'.
   (4) Change that to which.
   (5) No change is necessary.

5. Sentence 5: Those that oppose the sales tax offer another alternative.

   What correction should be made to the sentence?

   (1) Change Those to Them.
   (2) Change that to who.
   (3) Change that to whom.
   (4) Insert a comma after tax.
   (5) No change is necessary.

6. Sentence 6: He believes instead that the value-added tax is more fair than a sales tax.

What correction should be made to the sentence?

(1) Change he believes to they believe.
(2) Replace more fair with more fairer.
(3) Insert a comma after instead.
(4) Replace is with are.
(5) No correction is necessary.

7. Sentence 7: A value-added tax are those that tax each step of production.

What correction should be made to the sentence?

(1) Change that tax to that taxes.
(2) Replace are those that tax with is one that taxes.
(3) Insert a comma after value-added tax.
(4) Change are to were.
(5) No correction is necessary.

8. Sentence 8: For instance, a company that makes aluminum cans pays tax only on the value it's process puts in the cans.

What correction should be made to this sentence?

(1) Change it's to its.
(2) Omit the comma after instance.
(3) Replace pays with pay.
(4) Change pays tax only to pays only tax.
(5) No correction is necessary.

9. Sentence 9: Here's how it works.

What correction should be made to this sentence?

(1) Change it works to they work.
(2) Replace Here's with Hear's.
(3) Change Here's to Here are.
(4) Change Here's to Heres.
(5) No correction is necessary.

10. Sentence 10: Perhaps the sheet aluminum is worth $1.00 but the finished aluminum cans are worth $4.00.

Which of the following is the best way to write the underlined portion of this sentence? If you think the original is the best way, choose option (1).

(1) worth $1.00 but the finished
(2) worth $1.00. So the finished
(3) worth $1.00, or the finished
(4) worth $1.00 and therefore, the finished
(5) worth $1.00, but the finished

11. Sentence 11: After the process is finished the can maker pays tax only on the $3.00 valued added to the product.

   What correction should be made to this sentence?

   (1)   Replace pays tax only with only pays tax.
   (2)   Change after to since.
   (3)   Insert a comma after process.
   (4)   Insert a comma after finished.
   (5)   No correction is necessary.

12. Sentence 12: When the Beverage Company fills the $4.00 cans to make them worth $10.00, it pays tax on the $6.00 added value.

   What corrections should be made to this sentence?

   (1)   Insert a comma after cans.
   (2)   Change it pays to they pay.
   (3)   Change Beverage Company to beverage company.
   (4)   Replace fills with fill.
   (5)   No correction is necessary.

13. Sentences 13 and 14: When you and I buy the canned beverage, we pay no tax. Except, of course, indirectly through increased prices.

   Which of the following is the best way to write the underlined portion of these sentences? If you think the original is the best way, choose option (1).

   (1)   tax. Except,
   (2)   tax, but except,
   (3)   tax; except,
   (4)   tax, except,
   (5)   tax except,

14. Sentence 15: Will we ever have a value-added tax in the United States.

   What correction should be made to the sentence?

   (1)   Change Will we to Will they.
   (2)   Insert a comma after have.
   (3)   Substitute a question mark for the period at the end of the sentence.
   (4)   Change United States to united states.
   (5)   No correction is necessary.

15. Sentence 16: Its doubtful.

   What correction should be made to the sentence?

   (1)   Change Its to It's.
   (2)   Change Its to Its'.
   (3)   Change doubtful to more doubtful.
   (4)   Change doubtful to doubtfully.
   (5)   No correction is necessary.

16. Sentence 17: Because our nation thrives on interstate commerce any value-added tax plan would have to be national.

    What correction should be made to the sentence?

    (1) Change interstate commerce to Interstate Commerce.
    (2) Change national to National.
    (3) Insert a comma after plan.
    (4) Insert a comma after commerce.
    (5) No correction is necessary.

17. Sentence 18: The beverage company cant pay value-added tax in Georgia only to have their colorado customers pay sales tax in they're local store's.

    Which of the following is the best way to write the underlined portion of the sentence? If you think the original is the best way, choose option (1)

    (1) The beverage company cant pay value-added tax in Georgia
    (2) The Beverage Company cant pay value-added tax in Georgia
    (3) The beverage company can't pay value-added tax in Georgia
    (4) The beverage company cant pay value-added tax in georgia
    (5) The beverage company cant pay value-added tax in Georgia,

18. Sentence 18: The beverage company cant pay value-added tax in Georgia only to have their colorado customers pay sales tax in they're local store's.

    Which of the following is the best way to write the underlined portion of the sentence? If you think the original is the best way, choose option (1).

    (1) only to have their colorado customers pay sales tax in they're local store's.
    (2) only to have their Colorado customers pay sales tax in they're local store's.
    (3) only to have their Colorado customers pay sales tax in their local stores.
    (4) only to have their Colorado customers' pay sales tax in their local stores'.
    (5) only to have their Colorado customers pay sales tax in there local stores.

19. Sentence 19: At present every state sets its own tax rate and a few states have no sales tax at all.

    Which of the following is the best revision for the underlined portion of the sentence? If you think the original is the best way, choose option (1).

    (1) own tax rate and a few states
    (2) own tax rate, a few states
    (3) own tax rate but a few states
    (4) own tax rate, and a few states
    (5) own tax rate. And a few states

20. Sentence 20: It seems unlikely then that well ever reach a national agreement for such a tax.

    Which of the following is the best revision for the underlined portion of the sentence? If you think the original is the best way, choose option (1).

    (1) unlikely then that well ever reach
    (2) unlikely then that we'll ever reach
    (3) unlikely, then, that well ever reach
    (4) unlikely, then, that we'll ever reach
    (5) unlikely then, that we'll ever reach

ANSWERS

The following provides answers, explanations, and references (by chapter and part) to specific rules, hints, and warnings. By checking the references, you can see how the GED test applies what you have studied so far.

1. (3) Use *between* to talk about two items and *among* to talk about more than two. See Chapter 9.

2. (5) The sentence is correct as it stands.

3. (3) The comma after *percent* signifies the appositive that follows. See Chapter 13, Rule 4. The word *what* should never be used to introduce an appositive; use *that* to refer to non-persons. See Chapter 12, Part 2, Section C, Item 1c.

4. (2) *Are* agrees with its subject *states*. See Chapter 3, Problem 1, Situation B. *That* is the preferred word unless the adjective clause is explanatory or by-the-way information. See Chapter 12, Part 2.

5. (2) *Who* is used to refer to persons. See Chapter 12, Part 2, Section C, Item 1a.

6. (1) The pronoun *they* must agree with *experts*. So the verb must be *believe* to agree with *they*. See Chapter 5, Rule 10.

7. (2) *Tax* is singular, so all that follows must be singular: the verb *is*, the pronoun *one*, and the verb *taxes*. See Chapter 3, Problem 2, and Chapter 5, Rule 2.

8. (1) *It's* means "it is," not the intent here. See Chapter 5, Rule 10, and Chapter 9.

9. (5) The sentence is correct.

10. (5) The comma and joining word correctly join the two parts of a compound sentence. See Chapter 13, Part 2, Rule 3.

11. (4) Use a comma after an introductory clause. See Chapter 13, Part 2, Rule 5.

12. (3) Capitalize only specific company names. See Chapter 4, Part 3.

13. (5) *Except* is a preposition, and what follows is a prepositional phrase. There is no rule to separate prepositional phrases from the rest of the sentence unless they are introductory. See Chapter 13, Summary for Using Commas.

14. (3) Use a question mark at the end of a question. See Chapter 13, Part 1.

15. (1) *It's*, meaning *It is*, make up the subject and verb of the sentence. See Chapter 5, Rule 10.

16. (4) The comma after *commerce* marks the end of an introductory adverb clause. See Chapter 12, Part 3 and Chapter 13, Part 2, Rule 5.

17. (3) *Can't* means *cannot*. See Chapter 13, Part 3, Apostrophes.

18. (3) Capitalize names of states. See Chapter 4, Part 3. The possessive *their* instead of the pronoun-verb *they're* (for *they are*) is the correct use of the pronoun. See Chapter 5, Rule 10. *Stores* is plural, not possessive. See Chapter 4, Part 1, and Chapter 13, Part 3, Rule 1.

19. (4) Use a comma and a conjunction to join to sentences. See Chapter 13, Part 2, Rule 3.

20. (4) Use an apostrophe to show the omission of letters in *we'll*, meaning *we will*. See Chapter 13, Part 3, Rule 2. Set off interrupting elements with commas. See Chapter 13, Part 2, Rule 6.

SECTION II

Writing Sentences, Paragraphs, and Essays

So far you've studied words and phrases. Now you're ready to put these words and phrases together into sentences. Once you've mastered the basic sentence structures, it's only a matter of putting sentences together in a logical, coherent manner to achieve paragraphs. And of course, paragraphs are the chunks of thought that make up an essay—like the essay you'll be asked to write in the second part of the GED Language Arts, Writing exam. This section of the book teaches you to write effective sentences, paragraphs, and essays.

Basic Sentence Structures

The whole point of studying different kinds of sentences is to learn to write them. Why? One mark of good writing is the use of a variety of sentence structures, and people who evaluate GED writing samples look for that variety.

Only four basic sentence structures make up the entire English language:

simple sentence
compound sentence
complex sentence
compound-complex sentence

This chapter teaches you to identify each and then to write each correctly.

PART 1: SIMPLE SENTENCES

The basic sentence is the simple sentence. It has the following characteristics:

1. The simple sentence has one subject.

2. It has one verb.

3. It may or may not have words or phrases telling about the subject or verb.

    Example: Randall overslept.

                Subject: Randall

                Verb: overslept

                Words about the subject: (none)

                Words about the verb: (none)

Warning: Be sure the verb in your simple sentence can stand alone.

    Error: Randall oversleeping.

                (The sentence is incomplete because the verb cannot stand alone.)

    Revision: Randall has been oversleeping.

                (Now the simple sentence is accurate, with a single subject and a single verb.)

Hint: Since some verbs need helping words, a single verb may include more than one word.

    Example: Randall has been oversleeping.

                Subject: Randall

                Verb: has been oversleeping

                (The main verb *oversleeping* and its helpers *has* and *been* make up a single verb, sometimes called a verb phrase. See Chapter 2 for a review.)

ROAD MAP

- *Simple Sentences*
- *Compound Parts and Compound Sentences*
- *Complex Sentences*
- *Compound-Complex Sentences*

Although most sentences contain far more than a single subject and a single verb, many are still simple sentences.

> Example: Randall, my coworker, overslept yesterday morning.
>
> Subject: Randall
>
> Verb: overslept
>
> Words about the subject: my coworker (tells *who* about *Randall*)
>
> Words about the verb: yesterday morning (tells *when* about *overslept*)

> Example: Tomorrow evening, hoping to avoid oversleeping again, Randall will carefully set the alarm for 6:45 a.m.
>
> Subject: Randall
>
> Verb: will set
>
> Words about the subject: (none)
>
> Words about the verb: tomorrow evening (tells *when* about *set*); hoping to avoid oversleeping again (tells *why* about *set*); carefully (tells *how* about *set*); the alarm (tells *what* about *set*); for 6:45 a.m. (tells *when* about *set*)

As you can see, then, even though a sentence may be relatively long, if it has only one subject and one verb, it is still a simple sentence.

Sentence variety is a mark of the good writer, so as you write, you will want to vary your sentences. You have already seen that you can vary the length, but you can also vary the kinds of sentences you use. Now that you understand what a simple sentence is, let's talk about compound sentences.

REMEMBER

Length will not help identify the kind of sentence.

PART 2: COMPOUND PARTS AND COMPOUND SENTENCES

Anything compound is made of two or more parts, so a compound sentence is made of two or more parts. The parts work as a single unit. Simple sentences can have compound subjects or compound verbs. Two simple sentences can be joined to form a compound sentence.

COMPOUND SUBJECTS

Sometimes a simple sentence has two subjects. The sentence is then said to have a compound subject.

> Example: Maria and Sue Ellen are going to the movie tonight.
>
> Two subjects: Maria, Sue Ellen
>
> Verb: are going

> Example: Five neighbors, a police officer, and two business owners formed a neighborhood committee to work for better streets.
>
> Three subjects: neighbors, officer, owners
>
> Verb: formed

Warning: A plural subject is not a compound subject.

Example: Michael and David landed jobs at the same local supermarket.

Two subjects: Michael and David

Verb: landed

(The subject is compound because two nouns, *Michael* and *David*, are the subjects.)

Example: Two brothers landed jobs at the same local supermarket.

One subject: brothers

Verb: landed

(The subject is plural, not compound. Because only one noun, *brothers*, is the subject, the subject is not compound.)

COMPOUND VERBS

Sometimes a simple sentence has two verbs. The sentence is then said to have a compound verb.

Example: Smiles warm the heart and cheer the soul.

Subject: smiles

Two verbs: warm and cheer

Example: The supervisor praises and rewards good, speedy work.

Subject: supervisor

Two verbs: praises and rewards

COMPOUND SENTENCES

Sometimes a sentence is made by joining two simple sentences. The result is a compound sentence.

Example: Randall overslept, so he was late for work.

Sentence 1 Subject: Randall

Sentence 1 Verb: overslept

Sentence 2 Subject: he

Sentence 2 Verb: was

NOTE

When you join two sentences, add a comma at the end of the first sentence.

Notice the comma after *overslept* in the compound sentence above. (Review Chapter 8, Part 2, Rule 1 regarding conjunctions and their use with commas in joining two sentences.)

Example: Maria and Sue Ellen are going to the movie tonight, but Lennie or Carol will stay home to baby-sit.

Sentence 1: Maria and Sue Ellen are going to the movie tonight.

Sentence 2: Lennie or Carol will stay home to baby-sit.

As you can see from the above examples, when two simple sentences are joined together, they form a compound sentence.

Common joining words are as follows:

    and   but   or   nor   for   yet   so

Warning 1: Be sure to use the joining words correctly. Study the following meanings and examples.

And means "also" and joins two equal ideas: this idea *and* that idea.

> Example: Repairing the dented fender will be expensive, and I have no insurance.

> Remember: The comma replaces the period at the end of the first sentence, in front of *and*.

But shows a difference, an exception, a change: this idea *but* not that idea.

> Example: The storm damaged the roof, but the rest of the house was unhurt.

Or shows an alternative: this idea *or* that idea.

> Example: You should cover the windshield, or you will have to scrape off ice and snow in the morning.

Nor means "neither." Like *or*, *nor* shows an alternative, but both alternatives are negative: neither this idea *nor* that idea.

> Example: The doctor's report sounded bad, nor did the nurse have anything good to say.

For means "because" or "for this reason."

> Example: The turtle soup was nutritious, for it was thick with meat and vegetables.

So means "with the result that": this is true, *so* that is true.

> Example: Road construction narrowed the usual two lanes to one, so traffic slowed to a snail's pace.

Warning 2: Be sure to distinguish between joining words that merely connect two subjects or two verbs and those that connect two sentences. Use commas only with those that connect two sentences.

> Example: Company officials hope to cash in on the rising market trends *and* make significant profit gains as a result.

> One subject: *officials*

> Two verbs: *hope* and *make*

> (*And* joins two verbs, not two sentences. Use no comma.)

> Example: Company officials hope to cash in on the rising market trends, *and* they may make significant profit gains as a result.

> Sentence 1: Company officials hope to cash in on the rising market trends.

> Sentence 2: They may make significant profit gains as a result.

> Joining word: *and*

> (The comma appears at the end of the first sentence, in front of *and*.)

REMEMBER

Use a comma to replace the period at the end of the first sentence, in front of the joining word, when you hook together two sentences. (See also Chapter 13, Part 2, Rule 3, for a review.)

Warning 3: If you omit the joining word when you hook two sentences together, you commit a serious error. We call that error a *comma splice* or *comma fault*. In other words, you must not join two sentences with only a comma. Use *both* the comma and a joining word.

  Error: Rigorous walking strengthens the cardiovascular system, jogging does the same thing.

  (two sentences incorrectly joined with a comma)

  Revision: Rigorous walking strengthens the cardiovascular system, and jogging does the same thing.

  (two sentences joined with *and* and a comma forming a compound sentence)

PART 3: COMPLEX SENTENCES

The word *complex* generally means "complicated." Complex sentences, as you might guess, are indeed complicated. Complex sentences have the following characteristics:

1. A complex sentence contains at least two clauses.

2. One clause must be the independent clause.

3. One or more clauses must be dependent clauses.

INDEPENDENT CLAUSES

A clause is a group of words with a subject and a verb (Review Chapter 12).

  Hint: A simple sentence is a clause.

    Example: The race began.

      Subject: race

      Verb: began

When the subject and verb make a sentence, this clause is an *independent clause*. We call it "independent" because, like an independent person, it can support itself. It can stand alone. Sometimes we call the independent clause the "main" clause. It's like the "main" man or woman in a household.

DEPENDENT CLAUSES

Sometimes a group of words with a subject and verb does not make a sentence. That is, it cannot stand alone.

  Example: When the whistle sounded

      Subject: whistle

      Verb: sounded

      The clause cannot stand alone. It makes no sense alone.

  Example: Because the traffic had slowed to a stop

      Subject: traffic

      Verb: had slowed

      The clause cannot stand alone. It makes no sense alone.

A clause that cannot stand alone is called a *dependent clause*. We call it "dependent" because, like a dependent person, it needs support to survive. A dependent clause needs—depends on—an independent clause for its meaning. Remember this two-part comparison:

1. An independent clause (main clause) is like the head of the household—the "main" person.

2. A dependent clause is like a child—a dependent.

    Example: Because the traffic had slowed to a stop, I knew I would be late for work.

        Dependent clause: Because the traffic had slowed to a stop

        Independent clause: I knew I would be late for work.

Now the dependent clause has meaning. It explains *why* about the independent clause.

JOINED CLAUSES

When an independent clause and a dependent clause are joined in a sentence, the sentence is complex.

    Example: When the whistle sounded, the race began.

        Independent clause: the race began.

        Dependent clause: When the whistle sounded

Warning: If you write a dependent clause as if it were a sentence, you commit a serious writing error. We call that error a *sentence fragment*. Be sure every sentence includes an independent (main) clause.

Three kinds of dependent clauses appear in complex sentences:

    noun clauses
    adjective clauses
    adverb clauses

You may need to review the three kinds of clauses in detail in Chapter 12, but here are some examples:

NOUN CLAUSE

The noun clause functions any way a noun functions. It can be a subject, an object, or a predicate word.

    Example: The salesman talked to *whoever* would listen.

        Independent clause: The salesman talked

        Dependent clause: whoever would listen

        (The dependent clause *whoever would listen* is a noun clause that is the object of the word *to* in the independent clause.)

ADJECTIVE CLAUSE

An adjective clause functions the way adjectives function; it tells *which one*, *what kind*, or *how many* about a noun.

    Example: We joined Teresa, who was sitting alone.

        Independent clause: We joined Teresa

        Dependent clause: who was sitting alone

        (The dependent clause *who was sitting alone* is an adjective clause that tells *which one* about the noun *Teresa*.)

ADVERB CLAUSE

Adverb clauses modify verbs, adjectives, and other adverbs. They answer questions like *when? where? how? why?* and *to what extent?*

Example: After we ate dinner, we played softball.

(The clause *after we ate dinner* tells *when* about the verb *played*. Any word that tells *when* about a verb is an adverb.)

Warning: Sometimes what seems to be an introductory word is *not* followed by both a subject and a verb. In that case you do not have an adverb clause.

Example: After eating dinner, we played softball.

Independent clause: We played softball.

Dependent clause: (none)

(The sentence has no dependent clause. No subject or verb follows the word *after*, a word that often is an introductory word. *After eating dinner* is only a prepositional phrase.)

REMEMBER

A clause must have both a subject and a verb.

PART 4: COMPOUND-COMPLEX SENTENCES

The compound-complex sentence will be easy for you because it is the combination of two kinds of sentences you already know.

$$\frac{\text{simple}}{\text{sentence}} + \frac{\text{complex}}{\text{sentence}} = \frac{\text{compound-complex}}{\text{sentence}}$$

Example:

Simple sentence: My car made a funny noise.

Complex sentence: The mechanic used a computer to find out what was wrong.

Independent clause: The mechanic used a computer to find out

Dependent clause: What was wrong

Compound-complex: My car made a funny noise, so the mechanic used a computer to find out what was wrong.

Or to put it another way,

$$\frac{\text{independent}}{\text{clause}} + \frac{\text{independent}}{\text{clause}} + \frac{\text{dependent}}{\text{clause}} = \frac{\text{compound-complex}}{\text{sentence}}$$

The compound-complex sentence *must* include a dependent clause in one of its independent clauses, but it *may* include a dependent clause in *both* independent clauses:

Example:

Complex sentence: Since minimum wages increased, I need work only one job.

Independent clause: I need work only one job

Dependent clause: Since minimum wages increased

Complex sentence: Now I have time to take extra classes that will help me improve my skills.

Independent clause: Now I have time to take extra classes

Dependent clause: That will help me improve my skills

Compound-complex: Since minimum wages increased, I need work only one job; so now I have time to take extra classes that will help me improve my skills.

Rule: In a compound sentence, use a semicolon at the end of the first sentence if other commas appear in the first sentence.

Example: When you use a computer only for games, you miss the real capability of the technology; but after you put in a day's work at the keyboard, you may no longer thrill to the games.

First dependent clause: you/use

First independent clause: you/miss

Second dependent clause: you/put

Second independent clause: you/may thrill

To see if you understand what this chapter is about, try your hand with the following exercises.

PRACTICE
EXERCISE 1

Directions: Identify the following sentences as simple (S), compound (CD), complex (CX), or compound-complex (CC). Some simple sentences will have compound subjects or compound verbs, so be sure to identify those as such. Answers follow below, but don't peek until you've completed your answers. Then you can decide if you understand!

1. Walking is good exercise.
2. When conditions are right, I really enjoy fishing for bass.
3. The plant foreman and the union steward investigated the workman's complaint.
4. Job applications call for accuracy and neatness.
5. Seeking a new job, Leroy answered newspaper ads and applied in person.
6. The clothing department featured the newest styles, but Janice hoped to find something more conservative.
7. If you understand its operation, a wood lathe can be a useful tool; but if you are untrained, you can be seriously hurt by it.
8. As we studied the almost perfect reflections in the lake, we felt dizzy.
9. After studying the almost perfect reflections in the lake, we felt dizzy.
10. Hamburgers and fries are popular fast foods.
11. The vocal trio needed more practice, so the recital was postponed.
12. Sherry and Marcella wait tables at a local restaurant, but unless they can work shorter hours, they will feel obligated to find different jobs.
13. The secretary took Mr. Toon's calls while he was in the three-hour meeting.
14. The secretary took Mr. Toon's calls during the three-hour meeting.
15. After the three-hour meeting, Mr. Toon returned his calls.

EXERCISE 1—ANSWERS

1. (S) simple (walking/is)

2. (CX) complex (introductory word: *when*; dependent clause: conditions/are; independent clause: I/enjoy)

3. (S) simple with compound subject (foreman and steward/investigated)

4. (S) simple (applications/call)

5. (S) simple with compound verb (Leroy/answered and applied)

6. (CD) compound (department/featured; Janice/hoped; joining word: *but,* with comma at end of first clause)

7. (CC) compound-complex (introductory word: *if*; dependent clause: you/understand; independent clause: lathe/can be; joining word: *but*; second introductory word: *if*; second dependent clause: you/are; second independent clause: you/can be)

8. (CX) complex (introductory word: *as*; dependent clause: we/studied; independent clause: we/felt)

9. (S) simple (we/felt; *After* is not an introductory word since no subject follows.)

10. (S) simple with compound subject (hamburgers, fries/are)

11. (CD) compound (trio/needed; recital/was postponed; joining word: *so,* with comma at end of first clause)

12. (CC) compound-complex (independent clause: Sherry, Marcella/bus; joining word: *but*; introductory word: *unless*; dependent clause: they/can work; independent clause: they/will feel)

13. (CX) complex (independent clause: secretary/took; introductory word: *while*; dependent clause: he/was)

14. (S) simple (secretary/took)

15. (S) simple (Mr. Toon/returned; *After* is not an introductory word because no verb follows.)

EXERCISE 2

Directions: Put the following sentences together to make new ones. Be sure to use necessary punctuation.

Example: Join these sentences to make a complex sentence:

a. Cotton fields stretched as far as the eye could see.

b. I was surprised.

Answer: I was surprised that cotton fields stretched as far as the eye could see.

1. Put these sentences together to make a compound sentence:

   a.   We stopped to talk to the park ranger.
   b.   He warned us about the rattlesnakes along the trails.

2. Join the same two sentences into a complex sentence.

3. Join these sentences to make a complex sentence:

   a.   The logging trucks were loaded and chained.
   b.   Then the logging trucks rumbled down the highway.

4. Join the same two sentences into a simple sentence.

5. Combine these sentences into a complex sentence. Write two dependent clauses and one independent clause.

   a.   Over-the-road drivers travel long distances.
   b.   Over-the-road drivers sometimes do not take breaks.
   c.   They sometimes fall asleep at the wheel.

6. Use the same three sentences above to write a simple sentence with a compound verb.

7. Combine these sentences to make a complex sentence:

   a.   Maria rode the subway about thirty blocks.
   b.   Then Maria walked another eight blocks.
   c.   Maria reached the place for the job interview.

8. Use the same three sentences above to write a compound-complex sentence.

9. Join these sentences into one simple sentence. The sentence will have compound parts.

   a.   Julio had carpenter's tools.
   b.   He had plumber's tools.
   c.   He had electrician's tools.
   d.   He had all the tools stored in his truck.
   e.   He knew how to use them all.

10. Use the same set of sentences above to create a compound sentence.

EXERCISE 2—ANSWERS

1. We stopped to talk to the park ranger, and he warned us about the rattlesnakes along the trails. (Be sure you used a comma to replace the period at the end of the first clause.)

2. We stopped to talk to the park ranger who warned us about the rattlesnakes along the trails.

3. After the logging trucks were loaded and chained, they rumbled down the highway. (Did you use a comma after the introductory element? See Chapter 13, Part 2, Rule 5.)

4. The logging trucks, loaded and chained, rumbled down the highway.

5. When over-the-road drivers travel long distances or when they do not take breaks, they sometimes fall asleep at the wheel. (Did you use a comma correctly?)

6. Over-the-road drivers travel long distances, sometimes do not take breaks, and sometimes fall asleep at the wheel.

7. After Maria rode the subway for about thirty blocks and walked another eight, she reached the place for the job interview. (Check punctuation.)

8. Maria rode the subway for about thirty blocks; and after she walked another eight blocks, she reached the place for the job interview. (Did you use either a comma or a semicolon where you joined the two main clauses?)

9. Julio had carpenter's tools, plumber's tools, and electrician's tools stored in his truck and knew how to use them all. (Did you use commas to separate the items in the series? See Chapter 13, Part 2, Rule 1.)

10. Julio had carpenter's tools, plumber's tools, and electrician's tools stored in his truck; he knew how to use them all. (Be sure to use both the commas for the series and a semicolon between the compound sentences.)

EXERCISE 3

Directions: Most of the following sentences are incorrect. Some are joined incorrectly, some are incomplete sentences (dependent clauses without independent clauses), and some are correct. Correct any errors.

1. Cartoon character Bugs Bunny is now 50 years old and so is Mickey Mouse.

2. A computer keyboard looks very much like a typewriter keyboard, people who use one can use the other.

3. Air pollution and water pollution are big political issues candidates like to make voters believe they are all friends of the environment.

4. After the security officer made hourly checks.

5. Because they make money, movie sequels are popular among producers and actors.

6. While we were visiting the pet cemetery.

7. After we visited the pet cemetery near the edge of town but near our house.

8. As the gas station attendant made change, we recalled the days when "self-serve" was the exception, not the rule.

9. Microwave ovens are real time savers, they cook food in minutes.

10. Windmills used to supply most of the electricity on many western ranches, now more modern windmills still produce energy-efficient power.

EXERCISE 3—ANSWERS

1. Cartoon character Bugs Bunny is now 50 years old, and so is Mickey Mouse. (Two sentences put together with only a joining word; add comma. See Chapter 13, Part 2, Rule 3.)

2. A computer keyboard looks very much like a typewriter keyboard, *so* people who use one can use the other. (Two sentences joined with only a comma; add joining word. See Chapter 13, Part 2, Rule 3.) Also correct: A computer keyboard looks very much like a typewriter keyboard; people who use one can use the other.

3. Air pollution and water pollution are big political issues, *so* candidates like to make voters believe they are all friends of the environment. (Two sentences joined with nothing; use comma and joining word. See Chapter 13, Part 2, Rule 3.) Also correct: Air pollution and water pollution are big political issues; candidates like to make voters believe they are all friends of the environment.

4. Answers will vary. Suggestion: After the security officer made hourly checks, he filed a report. (No independent clause; add one.)

5. (Correct)

6. Answers will vary. Suggestion: I felt sad while we were visiting the pet cemetery. (No independent clause; add one.)

7. Answers will vary. Suggestion: After we visited the pet cemetery near the edge of town but still near our house, we decided to bury our own pet there. (No independent clause; add one.)

8. (Correct)

9. Microwave ovens are real time savers, *for* they cook food in minutes. (Two sentences joined without joining word; use comma and joining word. See Chapter 13, Part 2, Rule 3.) Also correct: Microwave ovens are real time savers; they cook food in minutes.

10. Windmills used to supply most of the electricity on many western ranches, *and* now more modern windmills still produce energy-efficient power. (Two sentences joined without joining word; use comma and joining word.) Also correct: Windmills used to supply most of the electricity on many western ranches; now more modern windmills still produce energy-efficient power.

EXERCISE 4

Directions: Now that you can identify kinds of sentences, try your hand at writing them. Below are directions for writing a variety of sentence structures. See what you can do with the skeletons provided. It is fair to warn you that the items become progressively more difficult, but with some practice, you'll be ready for the tough ones when you get to them! (That's a compound-complex sentence you just read!)

1. Write a simple sentence with *employees* as the subject and *work* as the verb.

2. Write a simple sentence with two subjects and one verb. Use *taking tests* as one subject.

3. Write a simple sentence with one subject and two verbs. Use *sunshine* as the subject.

4. Write a simple sentence with two subjects and two verbs. Use *Uncle Clyde* and *Aunt Thelma* as the two subjects.

5. Write a compound sentence with *watermelon* as one subject and *tastes* as one verb. Be sure to use a comma at the end of the first clause.

6. Write another compound sentence with *car* as one subject and *runs* as one verb. Use a different joining word than you did for sentence 5. Be sure to use a comma to separate the two sentences.

7. Write a complex sentence using *Cecil walked* as the subject and verb of the independent clause. Begin the dependent adverb clause with *because*.

8. Write a complex sentence using *Cecil walked* as the subject and verb of the dependent clause. Make the dependent clause an adverb clause and put it at the beginning of the sentence.

9. Rewrite sentence 8 and put the dependent adverb clause at the end of the sentence.

10. Write a complex sentence using an adjective clause to describe the subject *sister*.

EXERCISE 4—ANSWERS

The following answers are only patterns after which your own sentences should be formed. The italicized parts are required. Otherwise, you should have the same series of independent and dependent clauses. Above all, if you have similar patterns, you have proved that you can write some really sophisticated sentences. Good for you!

1. Good *employees* usually *work* beyond the minimum task.

2. Interviewing for jobs and *taking tests* make some people nervous.

3. *Sunshine* makes me happy and keeps me warm.

4. On Sundays, *Uncle Clyde* and *Aunt Thelma* usually eat dinner at a local restaurant famous for barbecue.

5. During hot summer afternoons, ice-cold *watermelon tastes* better than anything else, but during cold winter evenings, hot chocolate hits the spot.

6. The antique *car runs* only thirty-five miles per hour, so it can't enter most interstate highways.

7. *Because* he had a flat tire and no spare, *Cecil walked* the last three miles home.

8. Because *Cecil walked* three miles in the rain, he was soaked to the skin.

9. Cecil was soaked to the skin because he walked three miles in the rain.

10. Carolyn's *sister*, who won first place in the dance contest, hopes to compete in more dance contests.

Solving Common Sentence Problems

Sentences are the building blocks of any piece of writing, whether for your job, your personal life, or the GED essay. If you can write one good sentence, you can write two. If you can write two, you can write three. And if you can write three, finally you have a complete piece of writing—all of it good! By setting a series of goals for your sentence writing, we'll help you solve common sentence problems.

GOAL 1: USING SPECIFIC WORDS

Without specific words, an otherwise good sentence fails. Your goal is to write specifically.

IDENTIFYING VAGUE WORDS

When writing lacks specifics, usually the writer has used only vague words to try to get across his message. You have a picture in your mind of what you are trying to say. Try turning the tables, and imagine the message your reader is getting. Are you putting the picture in your mind into your reader's mind?

> Example: We toured a big building.

Your reader has no picture of "building." Is this an office building, a church, a school, or something else? What do you mean by "big"? Is it six stories tall, seventy-five stories tall, or just one story tall but spread across fifty acres?

> Example: Today is a miserable day.

Your reader needs specifics. Is the day miserable because of the weather—rain, ice storm, hot, humid, cloudy? Or is the day miserable because you have a bad cold or everything seems to be going wrong?

ROAD MAP

- *Using Specific Words*
- *Combining Sentences*
- *Placing Words Correctly*
- *Balancing Sets of Words*
- *Avoiding Run-ons and Comma Splices*
- *Avoding Sentence Fragments*
- *Checklist for Writing Effective Sentences*
- *Practice*
- *GED Practice*

REPLACING VAGUE WORDS

Let's use the same examples above and create good pictures for the reader's mind.

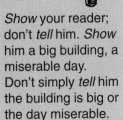

HINT

Show your reader; don't *tell* him. *Show* him a big building, a miserable day. Don't simply *tell* him the building is big or the day miserable.

Example:	We toured a big building.
Revisions:	We toured a seventy-five-story office building that had three floors underground.
	We toured a church that covers a city block and whose spire rises above all other buildings in the city.
	We toured a high school that sprawls across 80 acres.
Example:	Today is a miserable day.
Revisions:	With the temperature edging near 100 degrees, my shirt is clinging to me, the sweat running down my scalp, pasting my hair to my head and neck and burning my eyes.
	Today I lost my job, had a fender-bender accident on my way home, and then spilled a cup of hot chocolate on the white carpet.

Make sure when you write that you put the picture in your reader's mind.

GOAL 2: COMBINING SENTENCES

Good sentence variety comes in part from combining short sentences into a more effective longer one. But when you combine sentences, you have to do so correctly. Otherwise, you can create some really serious errors. The GED tests your ability to put sentences together correctly in two ways. One way is in questions like the following:

Sentences 1 and 2: The cost of new homes is high today. Many people are purchasing older homes in need of renovation.

The most effective combination of sentences 1 and 2 would include which of the following groups of words?

(1) Although many homes need renovation
(2) Although the cost of new homes is high today
(3) Because many people are purchasing older homes
(4) Because the cost of new homes is high today
(5) purchase older homes in need of renovation

The correct answer is (4).

The second way, of course, is in your essay response. So let's study some correct ways to combine sentences.

Method 1: Join Adjectives

Sometimes you can create new, improved sentences by joining adjectives.

Example:	The paper is wet.
	The paper is torn.
	The paper is useless for wrapping anything.
Combined:	The *wet, torn* paper is *useless* for wrapping anything.
	(See Chapter 13, Part 2, Rule 2, for comma rules.)

Method 2: Use Appositives

An appositive is a noun that renames another noun. You can join two sentences by making one an appositive.

Example: My uncle is a ten-year veteran in the fire department.

My uncle has made me conscious of fire hazards in the home.

Combined: My uncle, *a ten-year veteran in the fire department,* has made me conscious of fire hazards in the home.

Method 3: Use Phrases

Often two sentences can be combined by making one of them into a participial phrase (See Chapter 11, Part 3).

Remember that usually the participle is set off with commas, but participles that are necessary to identify the words they modify have no commas (See Chapter 13, Part 2, Rule 4).

Example: The package is lying on the counter.

The package belongs to me.

Combined: The package *lying on the counter* belongs to me.

(No commas are necessary since *lying on the counter* identifies which package.)

Example: My car is parked illegally.

My car may be towed away.

Combined: My car, *parked illegally,* may be towed away.

(The commas indicate added information. The writer has only one car, so *parked illegally* is not needed to identify which car.)

Method 4: Use Clauses

Clauses are groups of words that have both a subject and a verb (See Chapters 11 and 12). Using dependent clauses will help you combine sentences.

Example: Some bicycles have training wheels.

Some bicycles help beginners learn to ride.

Combined: Bicycles *that have training wheels* help beginners learn to ride.

Since some clauses are movable, consider the alternatives for combining these sentences:

Example: The snow was deep.

The depth was fourteen inches.

We could not move the car.

We had to shovel out the driveway.

Combined: *Because the snow was fourteen inches deep,* we could not move the car *until we shoveled out the driveway.*

Varied: *Until we shoveled out the driveway,* we could not move the car *because the snow was fourteen inches deep.*

Varied: We could not move the car *until we shoveled out the driveway because the snow was fourteen inches deep.*

Varied: *Because the snow was fourteen inches deep, until we shoveled out the driveway,* we could not move the car.

WARNING

Appositives are set off from the rest of the sentence with commas (See Chapter 13, Part 2, Rule 6).

HINT

Participles can appear at the beginning, in the middle, or at the end of a sentence. Hence, they give many ways to achieve sentence variety.

All of these sentences are equally correct; however, each carries a slightly different emphasis. How do you know how to put emphasis in the right place? Remember a simple rule:

> **Rule:** Put the main idea in the main clause.

The corollary to that rule is also simple:

> **Rule:** Put subordinate ideas in subordinate clauses.

Compare the following sentences to see how the emphasis changes:

Example 1: The robot, which was specially designed for the subassembly line, cost over two million dollars.

(The main clause is *The robot cost over two million dollars.* The main idea belongs in the main clause. The remainder of the sentence is an adjective clause—a subordinate clause—that modifies the subject.)

Example 2: A new design for the subassembly line, which is a two-million dollar robot, will replace three employees.

(The main clause is *The new design for the subassembly line will replace three employees.* The main idea focuses on the replacement of employees. The robot and its cost are secondary ideas.)

Example 3: Three employees lost their jobs as a result of a two-million dollar robot.

(The main clause is *Three employees lost their jobs.* The main idea supports the subordinating idea that the job loss was the result of a robot.)

Notice that there is nothing grammatically wrong with any one of these sentences. Each simply has a different emphasis and a different message. Be sure to put your main ideas in main clauses so that you communicate clearly.

GOAL 3: PLACING WORDS CORRECTLY

Sometimes a word or phrase is placed next to a word that it cannot describe in a way that makes sense. Correct the problem by changing or moving the word or phrase (See also Chapter 11, Part 3C).

Incorrect: Running around the block, the building came into view.

(The building is not running around the block.)

Correct: Running around the block, I saw the building come into view.

Incorrect: Rodney told Angela not to get upset calmly.

Correct: Rodney calmly told Angela not to get upset.

(*Calmly* talks about *told* and so should be placed as near to *told* as possible.)

Phrases or clauses that are misplaced are often called "dangling modifiers," or more simply, "misplaced modifiers." Sometimes the effect of dangling modifiers is unintentionally amusing, so check your work carefully. Compare these examples:

Misplaced Modifier: Hoping to land the job, his resume had been updated.

(His resume isn't hoping to land the job.)

Correct: Hoping to land the job, he updated his resume.

(He is hoping to land the job.)

NOTE: An introductory phrase or clause must modify the word immediately following it.

Misplaced Modifier: The company van came rattling to a stop painted red and purple.

(The stop is not painted red and purple.)

Correct: The company van, painted red and purple, came rattling to a stop.

GOAL 4: BALANCING SETS OF WORDS

When you put groups of words together, they need balance. To give them balance, write them with similar words. The technical word for that balance is *parallelism*.

Unbalanced: Carol likes *basketball* and *attending football games*.

Balanced: Carol likes *basketball* and *football*.

(The two nouns, both objects of the verb *likes*, are parallel.)

Unbalanced: Mark *studied* grammar and his answers *were checked*.

Balanced: Mark *studied* grammar and *checked* his answers.

(Each verb has its own object; thus, the verb phrases are parallel.)

Unbalanced: Sandra was *tall* and *with blond hair*.

Balanced: Sandra was *tall* and *blond*.

(The two adjectives *tall* and *blond* equally describe the subject. Thus the predicate parts are parallel.*)*

Unbalanced: *Working regular hours* and *to be able to pay the rent* were my goals.

Balanced: *Working regular hours* and *being able to pay the rent* were my goals.

(*Working* and *being* both end in *–ing* and have objects; the verbals are parallel.)

GOAL 5: AVOIDING RUN-ONS AND COMMA SPLICES

A run-on sentence occurs when two sentences are joined without a connecting word or any punctuation.

Run-on Sentence: The man ambled aimlessly through the crowd the woman walked with a purpose.

Corrected: The man ambled aimlessly through the crowd, but the woman walked with a purpose.

To correct a run-on sentence, use one of two methods:

1. Join the sentences with a comma and a joining word (Review Chapter 15, Part 2).

2. Use a period and a capital letter to form two sentences.

A comma splice occurs when two sentences are joined (spliced together) with only a comma.

Comma splice: The man ambled aimlessly through the crowd, the woman walked with a purpose.

To join two sentences correctly, use a comma and a joining word. Make sure, however, that the ideas in the two main clauses are closely related.

Corrected: The man ambled aimlessly through the crowd, but the woman walked with a purpose.

GOAL 6: AVOIDING SENTENCE FRAGMENTS

A sentence fragment is part of a sentence. If you punctuate part of a sentence as if it were a complete sentence, you make a serious error. There are two common kinds of fragments.

Type 1:   Phrase as fragment

Fragment: We saw the car. Speeding down the expressway.

Corrected: We saw the car speeding down the expressway.

Fragment: After working all day in the sun. He needed to drink plenty of liquids.

To correct the fragment, join the phrase to the main clause it describes.

Corrected: After working all day in the sun, he needed to drink plenty of liquids.

Fragment: The waves lapping against the shore in a quiet, sleepy rhythm.

To correct some fragments, change the verbal to a verb (See Chapter 11).

Corrected: The waves lapped against the shore in a quiet, sleepy rhythm.

Type 2:   Dependent clause as fragment

Fragment: I found my shop coat on the floor. When I arrived for work.

To correct dependent clause fragments, join them to a main clause.

Corrected: I found my shop coat on the floor when I arrived for work.

HINT

The best way to find fragments is to read your paper *backwards* sentence by sentence. In most cases, you will then be able to recognize pieces of sentences that cannot stand alone.

CHECKLIST FOR WRITING EFFECTIVE SENTENCES

Use the following checklist to evaluate your own sentences. You should be able to answer yes to each of these questions.

	YES	NO
1. Have I started each sentence with a capital letter?	❑	❑
2. Have I used an end mark of punctuation—a period, a question mark, or an exclamation point?	❑	❑
3. Have I written complete sentences?	❑	❑
4. Have I avoided comma splices and run-on sentences?	❑	❑
5. Have I used a variety of simple, compound, complex, and compound-complex sentences?	❑	❑
6. Have I used specific, concrete words?	❑	❑
7. Have I placed words and phrases correctly so that they are next to the words they describe?	❑	❑
8. Have I balanced sets of words?	❑	❑
9. Have I punctuated correctly?	❑	❑

PRACTICE
EXERCISE 1

Directions: Revise the following sentences to eliminate vague words. You will find more than one vague word in each sentence. As you revise, don't tell your reader; show him!

1. A tall man came into the room. (Clarify the vague words *tall, man, came,* and *room.*)
2. The child played with her toys. (Clarify *child, played,* and *toys.*)
3. The car wasn't running well. (Clarify *car* and *wasn't running well.*)
4. That man is really dirty! (Clarify *that man* and *dirty.*)
5. I was too busy to finish my chores. (Clarify *too busy* and *chores.*)
6. I ate too much. (You're on your own now. You decide what needs to be clarified.)
7. Mariann was dressed funny.
8. Wilma's present came in a big box.
9. The paint matched the gaudy wallpaper.
10. We had fun at the picnic.

EXERCISE 1—ANSWERS

The following are only suggested revisions for the ten sentences above. Obviously, yours will differ. If you've clarified the vague words in a similar manner, however, you know you're on the right track.

1. A seven-foot-tall basketball player ducked into the kitchen.
2. The toddler threw blocks across the room.
3. The 1967 jalopy clattered down the street in a cloud of blue smoke.
4. White spots where his goggles protected his eyes were the only places the miner was not covered with coal dust.
5. Because I worked until 11:30 last night, I didn't have time to do the laundry, wash the dishes, or iron a clean shirt.
6. I ate four hamburgers, three bowls of chili, a large pizza, and two combination salads.
7. Mariann wore men's hip boots, a fur coat, and a white ruffled sunbonnet.
8. Wilma's surprise birthday present came in a box the size of a 24-inch television set.
9. The purple paint matched the purple, pink, gray, and yellow wallpaper.
10. At the family reunion picnic, we played Frisbee, volleyball, and softball and ate off and on all afternoon.

EXERCISE 2

Directions: Vary the following sentences in at least three ways. You may use any sentence-combining technique you've learned.

1. Some men work in oil fields.
   These men are sometimes called "roughnecks."
   The name is appropriate for the job.

2. The highway crew arrived to clear the road.
   The road was strewn with boxes of nails.
   The nails spilled when a truck overturned.

3. Some people adore cats.
   Some people adore dogs.
   Few people adore both.
   Bitter arguments arise between the two.

4. Students are hard workers.
   Students are studious.
   Pupils merely attend classes.

5. Ona is on a diet.
   She ate chocolate chip cookies and ice cream.

EXERCISE 2—ANSWERS

The following are suggested variations possible from the above.

1. a. Men who work in oil fields are sometimes called "roughnecks," an appropriate name for the job.
   b. Men who work in oil fields are sometimes called, appropriately, "roughnecks."
   c. "Roughnecks" is an appropriate name for the men who work in oil fields.

2. a. The highway crew arrived to clear the road, which was strewn with boxes of nails when a truck overturned.
   b. After a truck overturned and spilled nails over the road, the highway crew arrived to clear the mess.
   c. The highway crew arrived to clear the road after a truck overturned and spilled boxes of nails on the highway.

3. a. Although some people adore cats and some adore dogs, few adore both, and bitter arguments arise between the two.
   b. Although few people adore both, some adore cats and others adore dogs, and bitter arguments arise between the two.
   c. Bitter arguments arise between the people who adore cats and others who adore dogs because few adore both.

4. a. While pupils merely attend classes, students are hard working and studious.
   b. Students are hardworking and studious while pupils merely attend classes.
   c. Pupils merely attend classes, but students are hard working and studious.

5. a. Even though Ona is on a diet, she ate chocolate chip cookies and ice cream.
   b. Even though she ate chocolate chip cookies and ice cream, Ona is on a diet.
   c. She ate chocolate chip cookies and ice cream, but Ona is on a diet.

EXERCISE 3

Directions: Rewrite these sentences to correct misplaced words or phrases.

1. Throwing the ball hard, the batter was struck by the pitcher.
2. To create the right color, the paint was mixed carefully.
3. Complaining of a headache, the doctor gave Jethro medicine.
4. My boss ordered me back to work angrily.
5. After learning the basic rules, the game went smoothly.
6. We heard the board elected officers on the late news last night.
7. The cat played with the ball running in circles.
8. The fans on the other side of the field, who are cheering wildly, are the team's loyal followers.

EXERCISE 3—ANSWERS

1. Throwing the ball hard, the pitcher struck the batter.
2. To create the right color, he mixed the paint carefully.
3. Complaining of a headache, Jethro received medicine from the doctor.
4. My boss angrily ordered me back to work.
5. After learning the basic rules, I smoothly played the game.
6. On the late news last night, we heard the board elected officers.
7. Running in circles, the cat played with the ball.
8. The fans who are cheering wildly on the other side of the field are the team's loyal followers.

EXERCISE 4

Directions: Rewrite these sentences so the pairs or groups of words are balanced (parallel).

1. Shelton likes to play basketball, going to movies, and skiing.
2. They traveled by plane, in boats, and by train.
3. Cathy promised that she would cut the grass and to trim the hedges.
4. The best way to study is to find a quiet room and concentrating on the lesson.
5. Her goal was to become an accountant and attending classes in ethnic cooking.
6. Jennifer carried the boxes carefully and with ease.
7. To be cheerful and showing optimism are good qualities.
8. Erin planned a shopping trip and to go on a short vacation.

EXERCISE 4—ANSWERS

1. Shelton likes basketball, movies, and skiing.
2. They traveled by plane, by boat, and by train.
3. Cathy promised that she would cut the grass and trim the hedges.
4. The best way to study is to find a quiet room and concentrate on the lesson.
5. Her goal was to become an accountant and attend classes in ethnic cooking.
6. Jennifer carried the boxes carefully and easily.
7. To be cheerful and to show optimism are good qualities.
8. Erin planned a shopping trip and a short vacation.

EXERCISE 5

> **Directions:** Correct these sentences as needed. Some may be correct.

1. As we write, we must avoid comma splices, they are serious errors.
2. Run-on sentences are just as bad they are serious errors, too.
3. Writing effective sentences takes care but makes sense.
4. The neighbor's dogs howled all night, they kept me awake until 3:00 a.m.
5. What he wants for his car is a new paint job, but what he will get for his car is just a good wax job.
6. In 1965 when gas was twenty-nine cents a gallon, we often took short family trips, now we take only one trip a year.
7. The table is too big for the room there is no room for any extra chairs.
8. The job of raking leaves kept Robert busy all day Saturday so he was happy to relax on Sunday.
9. The car windshields in the parking lot reflected the sunlight, and the reflection hurt my eyes.
10. The clothes dryer dries some of my shirts wrinkle-free, I iron most of them.

EXERCISE 5—ANSWERS

1. comma splices; they OR comma splices, *for*
2. bad; they OR bad, *for*
3. correct
4. night, *and* OR night; they
5. correct
6. trips, *but* OR trips; now
7. room; there OR room, *and*
8. Saturday, so
9. correct
10. wrinkle-free, but

EXERCISE 6

Directions: Rewrite the following sentences to correct any sentence fragments. Some sentences may be correct.

1. Tina knew she would find the answer to the problem. When she left work today.
2. This new printer is really fast. It can print a full page in less than five seconds.
3. Whatever you need to get the job done.
4. Having spoken, he sat down.
5. Harold called yesterday. Thinking it was my birthday.
6. Across the patio, through the yard, and out the driveway.
7. The cars parked in the lot across the street from our house.
8. A soft, gentle breeze sighing through the pines and across our picnic table.

EXERCISE 6—ANSWERS

1. Tina knew she would find the answer to the problem when she left work today.
2. correct
3. We will order whatever you need to get the job done.
4. correct
5. Harold called yesterday thinking it was my birthday.
6. I chased the new puppy across the patio, through the yard, and out the driveway.
7. The cars are parked in the lot across the street from our house.
8. A soft, gentle breeze sighed through the pines and across our picnic table.

GED PRACTICE

CROWDING THEM OUT

A

(1) *The term "economic development" brings a smile to most politicians' faces but some folks shudder in dismay.* (2) *Every year civilization pushes harder and harder on wild critters' habitat and on the balance of life.* (3) *Farmland which developers concrete over by the thousands of acres has fed the country for generations.* (4) *Shopping centers and houses in suburban developments spring up where forest, thickets of bushes, and wetland stood for thousands of years.* (5) *At the same time that the development leaps ever outward from cities' downtown areas, the already concreted downtown areas fall into decline.* (6) *Instead of fixing up or rebuilding, the trend is to move on, bulldoze more, concrete more, add more buildings, pave more parking lots.*

B

(7) *Surely the problem isn't as serious as some folks suggest.* (8) *After all the raccoons, snakes, foxes, birds, frogs, earthworms, and bugs can simply move someplace else, can't they?* (9) *Well, not really.* (10) *Critters are unlike people.* (11) *Humans will live in twenty-story apartment complexes sharing box-like quarters with several other people.* (12) *Other animals, on the other hand, when their habitat is destroyed, die.* (13) *They can't move on to other territory it's already claimed by another of their kind.* (14) *A hawk, for instance, may need a five-mile radius of grasslands in order to find enough to eat and feed its young.* (15) *The hawk can't encroach on another hawks' territory without a whopping big battle.* (16) *When a developer paves all or part of the five acres.* (17) *Only one hawk wins the other dies.*

C

(18) *Indeed, then, development means that critters that have lived there for thousands of years will die only because humans are too insensitive to this earth's balance.* (19) *In fact, a huge percentage of humans act as if they believe that the earth gives them the right to personal exploitation, that humans are superior to all other life and this shortsightedness will ultimately be this earth's demise.*

1. Sentence 1: The term "economic development" brings a smile to most politicians' faces but some folks shudder in dismay.

   What correction should be made to this sentence?

   (1) Change the word <u>but</u> to <u>and</u>.
   (2) Insert a comma after the word <u>but</u>.
   (3) Insert a comma after the word <u>faces</u>.
   (4) Change the word <u>but</u> to <u>because</u>.
   (5) No correction is necessary.

2. Sentence 2: Every year civilization pushes harder and harder on wild critters' habitat and on the balance of life.

   What correction should be made to this sentence?

   (1) Insert a comma after <u>habitat</u>.
   (2) Insert a comma after <u>pushes harder</u>.
   (3) Change <u>on the balance of life</u> to <u>on life's balance</u>.
   (4) Change <u>harder and harder</u> to <u>more and more hard</u>.
   (5) No correction is necessary.

3. Sentence 3: Farmland which developers concrete over by the thousands of acres has fed the country for generations.

   What correction should be made to this sentence?

   (1) Insert a comma after <u>Farmland</u>.
   (2) Change <u>which</u> to <u>that</u>.
   (3) Rewrite the sentence so that it begins <u>Developers concrete over by the thousands of acres farmland...</u>.
   (4) Rewrite the sentence to read <u>Because developers concrete farmland by the thousands of acres, it can no longer feed the country</u>.
   (5) No correction is necessary.

4. Sentence 4: <u>Shopping centers and houses in suburban developments spring up</u> where forest, thickets of bushes, and wetland stood for thousands of years.

   What correction should be made to the underlined portion of the sentence?

   (1) Change <u>houses in suburban developments</u> to <u>suburban housing</u>.
   (2) Insert a comma after <u>developments</u>.
   (3) Insert a comma after <u>centers</u>.
   (4) Change <u>Shopping centers and houses in suburban developments</u> to <u>Houses and shopping centers in suburban developments</u>.
   (5) No correction is necessary.

5. Sentence 4: Shopping centers and houses in suburban developments spring up <u>where forest, thickets of bushes, and wetland stood for thousands of years</u>.

   What correction should be made to the underlined portion of the sentence?

   (1) Change <u>where</u> to <u>in which</u>.
   (2) Omit <u>of bushes</u>.
   (3) Insert a comma after <u>wetland</u>.
   (4) Omit the word <u>and</u>.
   (5) No correction is necessary.

6. Sentence 6: Instead of fixing up or rebuilding, the trend is to move on, bulldoze more, concrete more, add more buildings, pave more parking lots.

   What correction should be made to the sentence?

   (1) Reword rebuilding to read putting up new buildings.
   (2) Move the phrase Instead of fixing up or rebuilding to the end of the sentence.
   (3) Insert the word and after buildings.
   (4) Reword add more buildings, pave more parking lots to read build more, pave more.
   (5) No correction is necessary.

7. Sentence 7: Surely the problem isn't as serious as some folks suggest.

   What correction should be made to the sentence?

   (1) Move the word surely to follow isn't.
   (2) Move the word surely to follow problem.
   (3) Insert a comma after the word serious.
   (4) Reword the sentence to that it begins As some folks suggest.
   (5) No correction is necessary.

8. Sentence 8: After all the raccoons, snakes, foxes, birds, frogs, earthworms, and bugs can simply move someplace else, can't they?

   What correction should be made to the sentence?

   (1) Insert a comma after all.
   (2) Move the word simply to follow else.
   (3) Reword the sentence so that it begins Shouldn't all the raccoons. . . .
   (4) Reword the sentence so that it begins When all the raccoons. . . .
   (5) No correction is necessary.

9. Sentence 9: Well, not really.

   What correction should be made to the sentence?

   (1) Rewrite it as Well, they really can't.
   (2) Rewrite it as Well, no.
   (3) Omit the comma.
   (4) Reword it to read Not really, no.
   (5) No correction is necessary.

10. Sentences 10 and 11: Critters are unlike people. Humans will live in twenty-story apartment complexes sharing box-like quarters with several other people.

    What correction should be made to these sentences?

    (1) Join the two sentences by omitting the period after people and writing humans in lower case.
    (2) Join the two sentences by changing the period to a comma.
    (3) Make the second sentence a subordinate clause so that the sentence reads Critters are unlike people, who will live. . . .
    (4) Change sharing to will share.
    (5) No correction is necessary.

11. Sentence 12: Other animals, on the other hand, when their habitat is destroyed, die.

What correction should be made to the sentence?

(1) Rewrite the sentence so that it begins When their habitat is destroyed.
(2) Rewrite the sentence so that it begins On the other hand, when their habitat is destroyed.
(3) Rewrite the sentence so that it begins On the other hand, other animals.
(4) Rewrite the sentence so that it begins Other animals, when their habitat is destroyed.
(5) No correction is necessary.

12. Sentence 13: They can't move on to other territory it's already claimed by another of their kind.

What correction should be made to the sentence?

(1) Insert a comma after territory.
(2) Add the word and and a comma after the word territory.
(3) Add the word because after the word territory.
(4) Insert a period after the word territory and capitalize It's.
(5) No correction is necessary.

13. Sentence 14: A hawk, for instance, may need a five-mile radius of grasslands in order to find enough to eat and feed its young.

What correction should be made to the sentence?

(1) Rewrite the sentence so that it begins A five-mile radius of grasslands.
(2) Rewrite the sentence so that it begins Because a hawk needs a five-mile radius of grasslands.
(3) Insert a comma after grasslands.
(4) Change for instance to therefore.
(5) No correction is necessary.

14. Sentences 15 and 16: The hawk can't encroach on another hawks' territory without a whopping big battle. When a developer paves all or part of the five acres.

What correction should be made to these sentences?

(1) Join the two sentences by beginning with When a developer paves all or part. . . .
(2) Join the two sentences by changing the period to a comma and writing when in lower case.
(3) Join the two sentences by changing the period to a comma and adding the word and after the comma.
(4) Join the two sentences by beginning with Without a whopping big battle. . . .
(5) No correction is necessary.

15. Sentence 17: Only one hawk wins the other dies.

What correction should be made to the sentence?

(1) Insert a comma after wins.
(2) Insert a comma and the word and after wins.
(3) Insert a comma and the word but after wins.
(4) Insert a comma and the word or after wins.
(5) No correction is necessary.

16. Sentence 18: Indeed, then, development means that critters that have lived there for thousands of years will die only because humans are too insensitive to this earth's balance.

    What correction should be made to the sentence?

    (1) Reword the sentence so that it begins <u>Critters that have lived there</u>. . . .
    (2) Reword the sentence to that it begins <u>Because humans are too insensitive</u>. . . .
    (3) Move the word <u>only</u> so that it is in front of <u>too</u>.
    (4) Move the word <u>only</u> so that it is in front of <u>humans</u>.
    (5) No correction is necessary.

17. Sentence 19: In fact, a huge percentage of humans act as if they believe that the earth gives them the right to personal exploitation, that humans are superior to all other life and this shortsightedness will ultimately be this earth's demise.

    What correction should be made to the sentence?

    (1) Revise the sentence so that it is three sentences.
    (2) Revise the sentence so that it is two sentences by inserting a period after <u>life</u>, omitting the word <u>and</u>, and capitalizing the word <u>This</u>.
    (3) Reword the sentence so that it begins <u>Because a huge percentage of humans act</u>. . . .
    (4) Reword the sentence so that it begins <u>Since humans are superior to all other life</u>. . . .
    (5) No correction is necessary.

GED PRACTICE—ANSWERS

1. (3) Use a comma and conjunction to join two sentences. See Chapter 15, Part 2.

2. (3) *On life's balance* is parallel with *on wild critter's habitat*. See Chapter 16, Goal 4.

3. (3) The main idea, *that developers concrete over farmland*, belongs in the main clause. See Chapter 16, Goal 2.

4. (1) *Suburban housing* is parallel with *shopping centers*. See Chapter 16, Goal 4.

5. (2) By omitting *of bushes*, the remaining parts are parallel. See Chapter 16, Goal 4.

6. (4) The revision creates parallel structures. See Chapter 16, Goal 4.

7. (2) *Surely* modifies the predicate word. See Chapter 16, Goal 3.

8. (1) The comma is essential for clarity. See Chapter 13, Part 2.

9. (1) All other choices are sentence fragments. See Chapter 16, Goal 6.

10. (3) The subordinate idea is now in a subordinate clause. See Chapter 16, Goal 2.

11. (2) The main clause is *other animals die*, so these words should appear together. See Chapter 16, Goal 2.

12. (3) *Because* makes the second part a subordinate clause. See Chapter 16, Goal 2.

13. (5) Correct

14. (1) The adverb clause is the best beginning for the sentence. See Chapter 12, Part 3.

15. (2) A comma and conjunction correctly join two sentences. See Chapter 15, Part 2.

16. (5) Correct

17. (2) The revision corrects the stringy run-on sentence. See Chapter 15, Part 2 and Chapter 16, Goal 5.

A Paragraph's Topic Sentence

The writing you will do for the GED test is called an essay. An essay is a short piece of writing that tells what you think about something and gives details to explain your thoughts. Most good paragraphs begin with a topic sentence. That sentence does just what its name says: it states the topic of the paragraph. Study the following examples:

Topic Sentence: Getting along with fellow workers is important but sometimes difficult. (The writer will explain *how* to get along.)

Topic Sentence: Regular exercise helps people feel better, think better, and work better. (The writer will explain *why* this is true.)

Topic Sentence: Farm subsidies needlessly increase the cost of our groceries. (The writer will support this *opinion* by giving details to show why he thinks so.)

Topic Sentence: There are both advantages and disadvantages to working at night. (The writer will give details to show both good and bad results from night jobs.)

ROAD MAP

- *Start with a Topic Sentence*
- *Write an Effective Sentence*
- *Practice*

GOAL1: START WITH A TOPIC SENTENCE

Why start with a topic sentence? Two reasons:

1. By starting with a topic sentence, you force yourself to say exactly what you are going to do in your paragraph.

2. By starting with a topic sentence, you tell your reader exactly what you are going to do in your paragraph.

GOAL 2: WRITE AN EFFECTIVE TOPIC SENTENCE

What makes a good topic sentence? In order to answer the question, let's compare some poor topic sentences with better ones:

Poor: Last month I began taking a computer training class. (We can only guess what the writer will talk about: the class? the instructor? the equipment? the homework? the exhaustion from taking classes after working all day?)

Better: Computer training classes provide job training for an expanding job market. (We know the writer will explain why the classes are beneficial in terms of job potential.)

Poor: At my age, I still have the energy to work hard and play hard. (We assume the writer is going to talk about working and playing.)

Better: At my age, I have the energy to work and play hard, but I lack the experience for better jobs. (We know now that the writer will compare the advantages and disadvantages of youth in the job market.)

So, what makes a good topic sentence? It should say in one sentence *exactly* what you are going to write about—exactly what you are going to explain—in your paragraph.

Example:

Poor: The purpose of this paragraph is to explain why I think drunk drivers should be imprisoned.

Better: Drunk drivers should be imprisoned.

Better: Drunk drivers should be imprisoned for three important reasons.

Before you write your own topic sentence, work through the following exercise to see if you recognize the difference between good ones and poor ones.

HINT

The topic sentence should *not* say, "The purpose of this paragraph is to. . . ." Rather, simply say what you are going to talk about.

PRACTICE
EXERCISE

Directions: Decide whether the following are good or poor topic sentences. Compare your answers with those that follow.

1. Autumn is my favorite time of year.
2. Three area houses are built of Bedford stone.
3. Last night's football game showed Bradford's defensive superiority.
4. The Otmans collect hornets' nests.
5. For safety's sake, automobiles should have regular maintenance.
6. Unannounced drug testing may be the only way to keep public transportation safe.
7. Passengers ride helicopters between the two major airports.
8. Summer repairs on streets and highways are well underway in July.
9. Feeding backyard wildlife creates both advantages and disadvantages for the birds and animals.
10. Radio stations, as one form of media, influence voters through advertisements as well as news stories.

EXERCISE—ANSWERS

1. Good. The writer will then explain why.
2. Poor. An improvement: *Although Bedford stone is beautiful, it has three disadvantages as a building material.* Then the writer will explain the disadvantages.
3. Good. The writer will then explain why.
4. Poor. An improvement: *Collecting hornets' nests is a challenging—and dangerous—hobby.* The writer will then explain how to collect—safely.
5. Good. Writer will then explain why maintenance keeps autos safe.
6. Good. Writer will then give details to support his opinion.
7. Poor. An improvement: *Helicopter service between the two major airports has vastly improved flight connections.* Writer will then give details to show why.
8. Poor. An improvement: *Summer repair jobs on streets and highways affect traffic flow.* The writer will then explain how to deal with the slowed traffic patterns.
9. Good. Writer will then give details to show both advantages and disadvantages.
10. Good. Writer will then tell how.

Paragraph Organization and Content

Writers' thoughts are put together into units we call paragraphs—one thought, one paragraph. The GED essay requires that you be able to write well-developed paragraphs. Good paragraphs come about when the writer does four things:

1. uses specific details to support the topic sentence;

2. puts the details in a logical order;

3. uses effective connecting words to show the logical order and to hold the paragraph together; and

4. stays on the subject.

Let's study each of these four points.

PART 1: ADEQUATE SUPPORT: USING SPECIFIC DETAILS

You learned in Chapter 16 to use specific words. We looked, for instance, at the difference between such words as "building" and "seventy-five-story office building." You practiced making vague words into specific words.

The same idea applies to details in a paragraph. The directions on the GED test will often say, "Be specific," "Support your explanation with specific details and examples," or "State specific reasons and examples." Your reader must find evidence of adequate support. Using specific ideas to explain your topic will make your essay sparkle.

Compare the following two paragraphs that attempt to explain why the Tuesday Market may startle first-time visitors.

THE TUESDAY FARMERS' MARKET

The Tuesday Farmers' Market may startle a first-time visitor. Vendors gather early and begin selling right away. They often buy from one another. All kinds of things are available for sale, some new and some old. All kinds of strange noises can be heard and all kinds of things can be seen. Even the people are a surprise. Yes, it's really a surprise to go to the Tuesday Farmers' Market if you've never been there before.

The topic sentence is clear: The Tuesday Farmers' Market may startle a first-time visitor. The reader is ready for some specific details to help him be startled—or at least understand why first-time visitors would be startled. Unfortunately, in this paragraph, the reader is only told that he should be surprised at all kinds of unnamed things. The writer is telling, not showing.

ROAD MAP

- *Adequate Support: Using Specific Details*
- *Organization: Putting Details in Order*
- *Transitions within Paragraphs: Using Connecting Words*
- *Unity and Coherence: Staying on the Subject*
- *Practice*

NOTE

Certain clue words help the reader follow the time, words like *when, first, then, after, since,* and *finally.* Such words are necessary to clarify the time order.

Now let's look at the same topic with specific details:

THE TUESDAY FARMERS' MARKET

The Tuesday Farmers' Market may startle a first-time visitor. Vendors gather by 5:00 a.m. every Tuesday, and by 5:30 the haggling begins. A bib-overalled, whiskered farmer bargains with a high school boy who has three pairs of pigeons for sale. They strike a deal, and the boy takes his cash to a stall selling fresh fried pork rinds and antiques. He buys the rinds, still warm. Nearby, Elvis Presley tunes squawk through a static-filled speaker, drowning out only temporarily the chickens squawking a few feet away. Across the aisle, a middle-aged woman displays old canning jars on the hood of her car, and a tobacco-chewing, black-aproned man puts new handles on old shovels, scythes, hoes, and axes. Rolls of carpet, jars of clear clover honey, loaves of banana bread, piles of clothes, coops of ducklings, pairs of beagles, boxes of hubcaps, all seek bargain hunters. Country music on a car radio, bleating goats, yapping dogs, and cajoling vendors compete for attention. At the Tuesday Farmers' Market, cabbages, gooseberries, soap, vacuum sweepers, porch swings, socks, pocketknives, country hams, sleeping bags, and tombstones go to the best haggler. For someone who's not been there before, it's a real surprise.

Now the reader has specific pictures in her mind! Notice that the writer has provided sounds as well as pictures as part of his description. Notice, too, that the second paragraph is longer than the first. Specific writing need not be long, and long paragraphs are not necessarily specific. On the other hand, if you must put a picture in your reader's mind, you can't do it with just a few splotches of paint. A good picture needs outline, color, detail, and shading. Be sure your paragraph paints a good picture!

PART 2: ORGANIZATION: PUTTING DETAILS IN ORDER

You must arrange the details in your paragraph so that your reader can follow them easily. Three kinds of arrangement are most common, and you will use the one that best fits the purpose of your paragraph. The three kinds of logical arrangements include time order, space order, and order of importance. Let's look at each of the three kinds of arrangement.

Time Order

HINT

Anytime your writing involves an explanation of something that has happened over a period of time, use time order to write about it.

We use time order when we tell about something that happened or will happen over a period of time. Items are presented in the order in which they occur. Study the following sample paragraph that explains why the writer reaches Jonathan's house late:

WE WERE LONG LOST, FRIEND

When we tried to reach Jonathan's house late last night, we faced a series of obstacles. First, some of the street signs were bent so that we couldn't read them. Then, after we made what we later learned were three wrong turns and came to a dead end, we decided we were lost. Since we didn't want to knock on anyone's door at 10:00 p.m., we drove south until we came to a 24-hour market. We asked directions there and found we'd driven nearly thirty blocks the wrong way. After we retraced our steps, we found the right street, but it was barricaded as a result of some utility repairs. By the time we followed the detour seven blocks east and seven blocks back west, we finally reached Jonathan's house only to discover "no parking" signs on both sides of the street. As a result, we parked around the corner and walked to his door, knocking as we heard his clock chime 10:30.

This paragraph is written in time order. The events are told in the order in which they happened.

Space Order

We use space order when we tell about something according to the way it is arranged in space. The common orders are as follows:

    left to right
    right to left
    top to bottom
    bottom to top
    front to back
    back to front

Look at the following paragraph organized spatially, left to right.

THE STOREROOM

The storeroom was a jumble of boxes, buckets, and useless debris. On the far left, stacks of old newspapers and scrap cardboard reached nearly six feet high. Next to them, empty boxes sat inside one another at unstable angles. To the right of the boxes, hundreds of buckets, most empty, some tipped over, were heaped pyramid fashion nearly to the ceiling. On the far right, an assortment of broken boxes, buckets, broom handles, rags, and rusted cans littered the floor. Certainly the storeroom needed a good cleaning.

This paragraph is written in space order, or as the reader sees the subject in space. In this case, the writer takes the reader around the room from left to right. Special words, called connecting words, offer clues to the reader: *on the far left, on the right, next to*. Connecting words tell the reader where to look in his mind's eye. They help establish relationships between one idea and the next. Be sure to use these special words to help your reader follow your ideas. (See also "Using Good Connecting Words" later in this chapter.)

Order of Importance

As the heading implies, this final method of arranging details offers more than one choice. Your paragraph details may be arranged by order of importance in one of three ways:

1. most important detail to least important detail

2. least important detail to most important detail

3. next most important detail to most important detail

In order to make more sense of these, we need to look at each of them individually.

Choice 1: Most Important to Least Important

The outline for such organization should be rather obvious. The most important idea or detail comes first. The order could be listed something like this:

1. most important idea

2. second most important idea

3. third most important idea

4. fourth most important idea

5. least important idea

The following paragraph states and supports the writer's opinion that the circus world is one of extraordinary work and organization. The paragraph is organized from most important to least important.

HINT

Anytime your writing involves an explanation of something your reader must do over a period of time—like repair his brakes, change his oil, prepare a gourmet dish—then use time order to write about it.

HINT

Anytime your writing involves an explanation of the arrangement of something—like parts of a carburetor, components of a stereo, furniture in a room, houses on a block—use the spatial method of organization so that your reader can follow your explanation.

HINT

A writer should use choice 1 when what he says first may be the only thing a reader reads. Newspaper writing usually follows such an organization. Often we read the first several paragraphs of a news item but fail to finish it. We know, however, that we have read the most important ideas.

HERE COMES THE BIG TOP!

From an adult's point of view, a circus is an impressive operation. While children may think the trained animal acts and the trapeze artists are most impressive, adults are most awed by the mere logistics of getting all the equipment and people from one site to another. Once the entourage has reached its destination by truck or train, the massive operation of erecting an entire city overnight amazes outsiders. The operation calls not only for putting up the big top but also for providing seating for thousands. In addition, the circus people and animals must be housed and fed. Imagine providing enough food for hundreds of lions, tigers, bears, elephants, and hungry working people. Finally, the fact that hundreds of costumes are ready for the performance impresses anyone who has had to prepare a single costume for a simple amateur performance. The circus world must be one of extraordinary work and organization!

As you can see, the paragraph begins with the writer's most important idea and ends with his least important idea.

Choice 2: Least Important to Most Important

This second method of order of importance is more common than the first. In this case, the organization is exactly opposite of the first example we considered. The list of details would look something like this:

1. least important detail
2. fourth most important detail
3. third most important detail
4. second most important detail
5. most important detail

Following is the same sample paragraph, this time reorganized to follow this second method of order of importance. Note the difference.

HINT

The writer should use choice 2 when he has no reason to believe his reader is antagonistic. Choice 2 lets the writer hit his reader at the end with the really big idea. The reader will be impressed! The reader will be apt to remember the impression longer!

HERE COMES THE BIG TOP!

From an adult's point of view, a circus is an impressive operation. The fact that hundreds of costumes are ready for the performance impresses anyone who has had to prepare a single costume for an amateur performance. In addition, the circus people and animals must be housed and fed. Imagine providing enough food for hundreds of lions, tigers, bears, elephants, and hungry working people. More impressive, however, is the operation of erecting an entire city overnight. The operation calls not only for putting up the big top but also for providing seating for thousands. Most impressive of all, however, are the mere logistics of getting all the equipment and people from one site to another. The circus world must be one of extraordinary work and organization!

Note that while the organization changed, the clue words remain, telling the reader what to expect next: *in addition, more impressive, most impressive of all.*

Choice 3: Next Most Important to Most Important

Finally, let's look at the most common of the three orders of importance. (Even this section of your book is organized by order of importance!)

The list of details for next-most-important-to-most-important organization should look something like this:

1. second most important detail

2. least important detail

3. fourth most important detail

4. third most important detail

5. most important detail

The same sample paragraph has been reorganized once again to follow this last method of organization by order of importance. Note the differences, and compare the paragraph with the outline list above.

HERE COMES THE BIG TOP!

From an adult's point of view, a circus is an impressive operation. For instance, imagine the operation required in erecting an entire city overnight. Not only does the operation call for putting up the big top but also for providing seating for thousands. Even lesser details are impressive. The fact that hundreds of costumes are ready for the performance impresses anyone who has had to prepare a single costume for an amateur performance. In addition, the circus people and animals must be housed and fed. Imagine providing enough food for hundreds of lions, tigers, bears, elephants, and hungry working people. Most impressive of all, however, are the mere logistics of getting all the equipment and people from one site to another. The circus world must be one of extraordinary work and organization!

This final method of organization by order of importance still uses clue words to help the reader follow the pattern: *in addition, impressive, most impressive of all.* How you arrange the details in your paragraph, then, should be determined in large part by the subject of your paragraph.

Remember: Certain subjects demand certain organization. Obviously, at times you will have two, perhaps three choices; but most of the time the subject and your purpose will dictate the organization.

PART 3: TRANSITIONS WITHIN PARAGRAPHS: USING CONNECTING WORDS

Throughout this chapter, you have read references to "clue words" and an occasional mention of "connecting words." Now that we have talked about how to support a paragraph effectively, let's talk about ways to tie that support together. The ties help the reader get through all the details in an orderly fashion. They help him know when you're moving from one idea to another or from one step to another. The ties, or clue words, we will call *transitions* or *connecting words*. Transitions serve two purposes:

1. Used within the paragraph, transitions tie sentences together. They serve as bridges from one sentence to another.

2. Used between paragraphs, transitions tie paragraphs together, still serving as bridges, but bigger bridges.

HINT

Choice 3 is the most common organization using order of importance. Its impact is probably the reason for its frequent use. By saving the most important detail until last, the writer can make a big impact.

HINT

By using the second most important detail first, the writer will have made a significant impact early as well. For this reason, such organization is especially helpful when the writer must convince the reader.

Below are listed some of the most common transitional words and phrases:

accordingly	consequently	in fact
also	after that	moreover
another	finally	last
first	at the same time	for instance
second	for example	nevertheless
next	otherwise	on the other hand
as a result	to begin with	similarly
at last	however	such
then	therefore	thus
but	and	

The words and phrases above serve as effective transitions, but they are not the only means by which a writer achieves smooth writing. Other means of connecting ideas include the following:

- repetition of a word or phrase
- synonyms (words with the same meaning)
- demonstrative pronouns (this, that, these, those)
- pronoun reference
- repetition of an idea or topic

The following paragraph explains why picket fences remind the writer of his grandmother. The transitions are italicized and illustrate most of the means of tying supporting details together or providing clues to the reader.

GRANNY'S PICKET FENCE

Seeing a white picket fence always makes me think about my grandmother. *She* had an immaculate *white picket fence* all the way around *her* yard. Every *slat* had a perfect inverted heart-shaped peak. *Those peaks* somehow made me think *Granny* was putting out *her* sign, because *she* literally opened *her* heart to all of *us* children, grandchildren, and neighbor children alike. *Whatever the case, that fence* was *her* pride and joy. Every time *she* cut the grass, *she* used scissors to trim around every single picket. *Along the front walk*, where the round-top *picket* gate swung in to visitors, *Granny* painted a pineapple design on each of the *slats. That* was a *symbol* of hospitality, *she* said. The *fence* even told of *her* generosity, for *she* removed two *slats* in the side so we *children* could run from the neighbor's wading pool to *Granny's* tire swing without going all the way around front.

Transitions and other connecting words abound! Without them, the reader is lost, and the writer's message is clouded.

PART 4: UNITY AND COHERENCE: STAYING ON THE SUBJECT

Whether writing a paragraph or an essay, a writer must stay on the subject. If he begins writing about hamburgers, he can't end up writing about ketchup. A paragraph that stays on the subject is said to have *unity*. In other words, it presents a unified idea, a single idea. Because all of the sentences in a well-written paragraph "stick together," the paragraph is said to be *coherent*. Your aim, of course, is to write paragraphs that demonstrate unity and coherence. You do that by making sure you stick to the subject you name in your topic sentence.

The following paragraph attempts to explain how communities try to combat problems caused by pigeons. Unfortunately, the paragraph gets off the subject. As you read, see if you can find the point at which the writer begins getting off the subject.

ENJOYING PIGEONS, NOT PROBLEMS
(a sample paragraph that gets off the subject)

Nearly every community tries to combat the problems pigeons create. While pigeons are docile and provide enjoyment in the parks for those who like to feed them peanuts and popcorn, they also create a health hazard where they most frequently roost. Some experts try simply to change the roosting place. Of course, that only causes the health hazard to relocate. In fact, one year, officials used chicken wire to close off a favorite roosting place; so the pigeons began roosting in our garage. They created not only a health hazard but a financial burden as well. We had to have the car repainted as a result of the frequent stains on the hood. In spite of that, I really like pigeons. In fact, we used to raise pigeons when I was a child. Some of them are quite beautiful, not only because of their colors but also because of the ruffs around their necks or the long feathers along their legs. Of course, these are special breeds. Other special breeds are racing pigeons and those that fly in groups called kits, tumbling and diving to the spectators' delight.

Obviously the writer lost track of his stated purpose, that communities try to combat the problems pigeons create. Where do you think he first loses unity? If you suspect the problem began when the pigeons moved into the garage, you're right! From that point on, the details no longer explain how communities battle the pigeon problem.

As you add transitions to your paragraph, you will improve the coherence. The transitions show your reader how the details are related to one another and how they fit together in the big picture. Thus, if you provide adequate detail, stay on the subject, and provide transitions within the paragraph, you will maintain unity and coherence.

HINT

As you write, keep your topic sentence in mind. Ask yourself this question: Does every detail I am writing explain or support my topic sentence?

PRACTICE
EXERCISE 1

Directions: Try your hand at making a vague paragraph into a specific one. Rewrite the paragraph below so that it creates a specific picture in your reader's mind.

SHOE SHOPPING

When Nan tried on nearly twenty pairs of shoes late Friday evening, the shoe salesman remained patient and helpful throughout the two hours. Nan told the clerk what kind of shoes she thought she wanted. The clerk brought out some for her to try on. Then Nan offered some additional explanation and the salesman brought out some more. After she tried some on, she changed her mind about what she wanted. So the salesman brought out still more shoes. Finally, after two hours, Nan decided on two pairs.

EXERCISE 1—ANSWERS

Although any revision of the above paragraph will necessarily differ from any suggested revision, you can examine your revision on the basis of the following questions:

1. Does your revision include details about what Nan asked to see when she went into the shoe store?

2. Does the reader know what color, style, or size shoe Nan is looking for?

3. Does your revision tell the reader what the shoe salesman first brought out for Nan to try on? How many pairs, what color, what style, what size? Are the shoes what Nan asked to try on?

4. Does your reader know how Nan reacted? Did she frown, scold, smile, try on all the shoes, or just look and shake her head?

5. Does your reader see the shoe salesman's reactions? Does he smile, frown, remain expressionless, ask questions, make any encouraging remarks, or agree with Nan?

6. When the salesman returns with more shoes, what does he bring? Are they different colors, different styles, different sizes? Does he ask any questions?

7. How many pairs of shoes does Nan try on? Does she walk in them, look in a mirror, wiggle her toes?

8. What is Nan like as a customer? Bold and bossy, kind and courteous, sharp and unkind, grouchy, concerned, or pleasant?

9. We know the clerk remains patient throughout. Does your reader see him struggle but remain patient?

10. Finally, and most important of all, do you *show* your reader rather than tell her about Nan's episode in the shoe store?

EXERCISE 2

> **Directions:** Put the following items in time order as if you were going to write a paragraph using the following topic sentence:
>
> Topic Sentence: The potholes on Elm Street have become rapidly worse.

1. In early April, the first cracks began showing along the tire tracks in the westbound lane.
2. Last week, most drivers swerved out of the westbound lane and across the centerline to avoid the basketball-sized potholes.
3. Four weeks later, the first cracks began crumbling, leaving bits of gravel scattered across the street.
4. For some reason, the eastbound lane remains relatively smooth.
5. Now Elm Street is a one-lane street.
6. The baseball-sized holes soon became basketball-sized holes.
7. Then dozens more baseball-sized holes appeared.
8. The crumbling worsened by early May, and holes began to grow, first to baseball-sized holes.
9. By the middle of May, the individual holes were beginning to grow into whole colonies.
10. As drivers avoided the holes in the tire tracks, holes began appearing across the entire lane, small at first, but quickly catching up with the basketball-sized holes in the tracks.

EXERCISE 2—ANSWERS

If you followed the clues within the sentences, you should have listed the sentences above in the following order:

Sentence 1 above will be 1 in chronological order.

Sentence 2 above will be 8 in chronological order.

Sentence 3 will be 2.

Sentence 4 will be 9.

Sentence 5 will be 10.

Sentence 6 will be 5.

Sentence 7 will be 4.

Sentence 8 will be 3.

Sentence 9 will be 6.

Sentence 10 will be 7.

EXERCISE 3

Directions: Rearrange the storeroom paragraph in Part 2 of this chapter (page 215) so that the organization is right to left instead of left to right. When you finish, compare your paragraph to the one below. Don't cheat yourself; do your own before you look below.

EXERCISE 3—ANSWERS

Your paragraph should look something like this:

THE STOREROOM

The storeroom was a jumble of boxes, buckets, and useless debris. On the far right, an assortment of broken boxes, buckets, broom handles, rags, and rusted cans littered the floor. To the left of that, hundreds of buckets, most empty, some tipped over, were heaped pyramid fashion nearly to the ceiling. Next to them, empty boxes sat inside one another at unstable angles. On the far left, stacks of old newspapers and scrap cardboard reached nearly six feet high. Certainly the storeroom needed a good cleaning.

EXERCISE 4

Directions: Determine which method of organization would be best for the following paragraphs. Choose time order (TO), space order (SO), or order of importance (OI). Answers follow below, but be sure you've made a decision before you consult the answer key.

1. An explanation of how to insulate a new house
2. An explanation of how to operate a drill press
3. A proposal supporting your opinion to eliminate billboards from the nation's highways
4. An explanation to a potential employer about why you are an excellent person for a particular job
5. The reasons for your building a fence around your property
6. The reasons why sunbathers should use sunscreen lotions
7. The reasons for using herbicides
8. A description of a farmer applying herbicides
9. The reasons we have tax laws
10. The process of implementing a new tax law

EXERCISE 4—ANSWERS

You should have the following answers for the exercise above:

1. TO
2. TO
3. OI
4. OI
5. OI (or TO if a series of events has led to the building)
6. OI
7. OI
8. TO (depending on whether the observer is with the farmer or watching from a distance)
9. OI
10. TO

EXERCISE 5

Directions: The paragraph below has no connecting words. Revise the paragraph to include effective connectors. A suggested revision follows below.

RAINY AFTERNOONS

I like rainy afternoons. Rainy afternoons help me relax. I can read or nap. I can work on my hobby. My hobby is building radio-controlled gliders. I know I can soon fly the gliders. Thinking about flying them helps me relax. Flying gliders takes my mind off everything else. I really like rainy afternoons.

EXERCISE 5—ANSWERS

The following paragraph offers a suggested revision for the exercise above. Obviously, your revision will be somewhat different from this one, but as long as you've used connecting words to provide good bridges between ideas, you have achieved the goal!

RAINY AFTERNOONS

I like rainy afternoons because they help me relax. On those lazy afternoons when I can't be working outside, I can read or nap. In addition, I can work on my hobby, building radio-controlled gliders. Even during rainy times, I know I can soon take the glider out to fly, and just thinking about flying it helps me relax. I imagine myself steering it, seeking lifts to keep it slipping through the skies for an hour or more. The fantasizing, just like actually flying, takes my mind off everything else. As a result, rainy afternoons provide real relaxation!

EXERCISE 6

Directions: From the list of details below, mark out the ones that will not support the topic sentence. These are the details that will cause the writer to get off the subject of his paragraph and destroy the paragraph's unity.

Topic Sentence: Neon signs flash messages through the night in many forms and colors.

1. Some neon signs are multicolored.

2. I especially like the ones that look like script, spelling out words in color.

3. Computerized marquees are beginning to replace neon signs.

4. In daylight, neon signs seem lifeless and dull.

5. After driving in darkness, coming up on a neon sign can be really startling.

6. Those little tubes of light can take on the most amazing shapes and designs.

7. Some of the most fascinating neon signs are in Las Vegas.

8. Las Vegas billboards and marquees compete with each other not only in size but also in brilliance.

9. I was overwhelmed by the excessive lights that made late night as bright as noon.

10. Some neon signs use only the sky as their backdrop.

EXERCISE 6—ANSWERS

Sentences 3, 4, 8, and 9 should be eliminated if the writer is to stay on the subject.

- In sentence 3, the writer should not talk about computerized marquees when his stated topic is neon signs.

- The topic sentence refers to *night*, so sentence 4 should not be included since it refers to daylight.

- Sentence 8 should be omitted because details about billboards and marquees are not part of neon signs.

- In sentence 9, the writer should not discuss *all* lights, only neon lights.

19

Paragraph Accuracy

After you have written a clear topic sentence and developed specific, organized supporting details with effective connecting words, you have 90 percent of the paragraph writing job done. GED essay evaluators, however, look for two other matters, and the GED writing skills questions address both of these matters as well:

>correct verb tense
>consistent point of view

This chapter shows you how to use both correctly.

PROBLEM 1: USING CORRECT VERB TENSE

A writer who uses verb tenses correctly helps his reader follow the paragraph's details. Tense, of course, shows time. Like time, tenses are relative. Their purpose is to show the time relationships among a series of events.

USING SIMPLE TENSES

The three simple tenses, past, present, and future, are the easiest ways to show yesterday, today, and tomorrow. (Review Chapter 2, Step 2, as well as Chapter 7.)

Example: (yesterday)   I *walked* home.   (past tense)
(today)   I *walk* home.   (present tense)
(tomorrow)   I *will walk* home.   (future tense)

When we speak of using consistent verb tense, we simply mean that if you begin a piece of writing in past tense, continue the piece in past tense. Do not switch from past to present to future and back to past, unless, of course, you are intentionally *showing* a change in time.

USING PERFECT TENSES

Even though we can easily recognize the simple yesterday, today, and tomorrow relationships, we must also recognize the difference between yesterday and the day before yesterday and the difference between tomorrow and next week. The perfect tenses allow us to be more exact—more perfect—in showing time relationships:

Example: (yesterday)   I *walked* home.
(day before yesterday)   Until yesterday, I *had walked* home only once.
(between then and now)   I *have walked* 3 more miles since then.
(today)   Instead of driving, I *walk* home now.
(tomorrow)   I *will walk* home every day this next week.
(after tomorrow)   By next week this time, I *will have walked* 25 miles.

ROAD MAP

* *Using Correct Verb Tense*
* *Using One Point of View*

Without going into all the details, let's just say that the perfect tenses are a combination of some form of the verb "to have" (*have, has, had, will have*) plus the *-ed* form of the verb.

had walked
has walked, have walked
will have walked

Summarized, the perfect tenses carry these meanings:

had + verb = a past action completed prior to another past action.

Example: The potter *had completed* the demonstration before I arrived.

has or *have* + verb = a past action that continues into the present

Example: I *have planned* a party for this Saturday.

will have + verb = action that will be completed at a specified time in the future

Example: WIKY radio station *will have been* on the air fifty years next month.

RECOGNIZING PROGRESSIVE FORM

Each of the six tenses can also appear in progressive form to show continuing action. Progressive form is characterized by the *-ing* ending.

Example: The latest MGM release *is* now *showing* at the theater.

Example: The line *was* already *forming* when we arrived.

Example: The line *had been forming* for almost an hour before we arrived.

Example: By next summer, I *will have been dieting* for a year.

SHOWING TIME RELATIONSHIPS

We've all heard the cliché that today is the tomorrow you worried about yesterday. The cliche suggests how complicated it can be to show clear time relationships in your writing. The following example explains why the writer's vacation was exhausting. The paper illustrates the use of all six tenses, including some progressive forms. Marginal notes identify the changes in time.

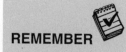

REMEMBER

Consistency of verb tense is achieved not by using the same tense throughout a piece of writing, but rather by using the same point of reference and allowing all events to take their respective time relationships from that point.

New-Car Phobia

Last summer's vacation *proved* really exhausting. Driving a brand- new car,	past tense (last summer)
I *worried* constantly that someone	past tense (still last summer)
would bang his car door into mine,	past tenst (last summer)
putting that first dent on the perfectly polished surface. As a result of my	
worry, I often *parked* blocks from	past tenst (last summer)
where I *wanted* to visit so I *could park*	past tense (last summer)
away from menacing two-door cars. In addition, because of frequent rain	
showers, mud often *spattered* the car's	past tense (last summer)
lower body. In the evenings, then, even though exhaustion *had* already	
hit, I *made* certain I *found* a place to	perfect tense (to show an earlier action)
hand wash my car. After all, the dirt	past tense (last summer)
will harm the paint, and those car-	future tense (to show what will happen)
wash places *will* scratch the finish. Or	future tense (to show what will happen)
so I *thought*. Now that my car *is* a	past tense (last summer)
year old, however, and already *is*	present tense (now)
scratched and dented here and there, I	
have been looking forward to this	perfect tense (shows past action continuing into future)
summer's more relaxing vacation. I	
will park as near to my destination as I	future tense (coming summer)
can. I *will leave* the mud, or I *will*	future tense (coming summer)
drive right into the nearest automated	future tense (coming summer)
car wash! By next summer's end, I	
will have enjoyed—finally—a relaxing	perfect tense (shows action to be completed at specified time)
vacation.	

HINT

Sometimes the second-person pronouns do not actually appear in print. Rather, they are understood.

PROBLEM 2: USING ONE POINT OF VIEW

A writer must use the same point of view throughout an essay. Point of view refers to the way the reader receives the message. If the point of view is first person, the reader learns about the writer's ideas through the writer's eyes. If the point of view is second person, the writer talks directly to the reader, giving commands or instructions. If the point of view is third person, both the reader and the writer are talking about a third party.

IDENTIFYING FIRST-PERSON POINT OF VIEW

Writers use the first-person point of view to tell about personal experiences or opinions. Certain words identify first-person point of view:

I   me   my, mine
we   us   our, ours

Those personal pronouns in the first row are singular and those in the second row, plural. All show first-person point of view. (You may need to review Chapter 5, Using Pronouns Correctly.)

Look at these sample sentences written in first-person point of view:

Example: During summer months, I usually try to get a part-time job working outdoors.

(The first-person pronoun *I* indicates point of view.)

Example: Since my sister gave me that book, it is especially precious to me.

(The first-person pronouns *my* and *me* indicate point of view.)

Example: Sometimes our neighborhood gets together for a block party, and we really learn to enjoy each other's company.

(The first-person pronouns *our* and *we* indicate point of view.)

HINT

If the first- or second-person pronouns do not appear, the writing is in third-person point of view. (But remember, second-person pronouns can be implied.)

IDENTIFYING SECOND-PERSON POINT OF VIEW

Writers use second-person point of view to give instructions, directions, or commands. Certain words indicate second-person point of view:

you, your, yours

Example: When you come in the house, take off your muddy boots.

(The second-person pronouns *you* and *your* show point of view.)

Example: Use extreme care when operating heavy machinery.

(second-person point of view for giving instructions; "you" is understood)

Example: Take Exit 33 off the Broadway Expressway.

(second-person point of view for giving directions; "you" is understood)

Example: Stop that noise!

(second-person point of view for issuing commands; "you" is understood)

IDENTIFYING THIRD-PERSON POINT OF VIEW

Of the three points of view, experienced writers use third-person point of view most frequently. It is also the most versatile. The following personal pronouns indicate third-person point of view:

he	him	his
she	her	hers
it	it	its
they	them	their, theirs

In addition to these personal pronouns, however, third-person point of view results when writers use proper names or common nouns. Consider these examples, all written in third-person point of view:

Example: The head of a single-parent family must be well organized to succeed as both parent and wage earner.

(Third-person point of view is indicated by use of common noun *head.*)

Example: Sometimes Rodney drives like a maniac.

(Third-person point of view is indicated by the proper noun *Rodney.*)

Example: When high winds toss the garbage cans about, debris litters the neighborhood.

(Third-person point of view is indicated by common noun *debris.*)

Example: During lunch hour, they ate quietly.

(Third-person point of view is indicated by pronoun *they.*)

CHOOSING POINT OF VIEW

We have hinted throughout this section that one point of view may be more appropriate than another for a specific purpose. Following is a summary of those points:

1. Use first-person point of view to tell about personal experiences or to give a personal opinion.

2. Use second-person point of view to give instructions, directions, or commands.

3. Use third-person point of view for any writing purpose.

4. Use third-person point of view for formal writing.

By now you should have a fairly good grasp of what point of view is all about.

In this chapter you have studied two kinds of consistencies: verb tense and point of view. If you can apply these two principles to your own paragraphs, you will be well on the way to passing your GED essay with high scores.

WARNING

Once you can identify the three points of view, you need only make sure that any given piece of writing uses the *same point of view throughout.*

PRACTICE
EXERCISE 1

Directions: The following paragraph does not use correct verb tense. Revise it so that tense is consistent and shows accurate time relationships.

THE MONEY BATTLE

In last year's financial statement, the company indicates a serious financial loss, a problem that had since affected negotiations with the union. While company officials tried in the last three weeks to convince workers to accept a wage reduction, only yesterday had they agreed that the reduced wages would eventually be repaid. That news sparks positive reaction among union leaders. Now, if company officials would agree to accept the same terms for themselves, the union will be finding a basis for agreement.

EXERCISE 1—ANSWERS

The following is a revision of the above paragraph. Verb tenses have been revised to show good time relationships.

THE MONEY BATTLE

In last year's financial statement, the company *indicated* a serious financial loss, a problem that *has* since *affected* negotiations with the union. While company officials *have tried* in the last three weeks to convince workers to accept a wage reduction, only yesterday *did* they *agree* that the reduced wages *will* eventually *be repaid*. That news *sparked* positive reaction among union leaders. Now, if company officials *will agree* to accept the same terms for themselves, the union *will find* a basis for agreement.

Explanation:

indicated (Use past tense, in keeping with "last year's.")

has affected (Use perfect tense to show past action that continues into the present.)

have tried (Use perfect tense to show past action that continues into the present.)

did agree (Use past tense to show "yesterday.")

will be repaid (Use future tense to show future action.)

sparked (Use past tense to show "yesterday.")

will agree (Use future tense to show future action.)

will find (Use future tense to show future action.)

EXERCISE 2

Directions: The following paragraph is not consistent in its point of view. Revise it first so that it is written in first-person point of view, and then revise it so that it is in third-person point of view. Suggested revisions follow, but be sure to try your own version before you look.

VACATION JOY(LESS)

Long vacation trips can really wear you out. My family, for instance, usually plans to hop in the car at an outrageously early hour, drive 700 miles, fall asleep in some faceless motel, and repeat the whole procedure the next morning. You do that for seven or eight of the fourteen days and call it fun. After the end of the first day, though, I've had all I can take of arguments about when we'll stop for lunch, where we'll stop for lunch, or if we'll stop before lunch. You get bored with the ride, the same scenery sliding past at 65 miles an hour, the same ribbon of highway rolling ahead and behind. If a person wants to enjoy his vacation trip, he should walk more, see more, enjoy more, and certainly drive less.

EXERCISE 2—ANSWERS

The following paragraph has been revised so that it maintains a consistent first-person point of view. Compare it with your own revision.

VACATION JOY(LESS)

Long vacation trips can really wear me out. My family, for instance, usually plans to hop in the car at an outrageously early hour, drive 700 miles, fall asleep in some faceless motel, and repeat the whole procedure the next morning. We do that for seven or eight of the fourteen days and call it fun. After the end of the first day, though, I've had all I can take of arguments about when we'll stop for lunch, where we'll stop for lunch, or if we'll stop before lunch. I get bored with the ride, the same scenery sliding past at 65 miles an hour, the same ribbon of highway rolling ahead and behind. If I want to enjoy my vacation trip, I should walk more, see more, enjoy more, and certainly drive less.

The following paragraph has been revised to maintain consistent third-person point of view. Compare this revision with your own.

VACATION JOY(LESS)

Long vacation trips can really wear a person out. Some families, for instance, usually plan to hop in the car at an outrageously early hour, drive 700 miles, fall asleep in some faceless motel, and repeat the whole procedure the next morning. They do that for seven or eight of the fourteen days and call it fun. After the end of the first day, though, some people have had all they can take of arguments about when they will stop for lunch, where they will stop for lunch, or if they will stop before lunch. They get bored with the ride, the same scenery sliding past at 65 miles an hour, the same ribbon of highway rolling ahead and behind. If they want to enjoy their vacation trip, they should walk more, see more, enjoy more, and certainly drive less.

The Conclusion

Think about a television commercial you've seen recently. What were the last words, the lingering idea you were left to think about? The last words we see or hear gain a few extra seconds' thinking time before our brains dart off on another thought. As a result, final words earn the writer's special attention for the emphasis they have. A good conclusion forces the reader to deal with the writer's message and give it a last, lingering thought. A good writer wants to be sure his conclusion makes the best of the extra time.

METHODS OF CONCLUDING

The conclusion should complete the paragraph. Use one of these three methods to write an effective conclusion:

Method 1: The conclusion may restate the main idea without repeating it word for word.

Example: Topic Sentence: Our long-awaited visit to Clingman's Dome, the highest point in Tennessee, brought nothing but disappointment.

Conclusion: As a result of the fog, rain, and wind, our visit to Clingman's Dome was disappointing.

Method 2: The conclusion may be a summary. It can help the reader pull the ideas together.

Example: Topic Sentence: Evaluating one day's activity on the stock market demands a thorough understanding of how world affairs affect international economics.

Conclusion: Whether war, famine, political unrest, industrial accident, or scientific discovery, all world affairs directly or indirectly affect the stock market.

Method 3: Sometimes, in a short paper, the conclusion may simply be the last statement.

Example: Topic Sentence: The last day of vacation brought both relief and regret.

Conclusion: When the two weeks were over, I headed home, unpacked my luggage, and stored it in the attic for another fifty weeks.

ROAD MAP

- *Methods of Concluding*
- *Model Paragraph*
- *Checklist for Writing Powerful Paragraphs*
- *Practice*

The last-statement conclusion can be effective and leave the reader with a sense of completeness. However, a conclusion cannot contain a new idea that needs development of its own. Look at the following example:

Topic Sentence: The last day of vacation brought both relief and regret.

Poor Conclusion: Now, two weeks later, I am enjoying my new exercise group.

The "new exercise group" has nothing to do with "the last day of vacation," so the reader is left wondering how it fits in with the statement of purpose. If you add a new idea, the reader loses the sense of completeness. He's trying to figure out what this new idea has to do with the rest of your paragraph!

MODEL PARAGRAPH

The following paragraph explains why offensive and defensive football players see the game so differently. The paragraph illustrates an effective conclusion, one that gives a feeling of completeness without introducing new ideas.

PLAYERS' JOBS

Offensive and defensive football players' jobs differ significantly. For instance, the defensive end and the offensive end have opposite jobs. While the defensive end is supposed to prevent the running back from getting around him, the offensive end is trying in turn to block the defensive end. Basically, the offense is trying to score while the defense is trying to stop the scoring. To make these plays semi-automatic for a well-practiced football player, even the practice sessions for the defense and offense differ. In fact, often each group has its own coach, a specialist in the most successful tactics. For example, the defense drill to hit and hit hard, react and react quickly while the offense drill to build strength and to bodily move defensive players from the runner's path. Even though offense and defense play for the same team, the players themselves have a different understanding of how to play the game.

The conclusion is a restatement of the main idea (method 1), and it emphasizes the differences between the offense and defense by saying that they "have a different understanding of how to play the game." The reader is left with a sense of completeness, knowing exactly what the writer has said.

As you write your own conclusion, choose the method that best suits the purpose of your paragraph.

CHECKLIST FOR WRITING POWERFUL PARAGRAPHS

Use the following checklist to evaluate your own paragraphs. You should be able to answer "yes" to each of these questions.

		YES	NO
1.	Have I written a good topic sentence?	❑	❑
2.	Have I used specific details to support the statement of purpose?	❑	❑
3.	Have I arranged the details in logical order?	❑	❑
4.	Have I included only details that support the topic sentence? In other words, have I avoided getting off the subject?	❑	❑
5.	Have I used good connecting words (transitions)?	❑	❑
6.	Have I used the right verb tenses?	❑	❑
7.	Have I used the same point of view throughout?	❑	❑
8.	Have I selected the most appropriate point of view?	❑	❑
9.	Have I written an effective conclusion?	❑	❑
10.	Have I written effective, powerful, and complete sentences?	❑	❑
11.	Have I used good sentence variety?	❑	❑
12.	Have I used specific, concise words?	❑	❑
13.	Have I checked for grammar, mechanics, and usage?	❑	❑
14.	Have I checked spelling?	❑	❑

PRACTICE
EXERCISE 1

Directions: Assume you have developed a paragraph supporting each of the following topic sentences. Now, write a concluding sentence for each. Of course, answers will vary widely, but some possible answers follow.

1. Refinishing the kitchen cabinets seemed at first an insurmountable task.

2. My first driving experience in big-city traffic nearly caused me to resign from ever driving again.

3. Uncle Earl has developed a foolproof technique for locating the elusive largemouth bass.

4. Hiking boots provide necessary protection for anyone tramping through back country.

5. Cross-country skiers experience the outdoors in a dimension the rest of us cannot share.

6. White wicker furniture combined with abundant green plants transformed the drab room into a sunny retreat.

7. Our neighbor, who sometimes seems eccentric, adheres to a strict daily routine.

8. Weekends offer a welcome respite from workday routines.

9. Contractors met unanticipated obstacles as they struggled to complete the apartment complex on schedule.

10. Community environmentalists fear the impact on clean air by the proposed paper mill.

EXERCISE 1—ANSWERS

The following statements will make suitable conclusions for the corresponding topic sentences above. Your answers will, of course, vary, but as long as you've used one of the three methods for developing a conclusion, no doubt yours will also be acceptable.

1. So, when the job was done, we realized the step-by-step process hadn't been so difficult after all.

2. As a result of such harrowing experiences, I almost refused to get behind the wheel again.

3. Uncle Earl's technique will certainly reap big catches for anyone who uses it.

4. Without hiking boots, then, the back-country adventurer risks more than he can afford to risk—a way back out.

5. No other mode of transportation can afford such a close-up look at the great outdoors.

6. Now we spend many pleasure-filled hours in a peaceful, restful atmosphere.

7. By the end of the day, our eccentric has exhausted himself from the routine.

8. Ah, what wonderful things, weekends!

9. With an added complication at every turn, contractors will be lucky to finish on schedule.

10. As a result, the community watchdogs will have ample support in fighting their battle.

Chapter

Practice, Chapters 15–20

Directions: Read the following essay and respond to the questions below. When you have finished, check your answers with those that follow. Review as necessary.

LANDSCAPING WITH WATER

A

(1) *In the landscaping business, most of your work is, obviously, with the land.* (2) *We plant trees, bushes, flowers, and grasses and designed the layouts so that these plantings created visual appeal.* (3) *We incorporate rocks and boulders as accents in the landscape.* (4) *We occasionally get calls to use our knowledge of plants and rocks to create yard ponds.*

B

(5) *Depending on the lay of the land, we usually begin a yard pond by outlining the shape of the intended pond, often with bright yellow ribbon tape staked into the soil.* (6) *Then we begin excavating, leaving a shelf-like terrace all around the perimeter.* (7) *After the excavation is complete, they use a heavy roofing-like material called pond liner to cover the bottom and the terraced sides of the pond-to-be.* (8) *We excavate for an in-ground biological filter and any special features the customer requests.* (9) *The tricky part, however, was to keep the top edges of the excavation level in all directions.* (10) *The final result will be lots of bare sides way above water level at one end of the pond.*

C

(11) *We use the rocks to cover any part of the liner that will not be underwater.* (12) *Fish and plants that come later also add to the attractiveness.* (13) *And that's where the shelf-like terrace comes in.* (14) *It's used as a base to stack rocks up the sides and over the edge so that after we fill the pond, no one ever sees bare liner.* (15) *Other rocks and boulders edged the pond and provided accents in the overall landscaping.* (16) *If the owner wants a waterfall or creek-like flow into the pond, we build those with rocks as well.*

D

(17) *We bring in the plants.* (18) *Pond edges will call for plants that droop and drape.* (19) *They call for low edging plants and tall grasses.* (20) *If ponds are in full sun, you can boast superb flowering perennials as well as colorful annuals along their banks.* (21) *If they are in mostly shade, they can support hostas and ferns in a mass of lush green.* (22) *We add dwarf cattails, arrow grass, tiger tail grass, water lilies, and irises.* (23) *In some cases, customers only wanted native plants both in and out of the water, but our overall plan is about the same with native or nonnative plants.*

1. Sentence 1: In the landscaping business, most of your work is, obviously, with the land.

    What correction should be made to this sentence?

    (1)   Omit obviously.
    (2)   Change your to our.
    (3)   Move In the landscaping business to the end of the sentence.
    (4)   Change is to was.
    (5)   No correction is necessary.

2. Sentence 2: We plant trees, bushes, flowers, and grasses and designed the layouts so that these plantings created visual appeal.

    What correction should be made to this sentence?

    (1)   Move so that these plantings created visual appeal to the beginning of the sentence.
    (2)   Change plant to planted.
    (3)   Change We to they.
    (4)   Change designed . . . created to design . . . create.
    (5)   No correction is necessary.

3. Sentence 3: We incorporate rocks and boulders as accents in the landscape.

    What correction should be made to this sentence?

    (1)   Change We to You.
    (2)   Change incorporate to incorporated.
    (3)   Insert Often, at the beginning of the sentence.
    (4)   Move as accents in the landscape to the beginning of the sentence.
    (5)   No correction is necessary.

4. Sentence 4: We occasionally get calls to use our knowledge of plants and rocks to create yard ponds.

    What correction should be made to this sentence?

    (1)   Insert Now, however, at the beginning of the sentence.
    (2)   Delete the word occasionally from the sentence.
    (3)   Change to use to to have used.
    (4)   Move occasionally to the end of the sentence.
    (5)   No correction is necessary.

5. Sentence 5: Depending on the lay of the land, we usually begin a yard pond by outlining the shape of the intended pond, often with bright yellow ribbon tape staked into the soil.

    What correction should be made to the sentence?

    (1)   Insert a sentence prior to this sentence that reads Before we apply our expertise with rocks and plants, however, we must first dig the pond.
    (2)   Insert a sentence prior to this sentence that reads We can apply what we know about rocks and plants to add the flash of fish and birds to your yard.
    (3)   Move Depending on the lay of the land to the end of the sentence.
    (4)   Delete often with bright yellow ribbon tape staked into the soil.
    (5)   No correction is necessary.

6. Sentence 6: Then we begin excavating, leaving a shelf-like terrace all around the perimeter.

What correction should be made to the sentence?

(1)   Omit the word Then.
(2)   Change we to you.
(3)   Change begin to began.
(4)   Move leaving a shelf-like terrace all around the perimeter to the beginning of the sentence.
(5)   No correction is necessary.

7. Sentence 7: After the excavation is complete, they use a heavy roofing-like material called pond liner to cover the bottom and the terraced sides of the pond-to-be.

What correction should be made to the sentence?

(1)   Omit the clause After the excavation is complete.
(2)   Change they to you.
(3)   Change they to we.
(4)   Insert the word however after the word complete.
(5)   No correction is necessary.

8. Sentence 7: After the excavation is complete, they use a heavy roofing-like material called pond liner to cover the bottom and the terraced sides of the pond-to-be.

The best position for this sentence is

(1)   at the end of Paragraph A.
(2)   at the beginning of Paragraph B.
(3)   at the end of Paragraph B.
(4)   at the beginning of Paragraph C.
(5)   The sentence should not be moved.

9. Sentence 8: We excavate for an in-ground biological filter and any special features the customer requests.

What correction should be made to the sentence?

(1)   Change excavate to excavated.
(2)   Change We to You.
(3)   Change requests to will request.
(4)   Insert the word also after the word we.
(5)   No correction is necessary.

10. Sentence 9: The tricky part, however, was to keep the top edges of the excavation level in all directions.

What correction should be made to the sentence?

(1)   Change was to is.
(2)   Move the word however to after the word keep.
(3)   Omit the word however.
(4)   Omit the sentence.
(5)   No correction is necessary.

11. Sentence 10: The final result will be lots of bare sides way above water level at one end of the pond.

    What correction should be made to the sentence?

    (1) Change will be to is.
    (2) Insert the word Otherwise at the beginning of the sentence.
    (3) Move at one end of the pond to the beginning of the sentence.
    (4) Move way above water level to the end of the sentence.
    (5) No correction is necessary.

12. Sentence 11: We use the rocks to cover any part of the liner that will not be underwater.

    What correction should be made to the sentence?

    (1) Insert a sentence before this one that reads Next, we add the rocks.
    (2) Insert a sentence after this one that reads That's why we use the rocks.
    (3) Move that will not be underwater to after the word rocks.
    (4) Change use to will use.
    (5) No correction is necessary.

13. Sentence 12: Fish and plants that come later also add to the attractiveness.

    What correction should be made to this sentence?

    (1) Insert a comma after later.
    (2) Omit the phrase that come later.
    (3) Omit the entire sentence.
    (4) Change add to will add.
    (5) No correction is necessary.

14. Sentence 14: It's used as a base to stack rocks up the sides and over the edge so that after we fill the pond, no one ever sees bare liner.

    What correction should be made to this sentence?

    (1) Change It's used to We use it.
    (2) Move after we fill the pond to the beginning of the sentence.
    (3) Change fill to are filling.
    (4) Change no one to you.
    (5) No correction is necessary.

15. Sentence 15: Other rocks and boulders edged the pond and provided accents in the overall landscaping.

    What correction should be made to the sentence?

    (1) Change edged . . . provided to will edge . . . will provide.
    (2) Change edged . . . provided to edge . . . provide.
    (3) Change edged . . . provided to have edged . . . have provided.
    (4) Change edged . . . provided to are edging . . . are providing.
    (5) No correction is necessary.

16. Sentence 15: Other rocks and boulders edged the pond and provided accents in the overall landscaping.

The best position for this sentence is

(1)   at the end of Paragraph B.
(2)   after Sentence 11.
(3)   after Sentence 13.
(4)   at the end of Paragraph C.
(5)   No repositioning is necessary.

17. Sentence 17: We bring in the plants.

What correction should be made to the sentence?

(1)   Change We to They.
(2)   Change bring to brought.
(3)   Insert Finally, at the beginning of the sentence.
(4)   Insert finally at the end of the sentence.
(5)   ·No correction is necessary.

18. Sentence 18: Pond edges will call for plants that droop and drape.

What correction should be made to the sentence?

(1)   Change will call to calls.
(2)   Change will call to call.
(3)   Change Pond edges to It.
(4)   Insert however after the word edges.
(5)   No correction is necessary.

19. Sentence 19: They call for low edging plants and tall grasses.

What correction should be made to the sentence?

(1)   Change They to We.
(2)   Change They to You.
(3)   Change call to called.
(4)   Change call to will call.
(5)   No correction is necessary.

20. Sentence 20: If ponds are in full sun, you can boast superb flowering perennials as well as colorful annuals along their banks.

What correction should be made to the sentence?

(1)   Change you to they.
(2)   Change can boast to will boast.
(3)   Change are to were.
(4)   Move if ponds are in full sun to the end of the sentence.
(5)   No correction is necessary.

21. Sentence 22: We add dwarf cattails, arrow grass, tiger tail grass, water lilies, and irises.

    What correction should be made to the sentence?

    (1) Change add to will add.
    (2) Insert Then, in the water itself, at the beginning of the sentence.
    (3) Insert in the water itself at the end of the sentence.
    (4) Change We to You.
    (5) No correction is necessary.

22. Sentence 23: In some cases, customers only wanted native plants both in and out of the water, but our overall plan is about the same with native or nonnative plants.

    What correction should be made to the sentence?

    (1) Omit In some cases.
    (2) Change customers only wanted to customers wanted only.
    (3) Change customers only wanted to customers only want.
    (4) Change customers only wanted to customers want only.
    (5) No correction is necessary.

23. Sentence 23: In some cases, customers only wanted native plants both in and out of the water, but our overall plan is about the same with native or nonnative plants.

    Which sentence should follow Sentence 23?

    (1) Thus, we build ponds.
    (2) Thus, we bring our knowledge of plants, rocks, and landscaping to the world of water.
    (3) Thus, you can have a pond with plants and rocks that attract birds and other wildlife to your yard.
    (4) Thus, customers can have a pond that attracts birds and other wildlife to their yards.
    (5) No additional sentence is necessary.

GED PRACTICE—ANSWERS

1. (2) Use a consistent point of view. The essay is written in first-person plural point of view. See Chapter 19, Problem 2.

2. (4) Maintain consistent verb tense. The essay is written in present tense. See Chapter 19, Problem 1.

3. (3) The transition is necessary to maintain coherence. See Chapter 18, Part 3.

4. (1) The transition helps maintain coherence. See Chapter 18, Part 3.

5. (1) The paragraph needs a topic sentence. See Chapter 17.

6. (5) correct

7. (3) Maintain consistent point of view, first-person plural. See Chapter 19, Problem 2.

8. (3) Putting the sentence at the end maintains time order. See Chapter 18, Part 2.

9. (4) The transition helps maintain coherence. See Chapter 18, Part 3.

10. (1) Maintain consistent present tense. See Chapter 19, Problem 1.

11. (2) The transition clarifies the relationship between the ideas. See Chapter 18, Part 3.

12. (1) The topic sentence is missing for this paragraph. See Chapter 17.

13. (3) The sentence is off the topic and destroys unity. See Chapter 18, Part 4.

14. (1) Maintain consistent point of view. See Chapter 19, Problem 2. Eliminate passive voice. See Chapter 17, Rule 5.

15. (2) Maintain consistent present tense. See Chapter 19, Problem 1.

16. (4) Moving the sentence maintains time order. See Chapter 18, Part 2.

17. (3) The transition helps maintain coherence. See Chapter 18, Part 3.

18. (2) Maintain consistent present tense. See Chapter 19, Problem 1.

19. (5) correct

20. (1) *They* refers to *pond edges.* See Chapter 5, Rule 9.

21. (2) The transition maintains coherence. See Chapter 18, Part 3.

22. (4) Maintain consistent present tense. See Chapter 19, Problem 1. Place modifiers next to the words they modify. See Chapter 6.

23. (2) This concluding sentence stays on the topic, adds nothing new, and ties the essay together. See Chapter 20.

Paragraphs into Essays

Once you can write paragraphs, you're ready to put them together into essays. While the next part of this workbook teaches you specifically about four kinds of essays that you might confront on the GED exam, this chapter tells you generically how to put paragraphs into essays.

You'll turn paragraphs into essays in five easy steps:

1. Write a thesis sentence that tells what your essay is about.

2. Write an introduction, which usually includes the thesis sentence.

3. Use a transition to move smoothly to the first body paragraph.

4. Use effective text divisions with a new topic sentence for each paragraph.

5. Write a conclusion.

Let's look at each of these steps.

STEP 1: WRITE A THESIS SENTENCE

The thesis sentence is to an essay what a topic sentence is to a paragraph. It tells the reader what each paragraph of the essay will discuss. Compare the following thesis sentences:

Thesis Sentence: On-location television crew members share responsibilities for lighting, sound, and transmission.

(The essay will include three paragraphs about various crew members' responsibilities: one about lighting, one about sound, and one about the television signal transmission.)

Thesis Sentence: The recycling operation involves advertising, sorting, and selling.

(The essay will include three paragraphs, one about how the organization advertises its operation, one about how the recycled materials are sorted, and one about how the organization sells the recycled materials.)

Thesis Sentence: Before choosing a new cell phone service, compare local minutes offered, roaming charges, long distance charges, and length of contract.

(The essay will include four paragraphs: one about local minutes, one about roaming charges, one about long distance service, and one about contract time.)

ROAD MAP

- *Thesis Sentence*
- *Introduction*
- *Transitions*
- *Text Divisions*
- *Conclusion*
- *Essay Skeleton*

It's clear from these examples that you must know what you're going to say before you begin writing. So how do you prepare to write a thesis sentence? Try these steps:

Make a List

On a sheet of paper, make a list of all the things you can think of that you might want to say about your topic.

Example: Topic: Stocking shelves

Seasonal Merchandise	Stock Always on Hand	Placement of Merchandise
pricing	bar codes	specials
oversupplies	appearance	line of sight
weekly or daily deliveries	damage control	inventory shrinkage
advertising	in-store specials	check-out lane promos

Look for Connections

Search your list for items that are closely related. Note that some ideas you listed above may not "connect" with anything else.

Example:

Stock Always on Hand	Seasonal Merchandise	Specials
weekly deliveries	weekly deliveries	monthly deliveries
placement	placement	placement
pricing	pricing	pricing
in-store specials	advertising	check-out lane promos

Pick the Key Ideas

Identify the terms on your list that represent the "big ideas." Pick out the three or four most important, or "big," ideas.

Example:

Stock always on hand   Seasonal merchandise   Specials

Write Your Thesis Sentence

The key ideas will help you generate your thesis sentence.

Example Thesis
Sentence: Stocking shelves demands first-hand knowledge of year-round stock, seasonal merchandise, and special promotions.

Notice two characteristics of a good thesis sentence:

1. It breaks the "big picture" into three or four key ideas.

2. It names the three or four key ideas in parallel structure. (See Chapter 16, Goal 4, to review parallelism.)

The models above illustrate these characteristics.

STEP 2: WRITE AN INTRODUCTION

The introduction to your essay usually includes your thesis sentence. It may also include some or all of the following:

Background information, especially if you need to identify who, what, why, when, or where. These details may not be important if you're writing about choosing a DVD player, but they are important if you're discussing an upcoming union vote.

Circumstances, especially if you're writing about a specific situation, like a tornado disaster or an American Cancer Society Relay for Life. You'll need to explain the circumstances of the event to your reader.

Definition, only if you're using a term your readers may not know. Always form definitions by way of explanation as well as example.

Attention-getter, so that your reader is enticed to read the entire essay. If a reader sees nothing in your introduction and/or thesis sentence that seems to apply to him, he'll likely doze off.

Study the model essays in the following part of this workbook to see how good introductions work.

STEP 3: USE GOOD TRANSITIONS

You learned about transitions in Chapter 18, Part 3. Review it now. Then remember that each paragraph needs to be connected to the next. You'll use transitions to do that. Study the model essays in the following part of this workbook to see how good transitions work.

STEP 4: USE EFFECTIVE TEXT DIVISIONS

Your thesis sentence is your guide to using good text divisions. Each part of your thesis sentence represents a separate paragraph. Each paragraph should focus on a single idea. (Remember the part about unity!) Thus, a new idea equals a new paragraph. Consider the thesis sentence we developed earlier and the topic sentences that spring from it:

Thesis Sentence: Stocking shelves demands first-hand knowledge of year-round stock, seasonal merchandise, and special promotions.

First Topic
Sentence: Year-round stock includes those items customers come to count on finding regularly on our shelves.

Second Topic
Sentence: On the other hand, seasonal merchandise, which we can't sell during off-season, tends to dwindle near the end of a season.

Third Topic
Sentence: When the store plans to advertise specials, we load up on those items just before the sale.

Each of these topic sentences suggests a new paragraph, a new text division. And all these paragraphs were evident in the thesis sentence.

Study the model essays in the following part of this workbook to see how text divisions correspond to the parts of the thesis sentence.

STEP 5: WRITE A CONCLUSION

Your essay should include a tight, pointed conclusion. Don't just stop writing. Consider, instead, the kinds of conclusions we described in Chapter 20:

- Restate the main idea (or refer to your thesis statement)

- Give a summary (especially by reiterating the key points in your thesis statement).

- Make a final statement (but avoid introducing any new material).

A good conclusion can also include anything that shows your reader how he or she can benefit from what you've said in your essay.

Study the model essays in the following part of this workbook to see how good conclusions work.

We've summarized here the five steps of turning paragraphs into essays. The next part applies these general steps and shows you annotated models. Then use the following skeleton to help you write your own essay.

ESSAY SKELETON

Your Title

First Paragraph: Introduction
Thesis Statement (suggesting three parts)

Second Paragraph: Transition
First Topic Sentence (from first part of thesis statement)
Details and Examples (connected by transitions)

Third Paragraph: Transition
Second Topic Sentence (from second part of thesis statement)
Details and Examples (connected by transitions)

Fourth Paragraph: Transition
Third Topic Sentence (from third part of thesis statement)
Details and Examples (connected by transitions)
Conclusion

Writing An Essay Explaining How

One of the four general kinds of topics you may be asked to write about on the GED essay test is one that asks you to explain how. An essay that explains how may, for instance, tell about the steps followed in landing a job or the steps needed to keep within a monthly budget.

The single most important part of writing a how-to paper is *organization*. If the steps for getting the task done are not in step-by-step order, the reader will be unable to follow them.

Here's how to write a paper that explains how.

ORGANIZATION

A paper that explains how will probably use the following general plan:

- The paper will begin with a thesis statement that names the process and says something about the task—how easy or how difficult, how simple or how time-consuming.

  Example: Packing a canoe for a trip through white water calls for certain precautions.
  (The writer will explain how to pack the canoe.)

  Example: Arranging for an office picnic requires careful planning.
  (The writer will explain the steps showing how to plan an office picnic.)

- The opening statement also shows the importance of the subject, telling why anyone would want to know how to do this.

  Example: Knowing how to shop wisely can save dollars for the comparison shopper.
  (explaining how to do comparison shopping)

  Example: If you sign your name on the wrong dotted line, you may end up renting an apartment for longer than you want.
  (explaining how to understand rental leases)

- The paper will be organized in time order (see Chapter 18, Part 2). The paper must show step-by-step how to do whatever it is that you are explaining: do this first, then do this, etc.

ROAD MAP

- *Organization*
- *Model*
- *Practice*
- *Checklist for Writing a Paper That Explains How*

- Connecting words should appear frequently. They help the reader follow the time order. Common how-to connecting words include the following:

first	next	at this time
second	then	following this
third	at this time	after
now	afterward	soon
thus	in addition	therefore
furthermore	hence	similarly
at this point	after this	

- The conclusion should summarize and restate the result of step-by-step procedure.

MODEL

The following example is a well-written how-to paper. It is similar in length and structure to the essay you will be expected to write for your GED exam. Study the notes in the margins as you read.

How to Eat Peas—Politely

Eating peas in polite company can be a real test of agility, and it's a test many employers like potential employees to take. In today's competitive job market, even table manners may determine who is hired and who is not. So how should a person deal with the peas? Courtesy denies the opportunity to mash the peas and scoop them up with a fork. Courtesy also disallows using a spoon to eat peas. Attempting to spear peas on the tines of the fork usually results in those little green spheres skittering across the plate into one's lap—or worse yet, onto a fellow diner's lap.

subject named; thesis sentence

opening statement shows importance to reader (to be polite, especially on a job interview)

third-person point of view established

A few simple steps will allow the polite diner to eat peas in relative comfort. First, the peas must reside next to a more solid food, like mashed potatoes or meatloaf. When the diner has the opportunity to serve the peas himself, he will, of course, want to situate them on his plate to his advantage. If the dinner plate is presented already filled, however, the diner has the tedious job of relocating the peas without appearing rude.

topic sentence referring to "simple" steps

connecting word introducing time order

Once the peas are situated next to a more solid food, however, the next steps are easy. By placing the fork beside the peas, tines against the plate, the diner merely shoves the fork under the peas. The solid food will prevent the peas from rolling with the fork. Finally, as one nears the end of his meal, he must be certain to leave sufficient solid food until the last of the rolling vegetables are safely hoisted away. In this manner, the polite diner wins the battle with peas without using his fingers or a dinner roll as a pusher.

connecting words showing continuing steps
topic sentence

third-person point of view used throughout

connecting word showing final step

connecting word signaling the conclusion

conclusion offers indirect challenge to reader

PRACTICE

Directions: To practice your own how-to writing, select a topic from those listed below, or choose your own topic. When you finish writing, use the checklist that follows to think through your paper.

Topic Selections

- How to play company politics
- How to start a car on a cold morning
- How to write a resume cover letter
- How to choose a restaurant/motel/vacation spot
- How to choose a restaurant/motel/vacation spot for children
- How to buy a used car
- How to buy the perfect birthday/Christmas/anniversary/wedding gift
- How to improve your golf game/bridge game/tennis game
- How to drive safely in heavy traffic
- How to win friends/enemies

CHECKLIST FOR WRITING A PAPER THAT EXPLAINS HOW

Use the following checklist to judge your paper. You should be able to answer "yes" to these questions.

		YES	NO
1.	Does my paper include a thesis statement that names the subject and suggests the ease or care with which the process can be completed?	❑	❑
2.	Have I shown the importance of the subject?	❑	❑
3.	Have I used plenty of specific details, clearly explaining each step in the process?	❑	❑
4.	Have I organized the paper in time order?	❑	❑
5.	Have I used clear connecting words (transitions) to help establish the time order?	❑	❑
6.	Have I omitted ideas not directly related to my topic? (That is, have I maintained unity?)	❑	❑
7.	Have I used the right verb tenses, especially as I developed my paper by time order?	❑	❑
8.	Have I maintained consistent point of view?	❑	❑
9.	Does my conclusion summarize, restate the result of the process, and challenge the reader?	❑	❑
10.	Have I used good, effective, complete sentences?	❑	❑
11.	Have I used good sentence variety?	❑	❑
12.	Have I used specific, concise words?	❑	❑
13.	Have I used good grammar and accurate mechanics and usage?	❑	❑
14.	Have I checked spelling?	❑	❑

Writing an Essay Explaining Why

We often ask "why?" Why am I grumpy after lunch? Why won't the car start? Why am I so short of money this month? Because explaining why is such a part of daily life, the GED essay topic may ask you to "Explain why and support your explanation with examples and specific details."

Explaining why can deal with causes: why something happened. It can also deal with results: why something is the way it is. The following samples illustrate what a writer does when he explains why:

Sample 1: The severe snow and ice storm caused especially serious problems in rural areas.

(The writer will explain why the problems were so serious: power failures, impassible roads, homes without heat or water, livestock stranded without food.)

Sample 2: The severe snow and ice storm resulted when the low-pressure storm system joined moisture from the Gulf.

(The writer, who must be familiar with the science of weather forecasting, will explain why the storm occurred.)

ROAD MAP

- *Organization*
- *Models*
- *Practice*

ORGANIZATION

A paper that explains why usually uses the following organization:

- The paper should begin with an attention-grabber that establishes the importance of the subject.

- The paper should include a thesis statement (See Chapter 22).

Example: In order to survive, workers in today's labor force must learn to deal with stress.

(The writer will explain the reasons why workers must learn to deal with stress.)

Example: The car failed to start because of a series of weather-related events.

(The writer will explain the reasons why the weather caused the car not to start.)

HINT

Decide on your plan of organization before you begin writing. Jot down the ideas you want to include and decide whether time order works better than an order of importance or vice versa.

- In a paper that explains why, the thesis statement is followed by specific examples and specific details (See Chapter 18, Part 1).

  Example: Workers must learn to deal with stress because they face stress on a daily basis.

  Detail 1: face stress keeping job (lay-offs, strikes, plant closings, cutbacks)

  Detail 2: face stress completing work (daily and weekly deadlines, work output per hour, meeting rates)

  Detail 3: face stress in labor-management relations (union policy vs. employee demands, demanding boss, personal conflicts)

  Example: Weather-related events caused the car not to start.

  Detail 1: sub-zero cold followed by very warm temperatures

  Detail 2: change brought condensation

  Detail 3: moisture in ignition system

- The supporting details may be organized in either of two patterns: time order or order of importance (See Chapter 18, Part 2).

For instance, in the first example above, order of importance will work best: some kinds of stress are more difficult to deal with than others. In the second example, however, time order is essential. The writer must explain the series of events that resulted in the car not starting.

- Strong connecting words must tie together details and show the reader time relationships and cause-effect relationships. Some useful transitions include *therefore, hence, consequently, accordingly, as a result, for this reason, thus,* and *so* (See Chapter 18, Part 3).

- The conclusion should relate directly to the thesis statement and tie together the logical steps presented (See Chapter 20).

MODELS

The following paragraphs explain why. Study them before you write your own.

Sun Worshipping

Everywhere, from beaches to back-yards, sun worshippers lie in the blazing heat soaking up rays. The resulting business in suntan lotions, sunscreens, beach towels, sunglasses, skin conditioners, hair conditioners, and medical bills for skin-cancer treatments adds up to big dollars. What causes apparently sane people to subject themselves to such discomfort and risk?	introductory statement attention-grabber that shows impact of subject thesis statement (in form of question)
First, some folks actually enjoy the sweltering experience. They like the feel of oil all over their bodies and the sun oozing sweat out of their every pore. They must see it as a kind of cleansing act that pays penance for whatever wrongs they have done. "Sweating it out" becomes almost heroic. Other folks, however, lie under Old Sol out of an apparent sense of duty. They don't like the oil-and-sand mixture on their skins, and they don't like to sweat. On the other hand, however, since all their friends soak in the sun, peer pressure indicates they, too, must soak in the sun. How could they make up an acceptable excuse not to join in?	connecting word and first cause (reason why) details supporting first reason why connecting word and second reason why specific details supporting second reason why
Finally, there are the folks who neither enjoy the sun nor feel a sense of duty to join the worshippers. They are the ones who think a tan is the absolute epitome of good grooming. A tan, they are convinced, makes them gorgeous; it attracts the opposite sex; it earns them better jobs; it authorizes them to be better than anyone else who doesn't have an equally golden tan. So they believe. The non-sun worshipper looks with raised eyebrows at any of these golden-bodied reasons, questioning the sanity and pointing to statistics about causes of skin cancer. On the other hand, stockholders in suntan-lotion companies cheer the golden business.	connecting words showing relationship of groups one and two to group three third reason why specific details supporting third cause conclusion in two statements (both referring to thesis statement and introduction and both suggesting writer's attitude about "logic" of reasons why) "golden" teases, makes final statement

The model above explains why a sunbather lies in the sun. The writer considers three possible reasons why people sunbathe.

The following model also is similar in length and structure to the essay you will be required to write for the GED exam. This model illustrates another kind of reason why. It shows why a situation brings certain results. Notice that the general principles and methods of organization are the same. The writer merely approaches the situation from a different direction, explaining why things are as they are. It's the difference between cause and effect. (Note: You have read other short models throughout the text that explain why. You may wish to review them as well.)

Sun Worshippers, Beware!

Sun worshippers embrace the blazing rays and welcome the golden tan. They usually forget, however, the other less desirable effects of sunbathing.

introductory statement
thesis statement showing paper will tell why sun-bathing is bad

First, the general discomfort from lying in the broiling heat must have some consideration. Sweat oozes from every pore; lotions with their heavy oily texture block the pores; and sand or grass mixes with the lotion to produce an on-skin sandpaper. Although these discomforts are only temporary, others may be more lasting. Folks who lie out too long soon experience painful sunburns, soon followed by itching and uncomfortable peeling. Certainly the splotches that result aren't very attractive, but, of course, that discomfort is only emotional.

connecting word introducing first effect
organization in order of importance, least to most
details to explain first reason why

connecting words

second part of first reason why

details explaining "more lasting"

Second, and more important, however, is the productive time a sunbather loses. If he spends only an hour a day seeking a golden tan, a sunbather loses seven hours a week, the equivalent of a full working day. Imagine the gain if such hours were spent doing something either personally or socially productive!

connecting words showing order of importance and naming second reason why

example supporting second reason why

challenge to the reader

Finally, dismissing the personal discomfort and the loss of productive time, the sunbather assumes a serious risk of physical problems. The problems may be as simple as nausea or headache from too much heat. They may be more complicated, such as an allergy to direct sun. Ultimately, the problems can be as serious as cancer. In fact, research is beginning to make many serious-minded people less and less interested in Old Sol's dangerous rays. In short, the effects from sunbathing range from general, short-termed discomfort to specific, long-termed physical problems, potentially fatal.

connecting word showing relationship of reasons one and two to three

third reason why

series of examples supporting third reason why
connecting word showing order of importance

connecting word and additional example of third reason why

connecting word and summary of ideas in concluding statement leaving reader with serious thought

PRACTICE

Directions: To practice writing a paper explaining why, select a topic from those listed below, or choose your own topic. Write your paper. Then, use the checklist that follows to check your paragraph.

SUGGESTED TOPICS

- Why I landed the job
- Why the accident occurred
- Why I/someone was late for work/appointment/class
- Why an industry leaves/closes/cuts back/lays off
- Why we should eat/exercise properly
- What brings about failure/success in class/career/society
- Why I/others respond to a specific advertising/political campaign
- What caused me to buy a certain car
- What causes me to shop at a certain shop/dine at a certain restaurant
- What causes me/someone to be rude/courteous/angry

CHECKLIST FOR WRITING A PAPER THAT EXPLAINS WHY

Use the following checklist to judge your paper that explains why. You should be able to answer "yes" to each of these questions.

		YES	NO
1.	Have I started with a thesis statement that names my subject?	❑	❑
2.	Have I included specific examples and details to support my reasons?	❑	❑
3.	Are my specific examples and details logical?	❑	❑
4.	Have I anticipated my readers' probable questions?	❑	❑
5.	Have I arranged the details of my paper either in time order or by some order of importance?	❑	❑
6.	Have I omitted ideas not directly related to my topic sentence? (That is, have I maintained unity?)	❑	❑
7.	Have I used good connecting words (transitions)?	❑	❑
8.	Have I used the right verb tenses?	❑	❑
9.	Have I used the same point of view throughout?	❑	❑
10.	Does my conclusion refer to the topic and tie together the logical steps in the paper?	❑	❑
11.	Have I written effective, powerful complete sentences?	❑	❑
12.	Have I used specific, concise words?	❑	❑
13.	Have I used good grammar, mechanics, and usage?	❑	❑
14.	Have I spelled all the words correctly?	❑	❑

Writing an Essay Stating and Supporting an Opinion

Everybody has opinions, but being able to state and support those opinions so that others understand them is the mark of an educated person. As a result, one of the four general kinds of essay topics on the GED test asks you to do just that: state and support an opinion. Being able to do so shows first that you can think clearly and second that you can communicate effectively—both important for success on the GED test. Here's how to write an effective opinion paper.

ORGANIZATION

The following pattern of organization is typical of an opinion paper:

- The opinion paper usually begins with a thesis statement (See Chapter 22).

- The supporting details must emphasize reasons for your opinion. Why do you think as you do? What examples can you give that help your reader understand why you think as you do?

  Note: The GED essay response directions will usually say, "Be specific. Give reasons and examples." If you do not, you will certainly receive a low score.

Phrases like *in my opinion* or *I believe* need not appear in an opinion paper. Your name appears on the paper, and that is sufficient to let the reader know whose opinion he is reading. Of course, if you express an opinion other than your own, it should be preceded by phrases like *in the opinion of some* or *some people believe that* to avoid confusing your reader.

If you need to soften certain points or limit their impact, you can use qualifying words like *in some cases, in most situations, occasionally, sometimes, perhaps, may,* and *probably*.

- The paper should maintain a consistent point of view (See Chapter 19, Problem 2).

- Opinion papers are usually organized by order of importance (See Chapter 18, Part 2).

The most effective organization plan for an opinion essay is the order of importance that uses the following pattern:

Detail one: second most important

Detail two: least important

Detail three: fourth most important

Detail four: third most important

Detail five: most important

Because the opinion paper may be read by someone who disagrees with your point of view, the paper should build to its most important detail.

- Good connecting words (transitions) help the reader follow the reasoning in an opinion paper (see Chapter 18, Part 3). Some typical connecting words for an opinion paper include *first, second, finally, on the one hand, on the other hand, in addition, as a result,* and *another reason.*

- The conclusion should help the reader understand your stated opinion.

MODEL

The following model shows what a good opinion paper should look like. It is similar in length and structure to the essay you will be required to write for the GED exam. Be sure to study the comments accompanying the model.

Do It Yourself: Fad or Fundamental?

"Making your own" has become the thing to do. Whether it's making clothes, baking bread, making yogurt, or building a car, the do-it-yourself fad appears destined to lose its fad status and become the mark of the well-rounded person. Originally, the do-it-yourselfers claimed their purpose was to save dollars. Save dollars they did. By building his own custom fishing rod, one do-it-yourselfer had a rod valued at $150 that he'd made for less than $50. Another made her own suit for less than $40, one she would have paid well over $100 for in a local department store.	introductory statement thesis statement first point in order of importance specific examples third-person point of view used throughout
While some do-it-yourselfers still talk about dollars saved, others are now more apt to point out the purity or quality of the homemade product. They can boast of vegetables organically grown and home-canned and home-baked products with no additives and no preservatives. The man who builds his own car boasts of enduring quality that will keep his car on the road years longer than those mass-produced.	connecting word to second point second reason for opinion specific example to support second reason third-person point of view; no reference to "my opinion" or "I think"

Even with the dollars saved and the purity and quality gained, perhaps the most important purpose in "making your own," however, is the resulting self-satisfaction. The mass-production society allows little room for self-satisfaction in the daily job. It's difficult at the end of a workday to see what's been accomplished, to point to a product of the day's labor. Then, at home, when the loaf of whole-wheat bread comes out of the oven, there, at last, is a product of one's labor, a product to touch, smell, taste, and enjoy. It feels good.

connecting word showing relationship of first two points to third point
connecting word showing "most important"

third reason for opinion

details explaining third reason

details explaining third reason

So begins the do-it-yourself concept. If making bread brings about such good feelings, maybe growing herbs will feel good, too. And then maybe growing a small vegetable garden will feel even better. As the good feelings intensify and assume a kind of ripple effect, they will guarantee a continuing "make your own" attitude. The fad idea will no doubt disappear and be replaced by a practiced part of personal development.

logical steps following

logical steps leading to conclusion

conclusion restating thesis sentence

PRACTICE

Directions: After studying the previous model paper you should be able to write your own opinion paper. To practice, choose from the suggested topics below or select your own. Then, when you've finished your paper, use the following list to check your paper.

SUGGESTED TOPICS

It is my opinion that . . .

- everyone should have flu shots.

- not everyone should vote.

- some people have a valid reason for not getting a high school diploma.

- everyone should spend an hour each month helping the community clean up litter.

- everyone should read a daily newspaper instead of watching the news on television.

- a parent can be a son's/daughter's best friend.

- the media influences voter reaction.

- women are effective wage earners.

- men make good househusbands as well as women make good housewives.

- computers can't replace the work force.

CHECKLIST FOR WRITING AN OPINION PAPER

Use the following checklist to think through your own opinion paper. You should be able to answer yes to each of these questions.

		YES	NO
1.	Have I written an effective thesis statement?	❏	❏
2.	Have I used specific details to explain why I hold my opinion?	❏	❏
3.	Do the details take into consideration possible reader apathy or opposition?	❏	❏
4.	Have I used effective organization, probably one of the orders of importance?	❏	❏
5.	Have I used good connecting words (transitions)?	❏	❏
6.	Have I omitted unnecessary phrases like "I believe" or "in my opinion"?	❏	❏
7.	Have I softened certain points or limited their impact with qualifying words?	❏	❏
8.	Have I stayed on the subject? (That is, have I maintained unity?)	❏	❏
9.	Have I used the right verb tenses?	❏	❏
10.	Have I used the same point of view throughout?	❏	❏
11.	Have I written an effective conclusion that helps the reader understand my stated opinion?	❏	❏
12.	Have I used effective, powerful complete sentences?	❏	❏
13.	Have I used good sentence variety?	❏	❏
14.	Have I used specific, concise words?	❏	❏
15.	Have I checked grammar, mechanics, and usage?	❏	❏
16.	Have I checked spelling?	❏	❏

Writing an Essay Showing Advantages and Disadvantages

Sometimes the GED essay topic will ask you to talk about the advantages (the good points) and the disadvantages (the bad points) about some topic. Such an essay will obviously have two parts: one part will talk about all the advantages; another part will talk about all the disadvantages. But be sure to read the directions carefully. The directions may ask that you address only advantages or disadvantages—not both. In either case, here is the general plan for writing a paper that discusses advantages and/or disadvantages.

ROAD MAP

- *Organization*
- *Model*
- *Practice*
- *Checklist for an Advantages/ Disadvantages Paper*

ORGANIZATION

The advantage-disadvantage paper will usually follow this plan:

- The paper begins with a thesis statement that tells the reader that you will be talking about two points: advantages and disadvantages.

  Example: Commuting an hour or more to work each day has advantages and disadvantages. (We know the writer will talk about both the good and the bad, but we have no idea of the specifics.)

You can write a better thesis statement if it does not repeat the words *advantages* and *disadvantages*.

  Example: Commuting an hour or more to work each day gives me both time to myself and added frustrations. (We know now that the writer sees "time to self" as an advantage, perhaps to read, finish up office reports, or think through what needs to be done at home or at work. But he sees "added frustrations" as disadvantages, perhaps because of the expense of commuting or the stress of fighting traffic or meeting bus, subway, or train schedules.)

If the directions ask that you write about only advantages or disadvantages, your statement of purpose must clearly state which you will be discussing.

  Example: Commuting an hour or more to work each day adds nothing but frustration. (The writer will show the disadvantages of the long commute.)

- The statement of purpose will be followed first by details about either all of the advantages or all of the disadvantages. Then will follow the details about the other.

  To decide whether to discuss advantages or disadvantages first, decide which you think are more important. For instance, if you think the advantages outweigh the disadvantages, talk about disadvantages *first*. Then you can end with your stronger point.

Example Topic: Driving a Small Car

Advantages:
good gas mileage
fits in small parking spaces
maneuvers well in traffic
quick acceleration, peppy
fits in garage with room for more
costs less to buy

Disadvantages:
only four people can ride
trunk too small (groceries, luggage)
expensive maintenance
noisy
insufficient power for air conditioner

Except for creature comforts (crowding, noisy, hot), the listed advantages seem to outweigh the disadvantages. So the plan may look like this:

Thesis
Statement:
Although the creature comforts are limited in a small car, the advantages make it a wise choice.

Disadvantages:
creature comforts (crowding, noisy, hot)
expensive maintenance

Advantages:
inexpensive to buy, insure, and drive
handles well in traffic and in parking
fits in garage with room for more

Of course, if you are writing only about either advantages or disadvantages, rather than both, then you will have only one part to your paper. Then you need only organize the details by some order of importance (see below and Chapter 18, Part 2). The best two choices:

- Choice 1: least important to most important

- Choice 2: second most important to most important

The paper will need strong connecting words (transitions) to help readers follow your points.

Use good connecting words (transitions) to tie together all the advantages, such as *one big advantage, another advantage, perhaps not as important but worth mentioning, the biggest advantage, yet another,* and *finally.* Use connecting words and phrases like *one major disadvantage, another disadvantage, perhaps less important but still worth considering, the biggest disadvantage, yet another,* and *finally* to tie together all the disadvantages.

Use a connecting sentence to tell your reader when you are changing from advantages to disadvantages or vice versa. One of the following may be useful:

Examples:

- While the advantages are numerous, the disadvantages are even more numerous.

- While the disadvantages may seem overwhelming, the advantages offer definite consideration.

- Even though the advantages sound beneficial, the disadvantages cause serious problems.

- Even though the disadvantages seem serious, the advantages are worth examining.

- The conclusion should acknowledge both advantages and disadvantages but reach a conclusion about which is the better choice.

    Example
    Conclusion: Even though it comes with a few creature discomforts, the small car brings two other important comforts: driving and paying the expense of driving.

Study the following model to see how a completed paper should look. Keep in mind that this model is similar in length and form to the essay you will be required to write for your GED exam.

MODEL

Advantages and Disadvantages of Small-Town Living

Small-town living cannot offer the variety of cultural events, comparison shopping, and job opportunities that city living offers, but it can guarantee a slower pace and the support of friendly neighbors.	thesis statement naming three disadvantages and two advantages, in order of importance writer uses order to imply advantages more important than disadvantages
Consider first what small-town living cannot offer. Those who enjoy the theater and concerts face a disadvantage living in small towns. A civic group or high-school orchestra may have performances, but small-town residents must travel to the cities to see equity actors or actresses or hear fine philharmonic concerts. Another disadvantage results from the relatively few businesses in small towns, reducing comparison shopping. When only one store sells boots, for instance, customers don't "shop around"; they either buy or not.	connecting words, disadvantages to be discussed first first disadvantage, least important supporting details to explain first disadvantage connecting words to introduce second disadvantage, second most important second disadvantage supporting details to explain second disadvantage
The biggest disadvantage to small-town living, however, is the lack of job opportunities. Since almost all small-town businesses are family owned, the family takes care of its own. So unless a person is already part of the family, or plans to open his or her own business, the chances are slim for successful employment.	connecting words to introduce third disadvantage, most important specific details to explain reasons why about third disadvantage

So why live in a small town? Those who live there say that the advantages outweigh the disadvantages. Small-town folks say they can always drive to the city for cultural events or a shopping spree. And they can commute to a job. They are willing to make the drive first of all because of the quieter, slower pace. Small-town traffic is minimal. No one hurries anywhere. A driver may stop along the street to chat with a neighbor-pedestrian, and no impatient honks shorten the friendly greeting.

Even though some folks commute to a job in a larger city, they look forward to returning to the friendly community they call home. That may be the biggest advantage: everyone knows everyone else, and help is always part of the neighborliness. Neighbors watch each other's pets, water each other's flowers and gardens, and take in each other's mail during vacations. And after a snowstorm, whoever has his grader blade on his tractor first cleans the neighborhood driveways. In short, the advantages of small-town living reduce stress and create a kind of life that makes the going easy—slow and easy.

connecting sentences to introduce second part, about advantages

direct answers to three disadvantages

connecting words to introduce first advantage
connecting words to introduce first advantage

specific examples to explain first advantage

connecting words to introduce second advantage

second advantage

examples to explain second advantage

more examples to explain second advantage

still more examples to explain second advantage
connecting words to introduce conclusion
conclusion emphasizes advantages, obviously writer's preference

PRACTICE

Directions: Write your own advantage-disadvantage paper using one of the topics below or a topic of your own. After you finish writing, use the checklist that follows to think through your paper.

Discuss the advantages and disadvantages of

- living alone.
- working nights.
- being the age you are.
- owning a car.
- renting a house/apartment/furniture/appliances.
- buying a used/new car.
- belonging to a union.
- adopting a child/children.
- owning a cat/dog/bird/other pet.
- having painted/papered walls.

CHECKLIST FOR AN
ADVANTAGES/DISADVANTAGES PAPER

		YES	NO
1.	Have I written an effective thesis statement?	❑	❑
2.	Have I put all the advantages together and all the disadvantages together?	❑	❑
3.	Have I put last the part (advantages or disadvantages) that I think is more important?	❑	❑
4.	Have I arranged the details in order of importance, probably with the most important last?	❑	❑
5.	Have I used good connecting words (transitions) to tie together the details about advantages and disadvantages?	❑	❑
6.	Have I used a good connecting sentence (or sentences) to move from advantages to disadvantages?	❑	❑
7.	Have I stayed on the subject? (That is, have I maintained unity?)	❑	❑
8.	Have I used the right verb tenses?	❑	❑
9.	Have I used the same point of view throughout?	❑	❑
10.	Have I included an effective conclusion that says whether advantages outweigh disadvantages or vice versa?	❑	❑
11.	Have I used effective, powerful, complete sentences?	❑	❑
12.	Have I used good sentence variety?	❑	❑
13.	Have I used specific, concise words?	❑	❑
14.	Have I checked grammar, usage, and mechanics?	❑	❑
15.	Have I checked spelling?	❑	❑

GED Practice, Chapters 15–26

PHYSICALLY FIT

A

(1) *The national physical fitness fad profits health clubs, exercise gyms, and fitness centers.* (2) *There is no question that fitness is important to good health.* (3) *The experts agree.* (4) *Some people, however, seemed to have the misunderstanding that fitness can result only from paid experiences.* (5) *They pay membership fees to sweat and feel pain.* (6) *They buy expensive outfits in order to be properly attired.* (7) *They may even buy home gym equipment seeking to maximize their time: weights, a stationary bicycle, and videos.*

B

(8) *Meanwhile, the yard grows up in weeds.* (9) *Therein lies the irony.* (10) *Our parents and grandparents stayed physically fit and at the same time accomplished something.* (11) *They mowed the grass, trimmed the shrubs, pulled the weeds.* (12) *Tended the garden, scrubbed the walls, cleaned the carpets, ironed the clothes, and washed the car.* (13) *The exercise cost them nothing but kept them physically fit.* (14) *Perhaps they need to be reminded, taking lessons, and to rethink their spending priorities.*

1. Sentence 1: The national physical fitness fad profits health clubs, exercise gyms, and fitness centers.

   If you rewrote sentence 1 beginning with Health clubs, exercise gyms, and fitness centers are the next words should be

   (1) national physical fitness fads.
   (2) profits of national physical fitness fads.
   (3) profiting from the national physical fitness fad.
   (4) profits from the national physical.
   (5) physical fitness fad profits.

2. Sentences 2 and 3: There is no question that fitness is important to good health. The experts agree.

   The most effective combination of sentences 2 and 3 would include which of the following groups of words?

   (1) Although the experts agree that
   (2) Experts agree that fitness
   (3) Because experts agree that there is no question
   (4) Good health is no question
   (5) There is no question that experts agree

3. Sentence 4: Some people, however, seemed to have the misunderstanding that fitness can result only from paid experiences.

   What correction should be made to this sentence?

   (1) Change result only to only can result.
   (2) Omit the commas before and after however.
   (3) Change can to could.
   (4) Replace seemed with seem.
   (5) No correction is necessary.

4. Sentences 5 and 6: They pay membership fees to sweat and feel pain. They buy expensive outfits in order to be properly attired.

   The most effective combination of sentences 5 and 6 would include which of the following groups of words?

   (1) membership fees and buy
   (2) feel pain and be properly attired
   (3) pain as well as to sweat
   (4) feel pain but buy
   (5) feel pain, therefore they buy

5. Sentence 7: They may even buy home gym equipment seeking to maximize their time: weights, a stationary bicycle, and videos.

   What correction should be made to this sentence?

   (1) Omit the colon after time.
   (2) Insert a comma after equipment.
   (3) Move seeking to maximize their time to the beginning of the sentence.
   (4) Change stationary to stationery.
   (5) No correction is necessary.

6. Sentences 8 and 9: Meanwhile, the yard grows up in weeds. Therein lies the irony.

The most effective combination of sentences 8 and 9 would include which of the following groups of words?

(1)   weeds; and therein
(2)   weeds, and therein
(3)   weeds, therein
(4)   weeds, because therein
(5)   weeds, but therein

7. Sentence 10: Our parents and grandparents stayed physically fit and at the same time accomplished something.

What correction should be made to this sentence?

(1)   Change Our to Their.
(2)   Replace accomplished with accomplishing.
(3)   Insert a comma after fit.
(4)   Change stayed to have stayed.
(5)   No correction is necessary.

8. Sentences 11 and 12: They mowed the grass, trimmed the shrubs, pulled the weeds. Tended the garden, scrubbed the walls, cleaned the carpets, ironed the clothes, and washed the car.

Which of the following is the best way to write the underlined portion of these sentences? If you think the original is the best way, choose option (1).

(1)   weeds. Tended
(2)   weeds; tended
(3)   weeds, and tended
(4)   weeds, tended
(5)   weeds; but tended

9. Sentence 13: The exercise cost them nothing but kept them physically fit.

What correction should be made to this sentence?

(1)   Insert a comma after nothing.
(2)   Change cost to costed.
(3)   Change kept them to kept us.
(4)   Replace kept with keeps.
(5)   No correction is necessary.

10. Sentence 14: Perhaps they need to be reminded, taking lessons, and to rethink their spending priorities.

What correction should be made to this sentence?

(1)   Insert a comma after Perhaps.
(2)   Change they to we.
(3)   Change need to needed.
(4)   Replace taking lessons with to take lessons.
(5)   No correction is necessary.

ANSWERS

1. (3) The progressive form of the verb shows ongoing action. See Chapter 19, Problem 1.

2. (2) The completed sentence should read "Experts agree that fitness is important to good health." See Chapter 16, Problem 2.

3. (4) The writer needs the present tense to be consistent. See Chapter 19, Problem 1.

4. (1) The combined sentence should read, "They pay membership fees and buy expensive outfits in order to be properly attired to sweat and feel pain." See Chapter 16, Goal 2.

5. (3) The participial phrase is not placed next to the word it talks about: *they*. The revision should read, "Seeking to maximize their time, they may even buy at-home equipment: weights, a stationary bicycle, and videos." See Chapter 16, Goal 3.

6. (2) To correctly join two sentences, use a comma and a joining word. See Chapter 15, Part 2.

7. (1) The point of view has been third person. *Our* is a switch to first person. See Chapter 19, Problem 2.

8. (4) The sentence is a series of balanced phrases. The comma is correct to separate items in a series. See Chapter 16, Goal 4.

9. (5) The sentence is correct.

10. (4) To write balanced phrases, use the series of three infinitives: *to be reminded, to take lessons,* and *to rethink their spending priorities.* See Chapter 16, Goal 4.

Writing The GED Essay

As you know by now, a portion of the GED Language Arts, Writing test is an essay response. The writing that you must do on that part of the test will be in response to a statement. You will have the opportunity to respond on the basis of personal experience, observations, and knowledge.

You will be asked to write something like the following:

Explain how to do something:

> how to control stress
> how to get along with people
> how to vote intelligently

Explain why (causes or effects):

> why people litter (causes)
> why the environmental issue is important (effects)
> why we should eat and exercise properly (effects)

State and support an opinion:

> about minimum wages
> about civil rights
> about single parenting

Show the advantages and/or disadvantages:

> of television programming
> of working nights
> of having children

You will be evaluated on five criteria:

1. Response to the prompt: Did you write with a clearly focused main idea that specifically addresses the prompt?

2. Organization: Did you start with a thesis sentence? Is your organization clear and logical? Did you use connecting words to help your reader follow your organization?

3. Development and details: Did you stay on the subject? Did you use specific details and examples? Did you maintain unity? Did you use good connecting words (transitions) to maintain coherence?

4. Conventions of English: Did you write effective sentences? Did you maintain correct usage? Did you punctuate, capitalize, and spell correctly?

5. Word choice: Did you use specific words and show a command of language?

ROAD MAP

- *Planning Your Response*
- *Writing Your Essay*
- *Checking Your Essay*
- *Model*
- *Practice*

PART 1: PLANNING YOUR RESPONSE

You have already studied how to develop each of these four kinds of responses (See Chapters 23–26). When you face the real test situation, however, you need a plan that will help you be successful. You have only 45 minutes to write your response (usually of about 200–250 words) to the essay portion of the GED test. Knowing that, some GED applicants rush into the task without taking time to think or plan. That can be a bad mistake.

Instead, use the SLOW approach:

S—Study the question.
L—List your ideas.
O—Organize your ideas.
W—Write your statement of purpose.

Let's think through the SLOW approach one step at a time. Remember that you will have 45 minutes to prepare your essay response. Plan to use 4 or 5 minutes to apply the SLOW Plan. We will use the following sample question to work through the steps and complete a model response:

Sample Essay Topic:

> Youth looks forward to being older, more mature, able to do everything promised for "when you're older." As the young grow older, however, they often reminisce about the joys of youth.
>
> What do you think are the advantages or disadvantages of being 25? Look forward or reflect back to give specific details to support your position.

STEP 1: *STUDY* THE QUESTION

You will probably be a little nervous when you first read the question, worried about whether you will have anything to say, worried about whether you can write an effective response. That's natural. So take a deep breath and think carefully.

> Remember: You will get no credit for responding to anything other than what the essay topic asks. Responding clearly to the prompt is one-fifth of your score!

Ask yourself:

- What am I supposed to do?
  (I'm supposed to explain advantages or disadvantages. I've noticed that the directions say advantages *or* disadvantages, not advantages *and* disadvantages. So I am supposed to explain only one idea.)

- What directions are included?
  (I am told to "give specific details." That means I must be sure to use examples that *show* advantages or disadvantages, not just tell about them.)

- How many things am I being asked to do?
  (Just one—to explain either advantages or disadvantages of being 25 years old.)

HINT

Some essay topics may ask you to do *two* things. For instance, you may be asked to explain *both* advantages and disadvantages. Be sure to read the directions carefully!

STEP 2: *LIST* THE IDEAS YOU WILL INCLUDE

For the question above, for instance, you first must decide whether to talk about advantages or disadvantages. Let's say you choose disadvantages. With that decision made, you're ready to list ideas.

Use a piece of scratch paper to write your notes. Write just key words about what you think you will include in your response to the topic.

Ask yourself:

REMEMBER

To let your readers see the picture, you must *show*, not *tell* about your subject.

- What do I want to say?
  For the question above, for instance, your list may look like this:

  Disadvantages of being twenty-five:
  lack work experience
  too old to act like a kid
  too young to fit in at work
  have lots of energy

- Have I included any ideas that do not belong?
  (Yes. Having lots of energy is not a disadvantage.)

  Revised list:

  Disadvantages of being twenty-five:
  lack work experience
  too old to act like kid
  too young to fit in at work

- Do I have enough ideas for a paper?
  (Yes. Three ideas, each with examples, will be adequate to support your response.)

- What details will I use to explain each of my ideas?

- Your list of details may look something like this:

  lack work experience

      only four years' experience
      only two positions
      others (older) have more and different

  too old to act like a kid

      others my age married
      singles scene too late (work early)
      other responsibilities (yard, apartment)

  too young to fit in at work

      others older, married, children, grandkids
      active in sports (they're couch potatoes)

With two or three examples to support each idea, you are ready for the next step.

STEP 3: *ORGANIZE* YOUR IDEAS

You have already studied three ways to organize ideas: time order, space order, and order of importance. You will need to choose the best way to put your list in order.

Ask yourself:

HINT

If there is no reason to use time or space order, then you will use the most frequently used order: order of importance.

- Is there a reason to use time order or space order?

- How can I organize these ideas by importance?

    Disadvantages of being twenty-five:

    > lack of work experience (most important disadvantage)
    > too old to act like a kid (second most important)
    > too young to fit in at work (least important)

Usually the most effective way to organize your ideas is from second most important to most important. As a result, the ideas above should go in this order:

1. too old to act like a kid

2. too young to fit in at work

3. lack work experience

- Number in order the items on your scratch list.

- In what order should I give my examples?

Again, review the three ways to organize. Then simply use letters to put the examples in order:

3. lack work experience

    b. only four years' experience

    a. only two positions

    c. others (older) have more and different

1. too old to act like kid

    b. others my age married

    a. singles scene too late (work early)

    c. other responsibilities (yard, apartment)

2. too young to fit in at work

    a. others older, married, kids, grandkids

    b. active in sports vs. couch potatoes

STEP 4: *WRITE* THE THESIS STATEMENT

When you write your thesis statement, you must make yourself—and your reader/evaluator—see clearly your main idea. In this example, your main idea is, of course, that there are disadvantages to being 25 years old. So your thesis statement might read like this:

> Thesis Statement: The three disadvantages to being 25 years old make me wish I were closer to 35.

Or, another version:

> Thesis Statement: At 25 a person is too old to act as he feels but too young to fit in at work or to have enough experience for a better job.

Or, another version:

> Thesis Statement: At 25 a person spends frustrating days thinking, "If only I were 30-something."

In each case, the thesis statement says or implies the following:

1. The writer is 25—or recalls being 25.

2. The writer sees age 25 as a disadvantage.

3. The writer will detail why it is a disadvantage to be 25.

Now you're ready to write. Just remember to follow the SLOW method to prepare:

S—Study the question.
L—List your ideas.
O—Organize your ideas.
W—Write your statement of purpose.

If you take the time to plan, you will write a far better essay.

PART 2: WRITING YOUR ESSAY

If you have worked according to schedule, you should have spent 4 or 5 minutes planning. That leaves 40 minutes. You will want to save time at the end for checking your paper and making some revisions—at least 6 or 7 minutes. That leaves 33 minutes to write:

> 5 minutes planning
> 33 minutes writing
> 7 minutes checking
> 45 minutes total

If you have 33 minutes to write and three ideas to cover, then you should spend 11 minutes on each topic:

> 11 minutes on "too old to act like a kid"
> 11 minutes on "too young to fit in at work"
> 11 minutes on "too young to have work experience"
> 33 minutes on writing time

Use your 33 minutes this way:

STEP 1: START WITH THE THESIS STATEMENT

Use the thesis statement in your introduction. Why? Three reasons:

1. By starting with the thesis statement, you force yourself to say exactly what you are going to do in your essay.

2. You have already written the thesis statement (from the planning steps above), so you can jump right into the writing task.

3. By starting with the thesis statement, you tell your reader exactly what you are going to do in your essay.

STEP 2: WRITE YOUR IDEAS

Write your ideas in the order in which you numbered and lettered them above.

Writing the essay should be almost like following a road map. You know where you must go, and your planning notes tell you the steps to take to get there. So go! Get your ideas down as quickly as possible. You can puzzle over punctuation, spelling, or a precise word later.

STEP 3: ADD A CONCLUSION

The conclusion, as you remember, is a simple summary or statement to help the reader feel a sense of completeness. Keep it short and snappy. Don't waste time here.

PART 3: CHECKING YOUR ESSAY

Checking takes two steps. Remember that you should have about 7 minutes to check. Use it this way:

4 minutes to check content
3 minutes to check spelling, mechanics, etc.
7 minutes total checking time

Here's how:

STEP 1: USE THE RS2C4 PLAN

RS2C4 is just a little trick to help you remember the important things you have studied about writing. You know about them, and you'll want to remember them as you check your essay response. The letters stand for five important ideas:

R—Response to prompt
S—Specific details
S—Sentence structure
C—Connecting words
C—Coherence
C—Consistency
C—Conclusion

• Ask yourself: Did I *respond* directly to the prompt and stay on the subject, following my plan and supporting my thesis sentence?

• Have I included *specific details*? Did I show, not tell?

• Have I used good *sentences*? Have I used a variety of sentences? Have I omitted sentence errors like run-on sentences, comma splices, and fragments?

• Have I used *connecting words* to move from one idea to the next smoothly?

• Have I maintained *coherence* by using connecting sentences between my main ideas?

• Did I use *consistent* verb tenses and the same point of view throughout?

• Did I add a *conclusion*?

STEP 2: USE THE GUMS PLAN

Again, GUMS is just a little trick to help you remember to check for:

G—Grammar
U—Usage
M—Mechanics
S—Spelling

MODEL

The following essay responds to this question:

> What do you think are the advantages or disadvantages of being 25? Look forward or reflect back to give specific details to support your position.

The model essay that follows is based on the plan outlined above. Furthermore, since the GED Writing Skills directions usually suggest an essay of about 200–250 words, this model falls within the suggested length. Study the model and the marginal notes to the right. Then use the topics at the end of this chapter to practice writing your own response.

Twenty-five or Thirty-Something?

Three disadvantages to being 25 years old make me wish I were 35. First, as a young single, I would like to do what I did at 18, but I'm too old. The late-night scene interferes with my early-morning work assignment. My friends are almost all married, and I feel silly doing alone the things we used to do together. And since I have a yard and an apartment to keep up, I can't act like a kid anymore, ignoring responsibilities.

It seems strange that while I'm too old for the activities of my youth, I'm too young for comfort at work. For instance, I'm too young to fit in with my fellow workers. All of them are at least 30, married, and have children or even grandchildren. They tease me about my youth, mostly because I like to play a fast game of racquetball, tennis, or basketball. They prefer to watch any sport for any number of hours from the living room couch. In short, we have practically nothing in common.

Marginal notes:

- thesis statement notes "three disadvantages"
- connecting word, introduces first disadvantage
- first example showing one disadvantage
- second example
- third example
- connecting sentence introduces second disadvantage
- connecting word introduces first example to explain second disadvantage
- details
- second example
- details explaining why
- connecting word for summary

The biggest disadvantage to being 25, however, is not social. Young adults simply do not have the work experience to move up the success ladder. Because my fellow workers are older than I, they are also more experienced. For instance, since I have held only two positions with my employer, I am told that I lack the understanding needed for a better job. In addition, since I have only four years' experience, I am the new man on the crew. Therefore, when a position opens, someone else always has more experience than I and beats me to the promotion. Being 25 often leaves me wishing I were thirty-something.

connecting sentence introduces third
    disadvantage
third disadvantage

first example to explain third disadvantage

connecting words to introduce details

connecting words to introduce more details

connecting word to show results

concluding statement

PRACTICE

Use the following topics to practice preparing GED essay responses. Aim for essays of about 200–250 words. Time yourself so you will get used to watching the clock and preparing an essay within the 45-minute limit.

Sample Topic 1

Internationally, people are voicing concern over environmental issues, like air and water pollution, the depletion of natural resources, and the extinction or endangerment of many plant and animal species.

Explain how an individual can alter his or her living habits to protect the environment. Give specific details and examples to support your explanation.

Sample Topic 2

Athletes in the United States enjoy high visibility and enormous salaries. Their images fill the television screen; their contracts are topics of general discussions. As a result, many children admire athletes as heroes and turn to them as role models.

Do you view this admiration as good or bad? State your opinion and give reasons to support your position.

Sample Topic 3

Credit cards provide the convenience of buying now and paying later. On the other hand, some people are caught up in the spending power that credit cards give them, and they destroy themselves financially.

Explain why you think credit cards are good or bad. Be sure to give specific reasons and examples to support your explanation.

NOTES

NOTES

Need Help Paying for School?
We'll Show You the Money!

Peterson's offers students like you a wide variety of comprehensive resources to help you meet all your financial planning needs.

Scholarships, Grants & Prizes 2002
ISBN 0-7689-0695-4, with CD,
$26.95 pb/$39.95 CAN/£18.99 UK,
August 2001

College Money Handbook 2002
ISBN 0-7689-0694-6,
$26.95 pb/$39.95 CAN/£18.99 UK,
August 2001

Scholarship Almanac 2002
ISBN 0-7689-0692-X
$12.95 pb/$18.95 CAN/£9.99 UK,
August 2001

The Insider's Guide to Paying for College
ISBN 0-7689-0230-4,
$9.95 pb/$14.95 CAN/£11.99 UK,
1999

Scholarships and Loans for Adult Students
ISBN 0-7689-0296-7,
$19.95 pb/$29.95 CAN/£16.99 UK,
1999

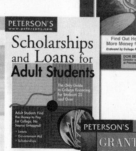

Grants for Graduate & Postdoctoral Study
ISBN 0-7689-0019-0,
$32.95 pb/$45.95 CAN/£25 UK,
1998

Scholarships for Study in the USA & Canada
ISBN 0-7689-0266-5,
$21.95 pb/$32.95 CAN/£16.99 UK,
1999

Visit your local bookstore or call to order: **800-338-3282.** To order online, go to **www.petersons.com** and head for the bookstore!

PETERSON'S
THOMSON LEARNING